THE**CALL**

Be and become the follower you are meant to be

Francois Carr

THE CALL—Be and become the follower you are meant to be

Copyright © 2021 by Francois Carr
Trade Paperback ISBN 978-1-77630-567-4
eBook ISBN 978-1-77630-568-1

Editor: Wilna Swart
Cover design: Megan van der Berg
Text design and layout: Megan van der Berg

First published in 2021 by The Connected Life Ministries.

This book is dedicated to

the Lord Jesus, who sets forth Himself as the object of our faith and the pattern of our life. His life is the illustration of what He wants all of us to be and become;

and to

my wife Dorothea and my daughter Leoné.

And He went up on the mountain and called to Him those He Himself wanted. And they came to Him. Then He appointed twelve, that they might be with Him and that He might send them out to preach, and to have power to heal sicknesses and to cast out demons.
(Mark 3:13–15)

And He went up on the hillside and called to Him [for Himself] those whom He wanted and chose, and they came to Him. And He appointed twelve to continue to be with Him, and that He might send them out to preach
[as apostles or special messengers] And to have authority and power to heal the sick and to drive out demons.
(Mark 3:13–15 *The Amplified Bible*)

He climbed a mountain and invited those he wanted with him. They climbed together. He settled on twelve and designated them apostles. The plan was that they would be with him, and he would send them out to proclaim the Word and give them authority to banish demons.
(Mark 3:13–15 *The Message*)

CONTENTS

ACKNOWLEDGMENTS

I am so grateful to God for calling me to Himself while I attended a weekend youth camp in Pretoria in April 1988. There is nothing sweeter and better than being a follower of Jesus.

There are many people to thank for this project, which began as a series of talks at the Reconnect Retreat for Spiritual Leaders and Pastors in South Carolina several years ago. I thank you all for your support and patience.

I thank Dr. Joe Youngblood, former Director of Church Health of the South Carolina Baptist Convention, and his team, who arranged these two-day retreats and for inviting me to share and teach on this important subject.

I thank those who attended these sessions in South Carolina, and other parts of the world, who so helpfully interacted with me about the ideas that I was trying to articulate. It helped me to 'test' and develop some of the thoughts, truths and principles captured in this book.

I want to thank those who walk in these principles and understand how important it is for me to walk in them also.

I want to thank my daughter Leoné Mostert for her assistance in finalizing the project.

Finally, Dorothea, my wife: thank you for your continuing role in my life and your support on my spiritual journey. Thank you for believing in me and modeling the truths shared in this book.

My hope is that this message and process positively impacts many.

Thanks be to God!

ENDORSEMENTS
AND
PRAISE FOR THE CALL

I've known Francois Carr for many years. His heart for the Lord and revival is exceptional. His life also testifies to this. Jesus commanded His church to make disciples—a matter sorely neglected by the church. This well-timed book by Francois will help you understand the personal calling that God has for you. You're going to become aware of the glorious presence of the Father and will experience changes in your life. You will be challenged to go live out your calling. In addition, you're going to be encouraged to make your own disciples. Thank you, Francois. I believe with my whole heart that this book is going to touch people's lives and be a blessing to the church of Christ.
Soli Deo Gloria!

Rev. Willem Badenhorst
Executive Director: Moreletapark Association and leader of Moreletapark Congregation, Pretoria, SA

'God assigned the prophet Ezekiel to be a spiritual watchman for God's people' (Ezekiel 33:1–20). In every age and in every country, God raises up those with a keen spiritual sensitivity to His activity. I have sensed that Francois is one of God's watchmen for our day. Francois has a hunger for God that is contagious. He has a ministry that God continues to use mightily. I am delighted with his latest book, *The Call*, in which he shares with readers the rich harvest he has gleaned from years of walking faithfully with God.

Dr. Henry Blackaby
Founder of Blackaby Ministries International, Jonesboro, Ga.
Author: *Experiencing God, Spiritual Leadership, Hearing God's Voice.*

I am proud to call Dr. Francois Carr a friend and a colleague in the faith for almost 20 years. The friendship that has grown through mission trips, revivals and conferences has led me to a deeper walk with Christ. In this book, Dr. Francois writes about the principles he shows in his own life as a true disciple of Christ. You will have a more intimate walk with the Lord after reading this book, as He teaches you about walking in obedience while your life is being transformed for the purpose of the Great Commission.

Dr. Charles Bishop
Pastor: Subligna Baptist Church, Summerville, Ga., USA

It was my privilege to meet my dear brother, friend and mentor Francois Carr 30 years ago. Preaching together on revival at revival conferences in South Africa, the Netherlands and Poland was an honor. Ever since the message has been the same: 'Jesus, all for Jesus,' following in the footsteps of Jesus. To have a friend like Francois, who always makes time for talking and praying together nearly every week is very precious. *The Call* is a living testimony of someone who does not just talk about Jesus, but also walks with Jesus. This I can tell you, because I know him well. My prayer is that this book will guide people to do what Jesus told His first disciples to do: change the world. *The Call* has changed my life and many others' in our congregation as we studied it together for many weeks. This book is meant for a time like this.

Rev. Johan Botha
Pastor: Evangelical Reformed Church, Pretoria East, SA

For any book to be of significant value to the reader it must be accurate, clear, and understandable. Dr. Carr has certainly achieved all three in his latest book titled *The Call*. Filled with supporting Scripture throughout, *The Call* is written in a simple manner that provides great clarity to the reader. It is replete with meaningful life illustrations that reinforce the basic premise of the book, which is that of connecting your life with God's purpose. Dr. Carr will awaken you to the joy of finding God's call on your life to become a fully devoted follower of Jesus Christ.

Dr. Gary Fleetwood
Pastor: Chime Bell Baptist Church, Aiken, S.C, USA
Vice President: Academic Affairs, Covington Theological Seminary, Fort Oglethorpe, Ga., USA

I greatly recommend the ministry of my dear friend Dr. Carr. He has been a great blessing to our revival work in Poland, and his book *Revival! The Glory of God* became the best and most-read publication regarding the topic of revival in Poland. No doubt the text that you hold in your hand is no different. It has the depth of great Puritan and revival writers of former centuries, but its anointed contemporary language makes it more understandable and practical. It is remarkably recommended for pastors, leaders, and laypersons who want to be used for the glory of God.

Pastor Dr. Kamil M. Halambiec (multiple PhDs, STM, MTh, MAR, BTh)
Associate Dean: College of Theology and Social Sciences, Warsaw, Poland

The power behind *The Call*, written by Dr. Francois Carr, is alignment to the model and the message of Jesus Christ as well as Dr. Carr's intention to model Jesus in his own life and work around the world. Dr. Carr's simple instructions reflect the model of the carpenter/stonemason, Rabbi and Lord, Jesus, who Himself was apprenticed by his Father, and who discipled and deployed ordinary men and women into His kingdom enterprise around the planet, began His training process with a 'call' to His followers. Dr. Carr captures the significance of the specific call to become a follower of Jesus and then to be launched into His work of 'fishing for people' and 'entering their lives' on a daily basis right where we are. I applaud Dr. Carr for this work, and I'm thankful for his life.

Dr. Carl F. Martin, Jr.
Executive Director of Real Champions Inc., Ridgeland, S.C., USA

I have known Dr. Francois Carr for about 20 years and appreciated his teachings from Scripture. In this book, *The Call,* he has captured the essence of where so many believers fall short. There is a great need for Christians to develop a deep intimacy with the Lord Jesus and Dr. Carr has laid out a road map for exactly that. It is worth reading and, more importantly, applying to life.

Rev. John McGregor
Former Executive Director: Canadian Revival Fellowship
Current Lead Pastor: Heritage Alliance Church, Regina, Canada

I have known Dr. Francois Carr for over 20 years. The messages that he was burdened with in the past, 'Revival, Intimacy with God and Discipleship,' are the same messages that he is still burdened with today. This latest book, *The Call,* continues to reflect this message of Jesus, namely, 'Come, follow me' (revival), 'Come, be with Me' (intimacy), 'I will send you' (discipleship). Jesus's last command, to go and make disciples (Matthew 28:19), must be our first priority if we are to make an impact toward ending gospel poverty. I highly recommend the reading of this masterpiece. The exegesis of the texts, coupled with personal, practical life experiences, will keep you wanting to read to the end, then regretting that you have come to the end. Francois has a hunger and thirst for the Word of God and this is reflected in his personal and family life. He has been a tremendous blessing to me personally and has made an impact on the lives of many in South Africa and around the world.

Rev. Kovilan Moodley
Moderator: Reformed Church in Africa, SA
Former Executive Director: Haggai International (South Africa)
International Faculty: Haggai International

I first met Francois Carr over 20 years ago while working with a mission in South Africa. Since then, I have hosted him in my home and church. I have been in his home and we have traveled to many locations around the world, sharing God's Word. I have always found him a man of passion for Christ, with an insatiable desire to know Jesus more deeply. Francois is a man truly hungry for God.

In his latest book, *The Call,* Francois shares practical insights into what it means to abide in Christ and in doing so fulfilling God's purpose. I recommend this book wholeheartedly.

Dr. Mark D. Partin
Director: Minister to Minister International
Senior Pastor: Grapevine Baptist Church, Madisonville, Ky., USA

The other day I took some time to read through *The Call* in one go. I must say, the more I read, the more I was blessed and, needless to say, challenged. Once again I learnt that: the intimate life with Jesus is not optional but really part and parcel of following Jesus and discipleship. In a world that emphasizes quick fixes, shortcuts to success, fast living and sensationalism, this book cuts past those transient things and ploughs into the inner soul, demands brokenness and full surrender to the Lord Jesus and His way by the working of the Holy Spirit. Ephesians 2:10 puts it so well, 'We are His workmanship created in Christ Jesus ...' What I, and all of us, need to do is to constantly step aside and let Him do His work in us! This will bring about authenticity, which is what the world is looking for. Jesus said, 'by this shall all men know that you are my disciples, if you love one another.'

Here's a book that can be studied carefully and could well be used as a study for groups, etc. I would therefore prayerfully but confidently recommend it to all who 'hunger and thirst after righteousness.' Thank you, Brother Francois, for these timely reminders and it is my sincere prayer that all who read it may become 'doers of the word and not hearers only' (James 1:22).

Dr. Harold Peasley
Former Director: Multi Ministries International, EE3, SA

Francois Carr's burden for revival is shown in an exemplary way in his new book, *The Call.* As he shows, revival is all about God's children spiritually moving back to normal Christianity so that, through awakening of the bride of Christ, the greatest salvation of the unsaved can occur. Carr exhorts that it is time for the followers of Christ to grow in obedient discipleship in the midst of an empty wasteland. He notes that as the 12 disciples learned intimately of Jesus, they became fishers of men. This revival consciousness of God's presence issues into the fulfillment of the Great Commission. This is Jesus's call today: out of daily obedience, relationship with Jesus becomes intimate, His love flows through us and into the work of God, and results in the salvation of a lost world. Spiritual power for this task comes from the Holy Spirit, all to God's glory. *The Call* is a book of compelling spirituality and obedience for all who are on this mission from God.

Dr. Tom Phillips
Vice President: Billy Graham Evangelistic Association, Charlotte, N.C., USA

Dr. Francois Carr has provided us with a wonderful resource in his book *The Call*. His words are filled with wonderful truths so needed by this generation. What makes this book different and so rich is its balance. He shows the importance of being *with Jesus, changed by Him, and sent for Him*. Francois intertwines the great truths of prayer, revival, and discipleship into one great work. I highly commend this book to every follower of Jesus. As you read it, you will discover God's original intent for your life. Read! Be blessed! Obey! And see the glory of God!

Sammy Tippit
Author and international evangelist at Sammy Tippit Ministries, San Antonio, Tx., USA

Francois Carr has now written a very needed and timely book, *The Call*, which will assist many people to learn how Christ connects people to His purpose and His plan for their lives. Far too many followers of Christ never learn how to connect their lives to Christ's purpose and plan and as such they remain unproductive in their Christian service. Dr. Carr uses the exegesis of Scripture, personal testimony and practical application to assist the reader with knowing and being engaged in Christ's plan and purpose for their lives.

Dr. Carr clearly shows, based upon Mark 3:13–15:

The Call to Communion (fellowship with Christ)
The Call to Conformity (transformation by Christ)
The Call to Commission (service with Christ)

I highly and enthusiastically recommend *The Call* to anyone who is seeking to connect their lives and ministry to the plans and purposes of God. I urge anyone who is desiring to be used by God to read and submit to the biblical truths of Dr. Carr's exegesis in his book.

Dr. Joe Youngblood
Director: Revival and Missions International, Aiken, S.C., USA

Foreword

I had the inestimable privilege of growing up in the home of a father who is widely regarded by people around the world as a great man of God. He did not earn that reputation because he was a great man per se. In many ways, he was exceedingly ordinary. As his oldest son, I have no doubt of that. But when it came to his walk with God and his life in the Spirit, he was extraordinary. When he preached, the Spirit of God would work so powerfully that people would stream to the altar before he had finished speaking. Often, after he sensed God leading him to take a step of faith, an unanticipated check would suddenly arrive in the mail. Other times God would alert him to a new ministry he should start, and someone would unexpectedly call and invite him to do the very thing God had revealed to him in prayer. When my father prayed for people, God powerfully set them free.

Now, I must confess that when I was a young child, I was unaware of how unusual my father was. I naively assumed all Christians routinely experienced the supernatural power of God working through their lives. I thought it was commonplace for God to speak to people and guide them to do surprising things that had amazing results. After all, the Bible was filled with examples of people doing just that. God told Noah to build a massive ship even though it is doubtful he had ever imagined such a craft before, let alone encountered a rainstorm. He inspired a teenaged shepherd boy to enter a grim battlefield and face down a lethal behemoth. He appointed Elijah to challenge 850 prophets of Baal and Asherah on the top of Mount Carmel, knowing that if a spectacular and unprecedented miracle did not occur promptly, he would suffer a gruesome death. Jesus invited a dozen ordinary working men to leave their careers and follow him. Before long they were healing people, casting out demons, and preaching before thousands. It's difficult to read very far in the Bible without seeing God do God-sized things through ordinary people. I might add that a cursory study of Church history reveals that there have been many who believed in God's mighty acts through ordinary people, and they, too, saw God accomplish spectacular things through their lives.

So, it is natural to assume Christians today should be experiencing a similar degree of heavenly power. But, sadly, they often do not. Many people today who profess to be Christians and have attended church services all of their lives have never heard God speak.

They have never experienced His power working through them. They cannot point to any experience in their life and exclaim, 'Only God could have done that!'

I eventually came to realize that my father, Henry Blackaby, author of *Experiencing God* and many other books, is unusual. At first, I assumed people like my father were extraordinary, while most Christians were ordinary. Later, I began to wonder if people like my father were normal Christians while all the rest were subordinary. Could it be that God intended for every Christian to hear His voice, know His will, experience His power, and bear much fruit?

I cherish many passages of Scripture, but my favorite is Ephesians 3:20–21: *Now to Him who is able to do exceedingly abundantly above all that we ask or think, according to the power that works in us, to Him be glory in the church by Christ Jesus to all generations, forever and ever. Amen.* I love that the passage begins with 'now.' Not 'in the New Testament.' Not 'in Martin Luther's day.' Not 'during George Whitefield's, Charles Wesley's, or Charles Spurgeon's age.' But *now!* 'To Him who *is* able.' Not *was* able. He *is* able! To do what? To do 'exceedingly abundantly.' The Greek word literally means 'superabundantly.' 'Above all that we ask or think.' I don't know about you, but I can think of a lot! And I have prayed for much. But God can do far more. Why? Because His work is not based on my effort, power, skill, resources, or the size of my church. It is based solely on *His* power. And He has a lot! Why does God work powerfully through us? So, Christ receives the glory due Him in the church before a watching world. God is looking for people who will trust Him to do what only He can do through their life and church.

I have often placed Ephesians 3:20–21 up against my life and ministry and asked, 'Do these verses describe my life?' If what I find in the Bible cannot be found in my life, then something is amiss. Sadly, many Christians witness this inconsistency and assume God's power is not available today. At least, not for ordinary Christians. Churches struggle and decline, yet they assume their challenges are normal for most churches in today's troubled times. But what might happen in the world today if ordinary Christians and average churches stood before the promises of Scripture and refused to accept that they were not intended for them as well? Our world desperately needs to encounter Christians who are living and ministering like first-century Christians.

I am delighted with Francois Carr's latest book, *The Call: Be and become the follower you are meant to be.* I thoroughly enjoy knowing and working with Francois. We have spent many hours discussing what God was teaching us as we traveled together across South Africa and spoke at conferences. We have also ministered together in the United States, the Netherlands, and Israel. I always enjoy my time with Francois, because I am inspired by his thirst to know God more deeply and to experience His power more dynamically. Francois is a zealous student of God's Word. He reads voraciously and has learned from many of the great Christian teachers of our day.

In this book, Francois compiles much of the rich spiritual food he has discovered over the years and presents it in a straightforward, engaging, and inspiring format. He has taught this material all over the world and it always has a profound impact on the audience. Francois has not only been teaching 'the connected life,' he has been living it. As a result, God is using him mightily.

As Francois underscores in his book, the key to a powerful, victorious Christian life is an intimate, growing, vibrant relationship with God. Such a walk with God is not restricted to famous saints and megachurch pastors. Christ invites everyone to come and follow Him. And, if you do, Scripture promises that you will experience God doing exceedingly abundantly more in and through your life than you could possibly have imagined.

Dr. Richard Blackaby
President: Blackaby Ministries International, Atlanta, Ga., USA
Co-author: *Experiencing God, Spiritual Leadership, Fresh Encounter.*

Note from the Author

Welcome to *The Call*.

Thank you for taking the time to pick up this book. I trust that you will enjoy reading it. The book that you are holding in your hands is part of my journey, some lessons learned, and insights gained on my walk with the Lord so far. And the journey continues as the Lord continues to teach me more about Himself. I believe that we are works in progress, on a quest to become the persons or followers of Jesus Christ that we are meant to be.

This book began as a series of talks at the Reconnect Retreat for Spiritual Leaders and Pastors in South Carolina several years ago. I was asked to share some thoughts from my book on quiet time, and how to have and enjoy meaningful quiet time. I initially thought to use some sermons and notes from my preaching arsenal. But at that particular time, I couldn't shake off the thought that I needed to do something new. Thinking about the invitation, I started to pray and fast for several days while I waited upon the Lord. I wanted God to speak to me and to the pastors in a new and fresh way. It was in that time that God led me to Mark 3:13–15:

> And He went up on the mountain and called to Him those He Himself wanted. And they came to Him. Then He appointed twelve, that they might be with Him and that He might send them out to preach, and to have power to heal sicknesses and to cast out demons.

So, I reflected on the reasons why Jesus called those Twelve into ministry. He wanted them to preach, do works of mercy and cast out demons. However, at first He did not call them to be preachers; He called them to be 'with Him.' Their lives and ministry had to flow out of their fellowship with Him. During the first three years of Jesus' ministry, the disciples simply traveled with Him. He did send them out to do some evangelistic work but that was not the main purpose of their time with Jesus. The main purpose was to get to know Him more intimately and to learn from Him.

Interestingly enough, the more they got to know Jesus, the more they got to know themselves and who they were in Christ. This resulted in their being changed and transformed.

The same is true and applies to us today. As I looked at that passage, it was as if God allowed me to see the process of transformation and the cycle of discipleship that Jesus followed with His disciples. The process of transformation consists of three main parts:

- Part One—the call to be with Jesus;
- Part Two—the call to be changed and transformed by Him;
- Part Three—the call to go out on His behalf.

In the cycle of discipleship, the disciples learned about the importance of being with Jesus, hearing Him speak, understanding His intentions, receiving His empowerment, understanding His concern, accomplishing His purposes, and receiving God's gift of rest. During this process they were also changed from mere converts of Jesus to being followers, workers and leaders. I presented some of those thoughts which God placed in my heart in the *Connecting with God* series at the retreats. Since then it has developed into *Connected—The Jesus Way*,[1] a 'disciple-based process' designed to equip and empower believers and churches to live and act like Jesus, become workers and leaders of influence who in turn transform their immediate environment.

In this book, *The Call*, we will cover some of those 'transformational moments' with Jesus and look at how those events affected the disciples and their impact on our lives today. Together we will discover how God uses encounters with old truths to generate a change in people's perspective of who He is, bringing about a change in their perspective of who they are, and what they can become with Jesus at the center of their lives. *Christianity is not about what we know about God but how what we know about God transforms us into His likeness.*

God has a purpose and a plan for your life.
That's right.

He wants you to see the potential of 'what you can be or become.' But we must be connected to His purpose and plan. God is still calling. He wants us to join Him today and experience Him like never before.

I should caution you here, though. If you respond to *God's Call* and *connect with His plan and purpose* for your life, you will undergo a life transformation, just as my life was transformed, and the lives of many others who chose to respond to God's call.

God has used many people over the years to shape my life. Some of them have already passed on to be with the Lord, while others are still alive and are having a continued impact on my life. I am deeply indebted to all of them for the example they set me and for every conversation and encounter that has helped me to become the person I am today. I am also thankful for all the quality resources,[2] books, commentaries and excellent teachings that have shaped my life and guided my thoughts as I write about this journey. Throughout *The Call* I will allude to some of these contributions that have become a part of my everyday life, message and mission. I am especially grateful to all the people whom God uniquely placed in my life to help me follow God's will and agenda for my life. I have received them as if I have received the Lord Himself. Did Jesus not say ...

> Most assuredly, I say to you, he who receives whomever I send receives Me; and he who receives Me receives Him who sent Me. (John 13:20)

It was not my desire to write one more book to add to the millions of books full of wonderful thoughts and ideas that already fill the shelves of bookstores. Although *The Call* is by no means a complete, detailed discussion on the topic, my desire, in writing this book, is to share some of my thoughts, a few truths and principles gleaned from my devotions that shaped my life and ministry. Looking back on my life, I celebrate those truths and encounters that have allowed me to gain a new perspective of God, and to develop a new perspective of myself, which helped me to rediscover the joy of fellowship with Him.

The Call consists of an introduction and eight chapters that take you on a journey through realizing your need to connect your life with God's Call and Cause. What would it be like to be at the feet of Jesus, listening, watching and learning more about His life, relationships, ministry and kingdom? What will happen if we follow Him wherever He leads and commissions us to go? In *The Call* we take a closer look at Jesus, the twelve disciples, and how they relate to our life. Here's a road map for *The Call*.

The Call: Introduction. I share how the Lord has called us into ministry and how two specific encounters with God, to know Jesus and be known by Him, and to follow His method, strategy and example, laid the foundation for me to write this book.

Chapter 1. The Cause: *Continue With What Jesus Started.* We take a look at Jesus' favorite mountain, the Great Commission and think back along with the disciples to where it had all begun before it spread throughout the world.

Chapter 2. The Connection: *To Be with Him Before we Work for Him.* We determine life's priorities, explore how Jesus stayed connected with His Father in the midst of a busy schedule and our call to be with Him. We also discuss four enemies of intimacy you should be aware of.

Chapter 3. The Communication: *To Hear Him Speak.* We establish that it is more important to listen to God than to speak to God. We elaborate on Why is God speaking? When does He speak? Why do so many struggle to hear Him speak? How does He speak to us? and How can I hear His voice?

Chapter 4. The Change: *To Understand and Realize His Intention.* God's purpose is to change and transform us and use us to accomplish His purposes. We take a look at the why, what and how God is doing in our following Jesus and becoming fishers of men.

Chapter 5. The Commission: *To Receive His Enabling and Empowerment.* We are called to 'go' and in this chapter we explore why we are sent out, what we have to do, where we need to go, when and how we do that. We share some powerful principles that will help and empower you to make a difference in your environment.

Chapter 6. The Commitment: *His Concern, Our Response and Obedience.* By the time you get to this chapter you will have the tools for a life connected to God's Call and Cause. However, in facing a crisis of belief, you will have to make the decision to obey. We also look at some enemies that you will face to prevent you from reaching your full potential.

Chapter 7. The Completion: *To Accomplish His Purposes.* We encourage you in this chapter to take some time out to behold and process following a season of ministry or encountering a truth from God's Word. We share some practical thoughts on when to do it, why to do it and how to do it.

Chapter 8. The Celebration: *To Rest and Be Refreshed.* We learn the importance of taking a break and practicing a rhythm of life.

The Conclusion: *An Invitation.* Jesus had called the disciples to be with Him, equipped and changed them and gave them all they needed to accomplish their mission. Then He invited and commissioned them to go, make disciples, baptize and teach them. We explain what it means to become a man or a woman on the move.

The Journey Begins

I am humbled that the Lord has encouraged me to share my heart, mind and prayers with you as you might find these writings valuable in your own walk with Him. I accept full responsibility for any shortcomings or weaknesses in this devotional book, but I am praying, however, that in what any of us render to God in sincerity, He finds something acceptable to use for His glory.

I am grateful that you have chosen to read this book, and I am confident that, as you read and allow God to speak to you, you will experience Him in a new and fresh way, your walk with Him will be refreshed as you rediscover the joy of fellowship with the things you already know, and so often take for granted. This could be more than the beginning of a book. It just might be the beginning of a changed and transformed life—a life connected to God's call and purpose. May God use it to help you change the world around you … to praise and glorify Him. This is my prayer and my heart's desire. May it be so!

This will be written for the generation to come,
that a people yet to be created may praise the
Lord. (Psalm 102:18)

PART ONE
Being with Jesus

The CALL

Introduction

You did not choose Me, but I chose you and appointed you that you should go and bear fruit, and that your fruit should remain, that whatever you ask the Father in My name He may give you. (John 15:16)

"Follow me" is the substance of the call in the power of which Jesus makes people his saints ... We may say, therefore, that in practise the command to follow Jesus is identical with the command to believe in Him. (Karl Barth)[1]

Our lives changed forever in 1999 when, on 30 June, I resigned from my role as Personnel Officer in the South African Defence Force in Pretoria, South Africa. My job, attached to the rank of Lieutenant Colonel, provided a good income and a secure future for our family but we were sure that God had called us to leave our secular jobs. My wife Dorothea and I had taken the major step of faith to leave behind a life filled with certainty and familiarity to believe in God and accept the call to follow Him.

Prior to my resignation from regular full-time employment, I used my evenings and weekends to plan and arrange revival meetings and evangelistic outreaches, and to complete my theological studies. The Lord helped us during those busy days and times of full-time work, studies and part-time involvement in the ministry. However, we knew that God was preparing us for a new season in our lives. We understood that God wanted us in full-time ministry. We accepted the call and responded by saying yes to His invitation to join Him and fulfil His purposes. One evening, shortly after I had resigned from my role, the Lord directed me to read from the book of Isaiah. The words of the prophet spoke to my heart:

Enlarge the place of your tent, and let them stretch out the curtains of your dwellings; do not spare. Lengthen your cords, and strengthen your stakes. For you shall expand to the right and to the left, and your descendants will inherit the nations and make the desolate cities inhabited. (Isaiah 54:2–3)

God was about to enlarge our borders. He was about to change our lives, routines, habits, thinking and even our view of Him. He was about to bring in people and opportunities, and open new doors in our lives. He was about to s-t-r-e-t-c-h us. When God tells you to *enlarge the place of your tent ... stretch out the curtains of your dwelling* and to *lengthen your cords* it means lengthen your reach. Wider tents require longer cords to keep them securely held in place. Once we lengthen our cords, we must also *strengthen our stakes*, and drive them deeper into the bedrock of God's Word and Truth.

If we are rooted in Him, we will be 'like a tree planted by the rivers of water, that brings forth its fruit in its season, whose leaf also shall not wither; and whatever he does shall prosper' (Psalm 1:3). We shall be like a tree—not a mere annual plant—with steady, progressive growth and increasing fruitfulness. Planted by the rivers of water, we shall drink from His deep and hidden sources and bear fruit. The wider the branches spread and the higher the tree grows, the deeper the roots must grow.

But be aware there is a difference between work and fruit. *Work is the outcome of effort, and fruit is the outcome of the way you live.* A bad person can do good work, but a bad tree cannot bear good fruit. We believe that God has chosen and appointed us to bear fruit (John 15:16). He is going to stretch us as we grow in becoming what He has in mind for us to be useful and fruitful in the ministry He will initiate. At the time my heart was filled with excitement, knowing that God was directing our lives on a new course.

Traveling with Jesus

The Lord strongly impressed on my heart to look at the life and ministry of Jesus, to recognize that during His time of ministry Jesus *went about all the cities and villages,* traveling from place to place (Matthew 9:35). I sensed that God wanted me ... just like Jesus ... to travel from place to place, to preach and teach in towns and cities in South Africa, and to go beyond these borders to other nations and countries. To me traveling was a foreign concept. I grew up in a small rural town and had never thought of or even cared much about traveling. Nor was I accustomed to being away from home for long periods of time, let alone being abroad.

Doors began to open for us to minister and expand to the east and to the west. The very next day after the Lord had given me the word about traveling to cities and villages, I received a phone call from a pastor inviting me to preach at his church in the state of Tennessee in the United States of America. Since then, I have crossed the Atlantic more than 40 times to teach and preach in North America. I have traveled many times to African nations, to Britain, Europe, the Middle East, Australia and New Zealand to speak and teach about prayer and revival. I have led more than 60 groups of Christian pilgrims, who walked in the footsteps of Jesus in Israel and other biblical countries, over the years. I have flown by airplane, and driven hundreds of thousands of kilometers along the roads of South Africa. God has been kind and gracious in blessing our ministry as people responded to the burden on us and our message, which He has given us to take out there.

I believe these open doors, expansions and growth were because of God's call upon our lives. God took the initiative. God did it. But God had to take us on mission with Him and put us through the *expanding*, the *stretching,* the *lengthening* and the *strengthening* of our faith and *trust* in Him. We surely felt the pressure and stress of it, and at times were afraid but we always found Him faithful. We stepped out by faith, without a fixed income or a promise from someone to help or provide for us. Looking back, we can truly say: 'Blessed be the Lord who daily loads us with benefits, the God of our salvation' (Psalm 68:20). By God's provision and grace, we have witnessed many miracles and I can honestly say that God has provided according to our every need as a family and that He has even spoiled us with special experiences, creating beautiful memories, throughout the journey. God has been kind to us as a family as He touched and used our lives in ways that we never could have dreamed possible.

It has been an incredible journey full of amazing, life-changing encounters with God. From the very beginning of my ministry, God has used my avid reading of the writings of Christian literature, which include biographies, revival accounts and more, to cause a stirring in my heart. It created within me a deep longing to really 'know' Him, grow closer to Him and to see Him work through me in revival.

Being Shaped for a Purpose

My life was deeply impacted by the friendship and mentoring of the Christian leaders who became companions on my Christian journey, those who have passed on and those still with us. God has used them directly or indirectly to impart values, principles and skills that have uniquely equipped and empowered me. None of us comes fully equipped to excel in life or ministry. The wisdom, experience, vision, example and direction of those who go before us can put us well ahead of where you and I would be if we were on our own. Not all of us are meant to be great but all of us have the potential to make a significant investment in the lives of others. I am thankful for those who have invested in me.

My life has moreover been shaped by touches of revival through my ministry when seeing how God works personally in the lives of His people. Those encounters have changed my perspective of ministry. It has had a major impact on me and changed my perspective and my life. It has become the 'front burner' of my heart, where God, yet again spoiling me, filled me with knowing that there is so much more that He can and wants to do in and through our lives and our churches (Ephesians 3:20).

How sad it would have been if I had not heard His call, perhaps misunderstood what He had said, or been unwilling to respond to Him? My life is so much richer because of that call. I remember two specific encounters with God that laid the foundation for the writing of this book.

To Know Jesus and Be Known By Him

First, several years ago, I had an experience that is still as fresh in my mind and heart as if it had happened this morning. I was listening to Dr. Henry Blackaby, well-known author of the *Experiencing God* materials, as He preached a message on the life of Jesus Christ. He explained that God's purpose for us is to be conformed to the image of His Son. He said that Christlikeness is the Father's personal and ultimate goal for us. In other words, God is seeking to develop the life and character of Jesus Christ in each of us. Not just in some of us but in all of us. Even me. The passage in Scripture that Dr. Blackaby quoted was from the letter of Paul to the Romans:

> For whom He foreknew, He also predestined to be conformed to the image of His son. (Romans 8:29)

Listening to the sermon, God reminded me of the words that Jesus spoke to His disciples when they were together for the last time. He said to them:

> If you abide in Me, and My words abide in you, you will ask what you desire, and it shall be done for you. (John 15:7)

Reflecting on these two passages of Scripture, the Holy Spirit spoke to me about the level of my own relationship and my walk with God. I realized that I was not as close to and intimate with Him as I thought I was. The Holy Spirit asked me:

- Do you look, act and speak like Jesus?
- Is there anything in your life that hinders God or prevents Him transforming your life into His likeness?
- What role does His words and Scripture play in your life?
- How does your abiding in Him or lack thereof affect your prayer life?

I realized that *the quality of my relationship with God will determine what God can do in me and through me.* My walk with God, the depth and character of my walk, or my not walking with Him, determined my assignments. God used that encounter to create discontent within my heart about my walk with Him and at the same time awakened an interest in studying the life and ministry of Jesus Christ, who is the author and finisher of our faith. If it is God's goal to change and transform me into the image of His Son, I need to take a closer look at and study the life of Jesus, consider and compare myself to Him (Hebrews 3:1–3). In doing so, we must lay aside every weight, and the sin that so easily ensnares us, and allow God to remove all things which are not Christlike. We are challenged in Hebrews 12:1–3 to do so:

> Therefore we also, since we are surrounded by so great a cloud of witnesses, *let us lay aside every weight, and the sin which so easily ensnares us,* and let us run with endurance the race that is set before us, *looking unto Jesus,* the author and finisher of our faith, who for the joy that was set before Him endured the cross … For *consider* Him … lest you become weary and discouraged in your souls.

Eugene Peterson, in his contemporary English version of the Bible, *The Message,* captures it in this way:

> Do you see what this means—all these pioneers who blazed the way, all these veterans cheering us on? It means we'd better get on with it. Strip down, start running—and never quit! No extra spiritual fat, no parasitic sins. Keep your eyes on *Jesus,* who both began and finished this race we're in. Study how he did it. Because he never lost sight of where he was headed—that exhilarating finish in and with God— he could put up with anything along the way: Cross, shame, whatever. And now he's *there,* in the place of honor, right alongside God. When you find yourselves flagging in your faith, go over that story again, item by item, that long litany of hostility he plowed through. *That* will shoot adrenaline into your souls! (*MSG*)

I want Jesus to be my all and be all for Him that I am meant to be. So, the words of the Apostle Paul to the church in Philippi became the focus of my heart and the determined purpose of my life:

> And this, so that I may know Him [experientially, becoming more thoroughly acquainted with Him,

7

understanding the remarkable wonders of His Person more completely] and [in that same way experience] the power of His resurrection [which overflows and is active in believers], and [that I may share] the fellowship of His sufferings, by being continually conformed [inwardly into His likeness even] to His death [dying as He did]; determined purpose to know Him, and become more deeply and intimately acquainted with Him, perceiving, and recognizing and understanding the wonders of His person more strongly and more clearly, and that I may be continually transformed into His likeness. (Philippians 3:10 *AMP*)

Not that I have achieved this, but it has become my determined purpose and goal as a follower of the Lord Jesus. I want to finish my race and the work that Jesus has given me.[2] I want to know Him … progressively become more deeply … and intimately acquainted with Him … perceiving … recognizing … understanding … while being continually transformed … experience His resurrection power and be His junior partner in my calling. I can only agree with Paul, press on toward the goal.

Not that I have already attained, or am already perfect; but I press on, that I may lay hold of that for which Chris Jesus has also laid hold of me. I press toward the goal for the prize of the upward call of God in Christ Jesus. (Philippians 3:12, 14)

God dramatically shifted my paradigm. His desire for me was to know Jesus and become more intimately acquainted with Him, to perceive, and to recognize the wonders of His person so that I may continually be transformed into His likeness.

That's true for you too.

Looking unto Jesus, considering Him and laying aside the weights and sin that so easily ensnares us is the key to becoming like Him.

In reading through the Gospels, I gave special attention to the 'red letters' in my Bible, which highlight the words spoken by Jesus. Since then, I have learned more about His words, example, relationships, conduct and character, conversations, teachings, preaching, and ministry. I took a special interest in His prayer life, relationship with His Father, love for the Word, obedience and character traits. In a casual reading of the Gospels and the red letters, a few things became clear to me:

- Jesus only spoke what He had heard from His Father.
- He only taught what the Father told Him to teach.
- He only did those things that His Father told Him to do.
- He only did what the Father showed Him to do.
- Jesus obeyed the Father in every area of His life.[3]

Then Jesus answered and said to them, "Most assuredly, I say to you, the Son can do nothing of Himself, *but what He sees, the Father do*; for whatever He does, the *Son also does in like manner.*" (John 5:19)

Then Jesus said to them, "When you lift up the Son of Man, then you will know that I am He, and that I do nothing of Myself; *but as My Father taught Me, I speak these things.* (John 8:28. See also John 12:48–50)

Can we honestly say that we only say and do those things that we have heard from the Lord or seen the Lord do? Can we honestly say that we obey the Lord in every area of our lives? I could not say that with a clear conscience, but I wanted to. We cannot truly expect to have the same impact and ministry that Jesus had and ignore the principles that directed and guided His earthly life and ministry. Many Christians try to live a good life while ignoring the way Jesus lived and ministered. Robert E. Coleman, in his book *The Mind of The Master*, says that Jesus presents Himself as the object of our faith and the pattern of our life.[4] His life is the illustration of what He wants all of us to be and become. I remember thinking: if I want to become a mature Christian, excel as a Christian leader, or be more like Jesus, I need to know Jesus Christ more intimately and be known by Him. In the life of Jesus I discovered a *pattern* in how we could and should live our lives and follow in His footsteps.

For to this you [*and I*] were called, because Christ also suffered for us, leaving us an example that you [*and I*] should follow His steps. (1 Peter 2:21)

That became my goal.
It should be yours too.

To Follow His Method, Strategy and Example

During this period in my life one of my preaching engagements was cancelled, and I ended up spending a full day reading, reflecting and praying in a coffee shop in Aiken, South Carolina. My extensive travel and other ministry-related opportunities and responsibilities had been keeping me very busy. Although I was sad about the cancellation of the meetings, I was also happy that I was able to catch my breath and enjoy a brief time of relief from a busy schedule. It gave me some time to think and to record my thoughts.

I have learned over the years that God plans the route and the course of our lives and that He purposefully allows certain things to happen in our lives.[5] Moses was minding the flock of his father-in-law when God spoke to him through a burning bush (Exodus 3:2–4). It was only when he turned away from his planned course of action, stopped to see what was happening and paid attention, that he heard the voice of God calling out to him. God had to disrupt Moses' normal, everyday routine to get his undivided attention.

This break in my schedule gave me some time of quiet for much-needed reflection and paying attention to what God was doing in my life. I was able to look at my life, my ministry in general and the church in particular. I saw things I didn't have the time to see before—because of 'busyness' or simply because I did not pay attention—to listen to God and think about what I was hearing.

God uses different means and ways to get our attention. He used the cancellation of my program to speak to me. He, right there in the coffee shop, told me the greatest need of the world today is a mighty manifestation of the Holy Spirit in revival power.

Revival Is The Need Of The Hour

Revival occurs when God sweeps through a region in great power and His people return to Him. This usually occurs when the church has become a weak minority. As I explained in my book *Revival! The Glory of God,* it is when individuals and churches find themselves caught in a 'low tide' and return to God that they are restored from recklessness, ineffectiveness and a state of spiritual decline.[6] Real and true revival always results in a new consciousness of God's presence and His holiness, a deep conviction of our own sinfulness, which leads to repentance and a changed life, as well as a hunger for God's Word and to pray. However, revival almost always brings a deep concern for and about others that would spill over into blessing of the millions who were without Christ, resulting in hundreds of thousands of lost, alienated, hopeless people being brought to Jesus. This is revival: when large numbers of people come alive to God. It occurs again and again in the Old Testament. Sadly, the effects of these revivals and awakenings often decline again.

In my book, I explained that it usually happens when sin creeps in or is allowed; if disunity, strife or indifference come into churches and amongst people; or when prayer does not play a central role anymore. Tragically, these revivals and awakenings usually fail to root out the perversities in society, and soon subside with the death or compromise of the revival leaders. However, in reflecting on the life and ministry of Jesus, I realized that another reason for the decline or fading of revivals is the failure to grow spiritually mature Christians who become effective laborers in the harvest (Matthew 9:37–38), 'which is engaged in winning the lost and building up the saved in obedience to the Great Commission' (Matthew 28:18–20).

The ministry of Jesus begins with His participation in the emerging revival of John the Baptist—the greatest religious awakening Israel had known in over 400 years. There Jesus was baptized and identified by the prophet as 'the Lamb of God, who takes away the sin of the world' (John 1:29, 36). With this introduction, Jesus could immediately enlist the following of John

11

the Baptist, who was willing to step aside so that Jesus could take over. He could easily have recruited the disciples of John and the thousands of people coming from Jerusalem and the land of Judea (Mark 1:5). He could easily have gathered a mighty army, started a movement, conquered the Romans, and taken the world by storm. However, He walked away. It strikes me as odd that Jesus walked away from an atmosphere of revival at the Jordan River.

A New Way of Living and Ministering

Jesus was led away by the Spirit into the wilderness (Luke 4:1). He was no longer actively involved in John's ministry and revival. He did not seek the following of the masses. He moved His home base from Nazareth to Capernaum (Matthew 4:12–17). He filled the vacuum in the leadership left by John the Baptist. He began to preach about God's kingdom. He called disciples to follow Him. He concentrated His attention upon a few men destined to reach out to and change the world through imparting His way of life and ministry to others. He traveled from place to place with His team.

A new way of living and a new way of ministering.
His life was controlled and directed by the Holy Spirit.
And so should ours.

When Paul arrived back in Ephesus, he met twelve men who professed to be Christian 'disciples.' Paul was able to witness in the synagogue for three months (Acts 19:1–10). However, hardness of heart had set in, so he left the synagogue and moved his ministry to a schoolroom, taking his disciples with him (Acts 19:8–9). Paul ministered in this way for about two years and 'so that all who dwelt in Asia heard the word of the Lord Jesus, both Jews and Greeks' (Acts 19:10). What a great, glorious and victorious ministry! Everybody knew what Paul was saying and doing. Fear fell upon them (Acts 19:17–20). Even his enemies had to admit that the Word was spreading, and people were being saved (Acts 19:26). There seems to be two main reasons for that: the witness of the believers as they went from place to place, and the 'special miracles' that God enabled Paul to perform in Ephesus (Acts 19:11).

Revival broke out in Ephesus. It is important to remember that Ephesus was the center of the occult and Paul was demonstrating God's power right in the midst of all the difficulties and persecution. God can do so much more than we can even think or pray about (Ephesians 3:10).

Why is it that we don't experience more of God in our lives and His working through our lives and churches? Could it be that hardness of heart is the reason (Hebrews 3:7)? It seems to me that our lives and churches are filled with programs, projects and the latest quick-fixes. We hope that it will bring the necessary growth and change but it is never as effective as we anticipated it to be. It does not take much to see that the church is struggling and that it is in serious trouble. If we look at history, it is fascinating to see that the early church flourished in difficult and dark times. The wickedness, apathy or darkness of the world surrounding the church are not the factors that determine the condition of the church—they only expose the true condition of the church. *The church will remain an effective and relevant entity, amidst a wicked and ungodly generation, if the church is unwavering in its devotion to God's truth and light.*

What a lesson for all of us to learn!

So, what is the problem?

The Forgotten Jesus Model

The problem is that the church has forgotten its intended purpose—to glorify God in making, training and equipping followers of Jesus Christ, who will in return invest in the lives of other people, who will then do the same (2 Timothy 2:1–2). Revival of the church and the Great Commission of Jesus Christ are two of the most important concerns of the day. What is the key to accomplishing these two great challenges that we face? I believe it is to accept the call to be and become the followers and laborers in the harvest that we are meant to be.

Jesus walked away from an atmosphere of revival to prepare His disciples to become instruments of peace, laborers in the harvest

13

that led to the revival in Jerusalem and Samaria, and then world evangelization. Paul walked away from preaching in the synagogue to teach and train his disciples to reach the whole of Asia (Acts 19:10) and laid the foundation for the revival in Ephesus (vv. 11–20). The methods Jesus and Paul used give us an example … of what every believer can and should do. Too often we relegate His work and His call to various organized programs and human effort. His work and call should direct the daily lives of all of us. It is a lifestyle—the way that He directed His life while He was among us—and now commands us to follow.

Jesus did not separate revival and discipleship, or discipleship and revival. Jesus followed a specific plan, method and strategy to train and develop His followers. He was led by the Spirit to walk away from revival into the wilderness because He was following the method and strategy of His Father. I want to call it the 'forgotten Jesus model.' The forgotten Jesus model is actually the 'forgotten Father's model.'

As I mentioned before, revival is still the front burner of my heart but since these two encounters with God's truth, I have become fascinated with how Jesus, and later on Paul, took 12 ordinary men and shaped them into greatness. We are not here by accident … you and I are here to accomplish the job that God has assigned to us from eternity past. The result of Jesus' example and obedience was that His Father brought eternal salvation to the human race. The result of Paul's example and obedience was that the Father took the good news of the Gospel into Asia Minor and Europe. As we, God's people, are obedient in responding to the call … God's call on our lives to make our lives available, He will also work through us to accomplish His purposes. *If we settle for less than God's best in our lives, we, our families, the church and the world will lose our contribution, and we will miss the excitement and exhilaration of reaching our full potential.*

The more I seek to be with Him and be like Him, the more I will know about Him—His love for me and His good plans and desires for me. Plus, the more intimate I become with God, the better I understand His ways, and this understanding leads to a deeper longing to know Him better. The more we get to understand His ways and plans for our lives and churches, the more we will be in step with Him.

We will be most effective and successful in reaching our full potential if we follow the method and strategy that Jesus Christ modeled.

The forgotten Jesus model!
The Father's model!

Let us begin where God has planted us … never settle for less than His best, believe in Him and accept the call to adjust our lives and follow Him. You'll be astonished at how much more God can and wants to do in and through your life or mine.

There is no limit to what God can do if He can find a man or woman whose heart and life is wholly yielded to Him.

He is calling. He is waiting …
He wants you and me to continue with what Jesus started.
We have a decision to make.
I have decided to follow Jesus. I have made my choice.
Why don't you join the Cause?
What is *your* choice?

1

The CAUSE

To continue with what Jesus started

Then the eleven disciples went away into Galilee, to the mountain which Jesus had appointed for them. (Matthew 28:16)

For I determined not to know anything among you except Jesus Christ and Him crucified. (1 Corinthians 2:2)

In November 1995 I traveled to Israel for the first time. Israel is a small country in the middle of the desert but, oh, was I surprised at all that Israel had to offer. Although Israel is a top tourist destination for many people all over the world, it is not its tourist sites that Israel is most accredited for. The one thing that makes Israel so special is its spiritual heritage. It is known as the Holy Land. My life was touched and changed forever during my first visit to Israel. As we visited the biblical sites throughout Israel, I could picture myself as one of the many followers of Jesus. The Scriptures that relate to the many sites came alive in my heart and mind.

In addition to the amazing experiences I had, my quiet time was also forever changed. Before, as I read the Scriptures, pictures of places, their smells and my knowledge of some of the cultural traditions that the Bible spoke of came to life in my mind. But a whole new dimension was added to my spiritual life during that first visit to Israel. Imagine following Jesus, along the dirt roads of Galilee, as He traveled between small villages.

I wish that I could travel back in time to Jesus' day and hear His words, listen to His conversations with the disciples, learn truths from the lessons He taught and watch Him as He related to all kinds of people. What would it feel like to be at the feet of Rabbi Jesus, sensing his power and learning at first hand about his kingdom? Ann Spangler and Lois Tverberg, in their book *Sitting at the Feet of Rabbi Jesus,* explain that we will enrich our understanding of the Bible and of Jesus when we immerse ourselves in the culture, customs, prayers, and feasts of the first-century Jews.[1] The Bible was written by Orientals. It is easy for us to overlook the fact that the Scriptures had their origins in the East, and that each writer was actually an Oriental.[2]

After my first trip to Israel, I felt as if I had shared in something sacred, as if God had met me at those sites and places linked with the past. I returned home from Israel with my faith in Jesus deepened but hungry for more. I wanted to know more about biblical archaeology, Bible-related backgrounds, oriental living and to know Jesus as His first disciples knew him. I began to explore the world of Jesus with a desire to grow and deepen my faith in Him.

Since then, I have had the privilege to lead more than 60 groups of people to the biblical lands. I enjoyed watching the people, all the while realizing that the Bible's stories are set in real time in the past and real places today. As they learn more about the land, the people, and the culture of the Bible, believers often say, 'I will never read the Bible the same way again.' Some even say, 'I read the Bible in 3D. I can actually see the places that I am reading about.' Every visit to Israel (and Egypt, Jordan, Greece and Turkey) has become a heart-engaging pilgrimage of walking in His (and the apostles') footsteps and learning from Him.

Jesus' Mountain

When speaking to people who have traveled to Israel, everyone is in agreement that Galilee was one of the highlights of their visit. This fascination with Galilee is not just because of the natural beauty of the lake and the surrounding upper and lower Galilee. This is a place that has mostly stayed untouched, and we can be sure that Jesus saw the same lake and the same mountains during His life that any visitor sees today. It is easy to imagine how scenes from the Gospels unfolded in these areas. Jesus would have taken most of the well-known routes stretching between towns in the Galilee area, as He spent a good amount of time in the parts surrounding the Sea of Galilee.

The Galilee area also had special significance in Jesus' life. Jesus grew up and began His public ministry in Nazareth, in the Lower Galilee. It was a small village of between 100 and 200 people. He was baptized by John (Matthew 3:13–7) in the Jordan River, 8 miles from Jericho, and after His baptism He was led by God's Spirit into the wilderness, where He spent 40 days in prayer, while He fasted and resisted the temptations of the devil (Luke 4:1–2). From the desert, Jesus returned to Galilee (Luke 4:14–15). He left Nazareth and lived in Capernaum (Matthew 4:13; 9:1). It is in Capernaum that Jesus began His 'Galilee ministry,' which lasted for three years. However, His life and ministry were not confined to His base in Capernaum. Although most of His miracles were performed around Chorazin, Bethsaida and Capernaum, His ministry and influence spread far beyond those places. He traveled to all the cities and villages in Galilee (Matthew 9:35; 11:1) and later on sent out His disciples 'to every town and place where He was about to go' (Luke 10:1). He had an itinerant ministry.

Jesus loved mountains. He often visited them.

There are lots of hills and mountains around northern Galilee. When Jesus looked to the north, He would have seen Mount Hermon about 70 miles away, which today borders Israel with Syria and Lebanon. Mount Hermon is also the highest peak in modern Israel, which rises 9,230 ft. above sea level. When Jesus looked across the lake, He would have seen the Golan Heights which borders Syria and Jordan, as well as Mount Arbel.

Mount Arbel has a sheer rock cliff in the northwest corner of the Sea of Galilee that is recognizable from any spot on the lake. Rising about 1,300 ft. above the water, Mount Arbel stands sentinel over the northern shore. The single most significant benefit of being on top of Mount Arbel is that you can easily see the places where Jesus spent most of His time, life and ministry: Migdal,

Tabgha, the Mount of the Beatitudes, Capernaum and other sites along the shore. You can also see the *Via Maris* (Way of the Sea), the popular trade route in Jesus' day that ran through Galilee and led travelers to the most powerful nations in the Middle East.

It was upon a mountain that He uttered the ethic of His Kingdom. It was on a mountain that He perfected His manhood in transfiguration glory. It was on a mountain that He uttered great prophecies. It was on a mountain that He wept over the doomed city He was about to reject. It was on a mountain that He gathered His disciples in Galilee, where He was about to utter three things: His claim, His commands, and His final declaration.

My favorite place is the little hill on the slope toward Capernaum on the Mount of the Beatitudes. Standing there, you can see what Jesus must have seen as He looked at the Sea of Galilee—the spot where He caught the fish and where He walked on the water. It is walking distance from Capernaum, which was the home base of Jesus' ministry. I believe it was also His favorite place. It was the desolate place mentioned in Scripture that Jesus regularly used to go to.

When Jesus became better known, and as He was popular, crowds of people were always thronging to see Him, wanting to touch Him, which was why He would often withdraw Himself to His *favorite* place.

> However, the report went around concerning Him all the more; and great multitudes came together to hear, and to be healed by Him of their infirmities. So He Himself often withdrew into the wilderness and prayed. (Luke 5:15–17)

When He became tired and needed His strength to be restored and refreshed, He would depart for His favorite place.

> Now in the morning, having risen a long while before daylight, He went out and departed to a solitary place; and there He prayed. (Mark 1:35)

When He needed to prepare Himself for the next day or just needed some direction and guidance from His Father, He would go to His favorite place, the mountains, to pray.

> Now it came to pass in those days that He went out to the mountains to pray and continued all night in prayer to God. (Luke 6:12)

It is also the place where He chose His disciples and where He taught 'Kingdom principles,' what we know today as the 'Sermon on the Mount,' which was delivered on the ridge at the back of the Mount of the Beatitudes.

> And seeing the multitudes, He went up on a mountain, and when He was seated His disciples came to Him. (Matthew 5:1)

What made this place so special to Him? This was His go-to place when He wanted to be alone. It was also the place where Jesus met with His Father. It was the place where His Father taught Him what to say and showed Him what to do (John 5:19; 8:28). That time alone with His Father was vital to His life and work. It was in these intimate moments that He was revived and restored. It was also during these times of solitude and quietness that wisdom and guidance were imparted to His heart. It became the source and secret of His spiritual power. This was the place where He received the courage and strength to complete His assignments and fulfil His mission. It was a place of rest.

Throughout the Gospels, we see that prayer and time alone with the Father structured Jesus's life. It was His habit to slip away into solitude, when He could pray. *When He disappeared, and they started looking for Him, they knew exactly where to find Him* (Mark 1:35). They would find Him at His favorite place: in the presence of His Father (Luke 22:39).

Even after His resurrection, having been with the disciples for almost 40 days, He summoned them to go and wait for Him on the mountain which He had selected for them to go to.

> Then the eleven disciples went away into Galilee, to the mountain which Jesus had appointed for them. (Matthew 28:16)

Which mountain is that? The Bible does not say which mountain. But they knew which mountain He was speaking about.
They knew exactly where they needed to go.

They would go to His *favorite place,* the mountain, where He met with His Father. The mountain with no name ... Jesus' mountain.

A Landmark Speech

On 12 September 1962 President John F. Kennedy delivered a landmark speech at Rice University in Houston, during which he reminded his listeners about the American goal to land a man on the moon and return him safely. Here's part of what he said:

> We choose to go to the moon. We choose to go to the moon in this decade and do the other things, not because they are easy, but because they are hard—because that goal will serve to organize and measure the best of our energies and skills, because that challenge is one that we are willing to accept, one we are unwilling to postpone, and one which we intend to win. It is for these reasons that I regard the decision last year to shift our efforts in space from low to high gear as among the most important decisions that will be made during the incumbency in the office of the Presidency.[3]

The decision to go to the moon required enormous commitment, time, sacrifice, hard work and courage. At its peak, the Apollo program employed thousands of people and relied on the support of many industrial firms. It cost the U.S. government more than $25.4 billion to land the first astronauts on the moon. On 20 July 1969 the task was completed when Neil Armstrong stepped off the lunar lander and announced, 'That's one small step for man ... one giant leap for mankind.'[4]

The mission motivated a nation to accomplish something that is still seen as a phenomenon today. The right mission can inspire people in amazing ways and motivate them to go above and beyond in completing whatever tasks they receive. President Kennedy's mission sparked the imagination and the perspiration of an entire nation.[5] Since then, America has returned to the moon several more times, and other countries have also been able to send teams to the moon, landing on it successfully. America saw the possibility of accomplishing the unthinkable, and they accepted the mission. They successfully finished what they had started. Jesus also wanted the Twelve, and us, to continue and finish what He had started.

- Jesus called His disciples to that 'special mountain' by prior appointment.
- He was going to set before them a vision of His power and authority.
- He was going to set before them a vision of His plan— to go reach and teach the nations.
- He was going to give them His assurance and promise to be with them.

The Great Commission

I would like to transport you back in time and place. It is 30–33 A.D. Picture yourself one of Jesus' first-century disciples. Just after Jesus' resurrection, He appeared to some people in Jerusalem and shortly thereafter called His disciples to meet Him in Galilee.[6] Imagine Jesus standing on the mountain with His disciples. Imagine yourself standing there, one of the disciples. You can see Mount Hermon, Mount Arbel, the Golan Heights, and the Sea of Galilee. As you see these places, you remember all the time that you have spent with Jesus over the previous three years.

Can you imagine the thoughts that must have gone through the disciples' minds and the emotions they must have felt at the time? They were just as human as we are. They had the same limitations, doubts, fears, and hang-ups that we have. What were they thinking as they reflected and remembered those moments, victories and even failures as they walked with Jesus during His three years of ministry? Maybe they were thinking about and remembering where it all began? It all started in the wilderness, near the Jordan River, where John baptized and ministered to the multitudes, when they met Jesus for the first time (John 1:35–51).

Bill Hull, in his book *Conversion and Discipleship*, explained that four distinctive phases marked Jesus' discipleship ministry and training of the disciples—turning them into some of the most influential men ever to live.[7] Jesus extended several invitations to them—which they chose to accept in response to His call.

First, *Come and See*, the invitation to explore and learn more about Him. Jesus invited them to join Him and, one by one, they were introduced to His life and ministry. They were all intrigued by the way Jesus spoke and wanted to learn more about His nature and ministry. They remembered the time at the lake, when they were fishing and mending their nets, that Jesus called them and began their training as apprentices. John, Andrew, Nathaniel, Peter and Philip responded first to the invitation to 'come and see.'

Second, *Come and Follow*, the invitation to watch and learn from Him. Simon, Andrew, James, John and Matthew left their jobs as fishermen to travel with Him.[8] He showed them how to become fishers of men. They remembered all the healings, debates and teachings about Jesus' identity and mission. They learned a lot and were changed because they had chosen to accept His invitation and follow Him. They learned, like people do in most apprenticeships, primarily by being with Jesus, assisting Him and being engaged in the ministry beside Him.

Third, *Come and Be*, when they also remembered the day when Jesus came down from His special, favorite place—after a night of prayer—when he had chosen them while they were sleeping. The Twelve, out of a crowd of followers, chosen to be with Him. They remembered how happy and proud they felt when Jesus chose them among a crowd of disciples (Luke 6:17). They remembered how He changed their status from disciple to apostle. He wanted them to be with Him and learn how to work with Him and serve with Him.[9] Not realizing it yet, they were about to enter the fourth phase, learning how to *abide* in Jesus and to multiply themselves (John 15:5).

Suddenly, Jesus appeared in their midst. He came to them, and when they saw Him, they worshiped Him.

When they saw Him, they worshiped Him; but some doubted. (Matthew 28:17)

The last few weeks must have been like a roller coaster ride. They entered Jerusalem on a spiritual high, saw miracles happen, watched how Jesus was taken prisoner and witnessed Him dying on a Roman cross. Since the resurrection of Jesus they had met several times, enjoying fellowship and even a fish meal on the banks of Lake Galilee. But now they found themselves standing with Him ... happy to see and be with Him once again, not knowing that it would be the last time and that their lives were about to change forever. I can only imagine what they must have been thinking.

What a ride! So, what's next?

> Will He deliver us from the rule of the Romans (Luke 24:21)?
> Will He restore Israel?
> Will we become the new leaders, endowed with special positions, authority and privileges?

They were eager to know more. Therefore, when they were together, they asked Him:

> Lord, will You at this time, restore the kingdom to Israel? (Acts 1:6)

Notice what Jesus did not say. He did not talk about a change in government. He did not tell them what He planned to do. He simply told them what they would do. He had been authorized and commanded by His Father to commission them. They needed to go out and train everyone they met, near and far, in this new way of living. Jesus was sensitive to His Father's instructions and obeyed without hesitation. He wanted the disciples to be as actively obedient to His Father during their time of ministry as He was.

Jesus was a man of action. Jesus had invested three years of His life in equipping the disciples for their future ministry. He lived with them and shared many of His daily activities with them. Jesus trained His disciples to make disciples, who would in turn continue to make disciples. They were always going, doing, praying, teaching and preaching. Looking back at the training they received from Him, Jesus knew that His life and message had become part of the disciples' lives. If the disciples told the story of Jesus' life, as seen from afar, it would have lacked authenticity and authority. They would merely have shared stories that were similar to many other fables and tales that prevailed at the time.

Jesus did not intend that the disciples should share with others information about His life and resurrection; He wanted them to share His actual, resurrected life. It was not a story to be told; it was a life to be lived. The disciples' lives had to resemble and reflect the life of Jesus before they could be messengers of the good news. Jesus knew exactly what the disciples would face in their respective ministries, and He knew that only a life conformed to God's will would succeed in the Great Commission. He knew they were ready but they had a decision to make. They had to accept the Great Commission, His final commission.

Imagine seeing Jesus standing there in His glorified body, delivering His final 'landmark' speech, revealing His power, plan and promise, as recorded in the Gospel of Matthew:

> And Jesus came and spoke to them, saying, "All authority has been given to Me in heaven and earth *[claim]*. Go therefore and make disciples of all the nations, baptizing them in the name of the Father and of the Son and of the Holy Spirit, teaching them to observe all things that I have commanded you *[command]*; and lo, I am with you always, even to the end of the age *[declare]*." (Matthew 28:18–20)

Jesus envisioned His followers joining His call to be on mission and reach every nation of the world. Instead of answering their question, He invited them to go on 'mission' with Him and to commit their lives to His kingdom mission. He simply instructed them to take His presence into the world. *They were called to play a part in developing others to think like Jesus, act like Jesus, and love like Jesus.* If they chose to accept and obey, it would change their lives.

> They accepted the commission and the world had been impacted and changed.
> Because of their obedience our lives had been impacted.
> Yours and mine.

Let's Continue With What Jesus Started

Jesus of Nazareth is unquestionably one of the most significant figures in history, a man with immeasurable influence in the world. Probably no one in history has fascinated people more, attracted people more, inspired people more, yet also angered people more than Jesus Christ. So, who was Jesus, and how did His influence grow? He was born into an ordinary Jewish family who lived in a tiny Middle Eastern state, under cruel military occupation. He spent His first 30 years in the shadows, doing what we all do— working, eating, laughing and sleeping. Jesus was also a faithful Jewish boy who worshiped God. Then one day, at the appointed time, Jesus stepped out of the 'shadow' onto the public scene, claiming God's kingdom had arrived and calling people to a radical new way of living.

Jesus poured light and guidance into the lives of His disciples for three years, after which He tasked them with a mission to reach the whole world for His glory and kingdom. Jesus then equipped them with all the spiritual gifts they would need for the task during Pentecost. Within two years after Pentecost, the disciples had reached the whole of Jerusalem with God's teachings.

> And when they had brought them, they set them before the council. And the high priest asked them, "did we not strictly command you not to teach in this name? And look, you have filled Jerusalem with your doctrine, and intend to bring this Man's blood on us!" (Acts 5:28)

Within four years the churches throughout all Judea, Samaria, and Galilee were multiplying and growing.

> Then the churches throughout all Judea, Galilee, and Samaria had peace and were edified. And, walking in the fear of the Lord and in the comfort of the Holy Spirit, they were multiplied. (Acts 9:31)

By the power of His Spirit and obedience to His Word, within just 19 years, they turned the world upside down.

> But when they did not find them, they dragged Jason and some brethren to the rulers of the city, crying out, "these

who have turned the world upside down have come here
too." (Acts 17:6)

Within only 20 years Jesus's followers had taken His message
to every major city of the Roman Empire as well as Africa and
India. Within 30 years, the gospel continued to grow and bear fruit
throughout the whole world.

... which has come to you, as it has also in the world, and is
bringing forth fruit. (Colossians 1:6)

Without Jesus there would be no Christian movement. Many
theories seek to explain the astonishing rise of this new faith.
Only one will do: Jesus is the founder and living Lord of the
movement that bears His name. Steve Addison, in his book
What Jesus Started, says that the world had never seen anything
like it.[10] By 300 A.D., Christians comprised around 10 percent
of the population throughout the Roman Empire —which
would be 5 to 9 million followers of Jesus.[11]

With all mainstream Christian denominations taken into
consideration, Jesus' followers today number more than 2 billion
around the world.[12]

Jesus' life inspired His disciples to labor without wavering
for His cause. The life work of one person, which only endured
for three years, resulted in the continuous multiplication of His
disciples around the world. During Jesus' ministry in Israel, He did
not obtain any form of stardom through writing a book or hosting
a TV show. It did not determine His success in His day.

So, what inspired the disciples to be men of action and to
follow their teacher?

They walked with a teacher who displayed an authentic life of
unwavering obedience to His Father—He lived what He taught.
Jesus' unobscured vision of His Father's plan to save sinners fueled
His every action. Jesus started a movement on that mountain. It
began with small, intimate conversations that changed ordinary
men into disciples, who went out into the world and seeded it
with God's kingdom vision. *If we look at the life of our Lord and the*

apostles He chose, led and trained, we find that the Holy Spirit painted a picture of an empowered church on the move.

Jesus called them to His favorite place. He revealed His power and plan and gave them a promise. Then He commissioned them to go. When they accepted the commission, not only did their lives change but it also had a lasting impact on the world. So, they left the mountain:

- remembering where it all began;
- with the Great Commission burning in their hearts;
- under the authority of the Word;
- with the Gospel on their lips;
- with Jesus Christ as the Lord of their lives;
- with the desire to continue and finish what Jesus had started.

What about Us?

Jesus' model remains the same today. Because Jesus extended His mission 'to the end of the age,'[13] His words and commissions apply to all of His followers throughout history—including us. It started with His disciples, and now their mission has become our mission. Life is full of decisions and choices. Can modern-day church leaders empower regular people to reach their full potential? The answer is yes—if we accept His invitation to explore, learn, follow, serve and multiply.

The disciples made their choice. They once accepted the initial call to be with Jesus, being changed, transformed and trained by Him, and being sent out for Him. They had accepted the call and the Great Commission to go into the world and make disciples. They made their choice.

What about You?

It's time to continue (and finish) what Jesus started on His favorite mountain.

Where do we Start?

We start where the disciples started ... by accepting the call to connect and be with Jesus.

The choice is yours!

2

The CONNECTION

To be with Him before we work for Him

And he went up on the mountain and called to him those whom he desired, and they came to him. And he appointed twelve (whom he also named apostles) so that they might be with him and he might send them out to preach. (Mark 3:13–14)

The purpose of the devotional life is to meet God ... to experience God ... to worship God ... to commune with God. (Bobby Moore)[1]

Jesus once arrived in Bethany on His way to visit Jerusalem briefly during the Feast of Dedication. It was only a short while before He would be crucified at the Feast of Passover. Bethany, a tiny hamlet of around 20 dwellings, was situated to the east of Jerusalem, on the eastern slope of the Mount of Olives. The distance between Jerusalem and Bethany is about 2 miles. He was welcomed into the home of Mary and her sister Martha. Their house was a sweet resting place after the journey from Galilee. He had been there before and established a loyal friendship with Mary, Martha and Lazarus. He felt welcome, comfortable and relaxed; it was 'home from home,' which He often visited and where He rested on His many travels into and out of Jerusalem. He also stayed with them during the week before He was crucified (John 12:1).

Luke described what happened when Jesus and His disciples arrived in Bethany.

> Now it happened as they went that He entered a certain village; and a certain woman named Martha welcomed Him into her house. And she had a sister called Mary, who also sat at Jesus's feet and heard His words. But Martha was distracted with much serving, and she approached Him and said, "Lord, do You not care that my sister has left me to serve alone? Therefore, tell her to help me." And Jesus answered and said to her, "Martha, Martha, you are worried and troubled about many things. But one thing is needed, and Mary has chosen that good part, which will not be taken away from her." (Luke 10:38–42)

When Jesus began to speak, Mary had rushed to sit down at the feet of Jesus and listen to His words. She was eager to learn from Him and to understand His ways. She is found at the feet of Jesus on three occasions throughout the Gospels. Apart from this passage, she fell at Jesus' feet in grief in John 11:28–37 and worshiped Him by anointing His feet in John 12:3. Ann Spangler and Lois Tverberg, in their book *Sitting at the Feet of Rabbi Jesus,* recognize the significance of that in this story.[2] It was customary for a rabbi to sit on a cushion or a chair while he was teaching. His disciples would sit on the ground around them as they taught. Paul wrote about being 'brought up at the feet of Gamaliel' (Acts 22:3). Just like his Master before him, he sat in the midst of learned men, teaching and answering questions (Luke 2:46). So when Mary was described as 'sitting at Jesus' feet,' she was being described as a disciple. Even King David sat 'before the Lord and listened to His voice' (1 Chronicles 17:16).

All was well. Mary was sitting down, eagerly listening to the words of life that came from the Saviour's heart and lips, but Martha was distracted because she was preparing the meal. She was not wrong to be concerned with preparing food for Jesus and His disciples. However, the more she worked, the more irritated and agitated she became with Mary. Poor woman! Martha's mind was pulled in every direction. Maybe she was thinking, 'How will I ever be able to take care of all the details of this meal: the appetizers, the salad, the meat, the vegetables, the rolls, the dessert, arranging the guests at the table ...?'

30

All this work, and Mary was just sitting there ... doing nothing! In her outburst, she not only found fault with Mary but also with Jesus for allowing Mary to just sit there with Him. It was Martha's attitude and the anxiety in her heart which meant that she, unlike Mary, did not give priority to the presence of Jesus.

She came to Jesus and said, 'Lord, do You not care that my sister has left me to serve alone? Therefore, tell her to help me' (Luke 10:40). But the Lord answered, 'Martha, Martha, you are worried and troubled about many things. But one thing is needed, and Mary has chosen that good part, which will not be taken away from her' (Luke 10:41–42). Martha had a legitimate case, yet Jesus gently rebuked her. He disapproved of her attitude but responded in a gentle, affectionate manner. She was inwardly worried and outwardly upset but Martha learned a valuable lesson that day.

> What did Jesus mean when He said, 'But one thing is needed?'
> What exactly is that one thing?

Jesus was actually saying, *The one thing that is important is to be with Me, and to listen to My words.*

Can there be anything greater in value than wholehearted devotion to and adoration of the Lord Jesus? The *one thing* referred to in the passage is a living, intimate relationship with Jesus, where we sit at His feet, with a willingness to listen to His voice and hear what He has to say to us. The response of Jesus here helps us to reflect on and understand what is truly important. It is a call to settle life's priorities and determine what is really important.

But One Thing Is Needed

First, the Lord should always be our *first priority,* before anything else. When Jesus entered the house, the first thing Mary gave Jesus was her undivided attention. She stopped what she was doing because the Master had arrived. It reminds me of the words of the Lord to Joshua, 'No, but as Commander of the army of the

Lord I have now come' (Joshua 5:14). The Lord came not to serve but to lead. It is a reminder that all of us are second in command to Jesus and that without Him we can do nothing.

Nicolas Herman was a monk who worked in the kitchen of a monastery in Paris. He became known as Brother Lawrence, who inspired a little book titled *The Practise of the Presence of God*. He said, 'I have looked on God as the *goal* and end of all the thoughts and affections of the soul.'[3] He continues, 'I have come to see that my only business is to live as though there were none but He and I in the world,'[4] and 'I have sought only to live for Him.'[5] Hundreds of years later, Joy Davidman, wife of C.S. Lewis, put it this way, 'to want God so much that everything else becomes irrelevant.'[6] He comes first. Watchman Nee, Chinese pastor and author once quoted, 'Not until we take the place of a servant can He take His place as Lord.'[7]

Jesus taught that we must always seek first the kingdom of God (Matthew 6:33). When He was asked which is the greatest commandment of all, He replied in no uncertain terms, 'You shall love the Lord your God with all your heart, with all your soul, and with all your mind.' 'This the first and great commandment' (Matthew 22:37–38).

Second, giving priority to the Lord means *hearing and listening to His voice and His words*. Roger Ellsworth, in his book *When Heaven Calls Your Name*, says that when we come to this matter of hearing and heeding the words of our Lord, we are dealing with an issue that is at the very core of the life of the church. According to Ellsworth worship services are designed to place the Word of God, the Bible, before us. When we have the opportunity to hear the words of our Lord, what do we do with it? If we place the fleeting, trivial concerns of this life, no matter how legitimate they may be, above hearing the words of the Lord, we might as well call ourselves 'Martha'! It does not matter whether the concern comes in the shape of baseball, basketball or football, or in the form of picnics, fishing, hunting, movies, concerts or television shows, when we put it above the words of the Lord, we have joined Martha in the kitchen. What is the name of your 'kitchen?' That thing, legitimate in its own way, that you use to excuse yourself from being with Jesus? That thing that keeps you from hearing, listening to and heeding the words of the Lord?[8] When Joshua discovered his visitor was the Lord, he fell at His feet and waited for His orders (Joshua 5). Moses turned aside to look at the bush that was burning and heard the voice of God (Exodus 3). Charles Wesley, English clergyman, poet, and hymn writer wrote:

> Oh, that I could forever sit, like Mary, at the Master's feet:
> Be this my happy choice: My only care, delight and bliss,
> My joy, my Heaven on earth be this, to hear the Bridegroom's voice.[9]

Third, if we give priority to Jesus, and to listening to His Word, *we will receive a blessing, that good part, which will not be taken away from her.* Mary, sitting at the feet of Jesus, received a deep sense of peace, security and assurance in her heart (Colossians 3:15–16). It also gave her the spiritual strength and direction she needed for the day. She learned the importance of hearing from Jesus before hearing from anyone else! Didn't God promise, 'When He gives quietness, who then can make trouble' (Job 34:29)? God will give us a blessing that cannot be taken away, whether it is peace, wisdom, guidance or insight. Listen to these words from the book of Isaiah: 'You will keep him in perfect peace, whose mind is stayed on You' (Isaiah 26:3).

The victory Joshua had over Jericho started with giving his undivided attention to the Lord. When the Lord appeared to Joshua all he had to do was listen to God's Word and obey His orders, and God would do the rest. God had already given Jericho to the nation of Israel (Joshua 6:2). They just had to step out in faith and claim the victory by obeying the Lord. Jesus Himself lived in this same way. He listened to His Father and obeyed what He heard. Jesus also wanted His disciples and followers to live in that way. *It was always God's intention for His children to be with Him and live life in the rest that He provides.* He wants you and I to settle life's priorities, in order for us to 'be' with Him before we starting 'doing' for Him. This is how He wants us to live. If we do, we will understand the connection between rest and work, His work and ours, and His burden and ours.

A Celebrity or Obedient Servant?

Jesus began His life and ministry as a missionary, sent by His Father. He didn't start an organization; He didn't write a book; He didn't broadcast at a local radio station or host a TV show. He was born into an ordinary Jewish family in Galilee. He grew up as a carpenter's son and received a basic education. He was not formally trained as a rabbi. He was without social status and wealth. He was not known for His reputation or power. And yet He became one of the greatest figures in history, a Man of immeasurable influence in the world. Today, as I have said, His followers number more than 2 billion around the world.

Jesus, in His ministry, traveled from town to town and demonstrated the compassion and power of God as He healed the sick and cast out demons, preached in synagogues (Matthew 9:38–42), spoke to crowds in the open air (Matthew 5–7), talked with individuals (John 4), and taught on the shore of a lake (Luke 5). He shared truths over a meal and sought out people who were responsive to His message: fishermen, tax collectors, farmers, soldiers, beggars and sinners. He clearly understood His mission to seek and save the lost.[10] He was welcomed everywhere. Everyone wanted to see the miracles—and Jesus performed many of them.

The power of God was at work as thousands of people were healed and many were set free from evil spirits. The lives of people were changed, and many followed Him. As a result of that, no matter where He went, crowds thronged about Him.[11] His fame spread and people came from all parts of the country, and in great numbers, to see Him, listen to Him and witness how He performed miracles.[12]

The masses wanted to crown Him king (John 6:15). Others were hoping that He would overthrow the Roman Empire (Luke 24:21). Even His own disciples supported the notions of the crowds (Mark 1:37). I am certain that Jesus faced the temptation to 'sell out' and enjoy stardom, with so many people who respected and idolised Him. There were many opportunities to build a ministry, a movement and a name for Himself. Had Jesus been a 'celebrity' and not a loving and obedient servant,

He would have succumbed to the call of the crowds and tried to please them (Matthew 11:7–15). However, *He resisted the 'pull of popularity' to increase His position and influence and walked away from it.*

One Busy Day in Capernaum

We read in the Gospel of Mark:

> Now in the morning, having risen a long while before daylight, He went out and departed to a solitary place; and there He prayed. And Simon and those who were with Him searched for Him. When they found Him, they said to Him, "Everyone is looking for You." But He said to them, "Let us go into the next towns, that I may preach there also, because for this purpose I have come forth." (1:35–38)

It was still dark when He left the house the next morning. The day before had been a long day that stretched late into the evening hours. It had been an awesome day. Years later, Peter could still remember it as though it had happened the day before. He told his young disciple Mark about it, and Mark wrote about it so that we could read it today. Jesus went to bed that night. He had a body of flesh and needed to rest. So, He went to bed. But He was up again a few hours later. Quietly, He put on His robe and sandals and slipped out of the house. He needed to be alone with His Father. His outer man had been refreshed and renewed by a few hours' sleep and now His inner man had to be renewed too. Most of all, He needed guidance for the day. What did Jesus do and why? (I explain this in more detail in my book *Running on Empty*.)

The Reason

Jesus wanted to be alone with His Father and have some time to pray. He understood His call and assignment to reconcile the world to His Father. He said, 'As long as it is day, we must do the work of Him who sent Me' (John 9:4). He needed to prepare Himself for the day, refresh and renew His spiritual 'batteries' and receive direction for the day.

His Mental Condition

Jesus was fully awake. He was dressed, and His mind was clear. One of the reasons why few people don't get anything from their devotional time is simply because they are mentally tired. When we are tired, we are unable to concentrate or retain anything that we have learned or received from Him. G.H. Lang became an evangelist who traveled all over the world and was greatly used by God. Being British, he was not used to the pace set by his mission partners, American missionaries with whom he sometimes worked in the mission field. He explained:

> The life was typically American, one steady rush all day, with visitors, letters, prayer sessions and at nights the meetings in Cairo five days a week, from which we did not return until 11.00 p.m. City life in England, with its late hour, had caused me to forgo my boyhood's habit of early rising. I now saw that unless it could be resumed there would be no leisure for indispensable privacy with God and soul-nurture. But how resume early rising with days so taxed with retiring so late? I besought the special help of the Lord. Who, in the days of His flesh had Himself been an early riser (Isaiah 50:4) and immediately I found myself able to rise at 05.00 am. ... the invention of artificial lights had turned night into day; the world sits up late and cannot rise early.[13]

Jesus gave His best time of the day to His Father, and so should we.

The Place

Jesus needed some solitude and silence and went to a solitary place, one with few distractions. He went to His favourite place. In order for Him to concentrate on prayer and to hear from His Father, He needed some solitude and silence. He needed a place without noise and distractions. He could find none in Peter's crowded house. Before long, Peter's mother-in-law would be up and about, lighting the fire and starting breakfast. Peter would be calling on his friends to come down to the beach and see the night's catch. Jesus slipped away before the events of another day could come crowding in.

He wanted and needed to be alone with God. When we study the life of Jesus, we see clearly that He often withdrew to such a quiet place. He withdrew ... to the Mount of Olives, to Gethsemane, to the desert and sometimes He simply pulled His outer garment over His head, as is customary among the Jews, in order to create a quiet place. When deep in prayer, Jewish men pull their prayer shawls over their heads to shut out the world and enter the presence of God. Therefore, praying under this garment, or prayer shawl, a tallit, is like covering yourself with the presence of God, enabling a person to get away from the people, to pray in secret.[14] Jesus once taught, 'When you pray, go into your room, close the door and pray to your Father, who is unseen. Then your Father, who sees what is done in secret, will reward you' (Matthew 6:6). This passage speaks about a place where it is quiet and conducive to spending time with the Father.

This reminds me of Susanna Wesley, mother of the well-known John and Charles Wesley. She was the youngest of 25 children and the mother of 19. She had many family responsibilities: she had to prepare food, make clothes and homeschool her children. She was a Sunday school teacher and she also hosted a weekly prayer meeting in their small home in Epworth. This was before the convenience of modern technology such as microwave ovens, washing machines and the like. She practised what she preached. She sat aside two hours of each day for private devotions. She made that decision when she already had nine children. No matter what intervened, at the stroke of the clock she retired to have spiritual communion with the Lord. In the biography *Susanna Wesley, The Mother of Methodism,* Mabel Brailsford comments on this:

> When we ask ourselves how twenty-four hours could hold all normal activities, which she, a frail young woman of thirty, was able to crowd into them, the answer may be found in these two hours anywhere and at any time to create a sanctuary. He also taught that to His disciples. Jesus was referring to this when He told of daily retirement, when she drew from God, in the quietness of her own room, peace and patience and indefatigable courage.[15]

The Time

Jesus set the example when 'a great while before day' He was with His Father, gaining strength for the day. It was His only time to be alone, for when the morning sun rose, the multitudes would be thronging around Him all day long, and His disciples would be desiring His fellowship. *Time with Jesus is essential. It must be quiet, unhurried time, when one can quietly listen and think.*

Hudson Taylor, a pioneer missionary, founded the China Inland Mission in 1865, and by the time he died at the age of 73, he had traveled to China 11 times, over 18 000 Chinese Christians had been baptized, and the mission had 825 members. What was it that made Hudson Taylor the man he was, right to the end? It is clear from reading his biography that his life, and life's work, was motivated by a love for God and a love for his fellow man. His heart's desire was to see Christ glorified in people coming to faith. His son and daughter-in-law, who regularly traveled with him in his later years, testified that their travels weren't always easy. They often traversed uneven cobblestone roads for many hours in a cart without springs to arrive at a Chinese inn late at night. They would then endeavor to obtain a little corner in a room for Mr Taylor, because usually in those inns there was just one large room in which everybody slept. He was an aged man but, without fail, every morning just before dawn there would be the scratch of a match and the lighting of a candle, and he would spend some time with the Lord. It was said that every day, before the sun rose on China, he was already worshiping the Lord. This was the key to his life. He loved his Lord and continued to cultivate that love by spending time in daily fellowship and communion with the Lord.[16]

The Heart

His heart was quiet and at peace. We see that Jesus was quiet within the confused noise of the crowds and busyness of ministry. He found rest in the midst of the growing pressures upon Him. God promised:

> You will keep him in perfect peace, whose mind is stayed on you. (Isaiah 26:3)
>
> When He gives quietness, who can then make trouble? (Job 34:29)

Lord, my heart is not haughty, nor my eyes lofty. Neither do I concern myself with great matters, nor with things too profound for me. Surely, I have calmed and quieted my soul, like a weaned child with his mother; like a weaned child is my soul within me. (Psalm 131:1–2)

If Christians experience anxious and troubled hearts today, it is a direct consequence of failing to sit at the feet of Jesus. Just like Martha, we will also feel overcome with worry over the things of the world if we do not keep to our daily fellowship with the Lord.

Being With His Father

What was the motivation for Jesus to walk away from the crowds? Jesus knew that most of the people who pushed to get near Him were shallow, insincere and driven by their own agendas and ambitions. Even when He was led into the wilderness to be tempted by Satan, He did not give in to self-gratification, public recognition or the misuse of His power (see Matthew 4:1–11). What mattered most to Him was His relationship with His Father. Jesus is the perfect example of how one can live for God and for Him alone. Jesus knew that the Father had put all things under His power, and that He had come from God and would return to Him (John 13:3).

The Passion

The passion that drove Him was love. Jesus loved the Father. Jesus was also aware that the Father loved Him. He said that the Father showed Him everything He did (John 5:20). Jesus revealed the Father and His love to the disciples (John 17:26). Jesus asked His Father to show the disciples their special, intimate relationship before creation (John 17:26). Jesus basked in His Father's love and wanted to please Him in all things, 'And He who sent Me is with Me. The Father has not left Me alone, for I always do those things that please Him' (John 8:29). He also declared, 'But that the world may know that I love the Father, and as the Father gave Me commandment, so I do. Arise, let us go from here' (John 14:31). He set the example and demonstrated His love for the Father through obedience.

Your love for God and your obedience to Him and His commands go hand in hand. This love relationship with the Lord is not one-sided. As we accept His love and obey His instructions, we get to know Him more intimately. Jesus said, 'He who has My commandments and keeps them, it is he who loves Me. And he who loves Me will be loved by My Father, and I will love him and manifest Myself to him' (John 14:21).

The Purpose

He knew that His ministry was not to attract a crowd and become popular and successful but to 'work the works of God' (John 9:4) and remain obedient and to do the will of the Father. *Jesus lived His life moment by moment in conscious cooperation with the known will of His Father.* He said, 'My food is to do the will of Him who sent Me, and to finish His work' (John 4:34). He had a task to perform and measured all of His activities against the sense of His call and mission (John 17:4). By putting the Father's will above His own, Jesus dwelt in that serene place where ego, prestige, and position had no dominion. It was His passion that led Him to seek, know and do the will of the Father.

The Plan

Everywhere He went, there were so many sick to be healed, people to be set free of demon possession, and so much preaching needed (Mark 3:7–15), it was normal to think that Jesus would stay and help them, but He did not. A casual reading of the Gospels show that Jesus constantly walked away from people, crowds, success and ministry opportunities because He was obedient to and depended on the guidance of the Father. Everything that Jesus said and did the Father had taught Him.[17] In order for Him to know and do the will of His Father, He needed to spend time in His presence and hear from Him. He prayed to the Father for guidance (John 11:42; Mark 1:35) and meditated on the Word.

What the Father taught Jesus, He shared with those who needed help and encouragement. What the Father revealed to Him, Jesus obeyed! The Father was the ultimate authority and primary audience of His life. In their book *Lead like Jesus,* Ken Blanchard and Phil Hodges explain that our audience is the one we trust and look to above all else. If we choose to follow Jesus, we are no longer our own. He is the only authority and audience in every life decision we make.[18]

This helps us to understand what our created identity and life purpose is. Jesus was able to answer the questions *Whose am I?* and *Who am I?* and as a result He was ready for His next assignment—leading and training the Twelve.

The Twelve

It was time for the next step to accomplish the call upon His life. As we have already seen, Jesus came to reveal the Father's love to all mankind (John 3:16) and His purpose to reconcile the world to Himself and to send out others as ministers of reconciliation (2 Corinthians 5:18–20). Jesus clearly understood His own physical limitations in accomplishing the call and mission of His life. When He came to the earth as the incarnate Son of God, He set aside certain rights, and accepted, for a time, certain physical limitations in order to identify fully with us. And because of that, He needed to train others and duplicate Himself in others in order to reach out and impact the world with the Father's mission. He could only be in one place at a time but through His workers more places could be reached and more people could hear the gospel. So, the next step was to invest His life and time in the men who could carry on long after He had gone away to be with His Father.

It was during this time in His life that the Father summoned Jesus to meet with Him. Jesus went to a nearby mountain. Luke tells us that He spent the night in prayer (Luke 6:12). By morning He was ready to choose the Twelve. Mark wrote:

> And he went up on the mountain and called to him those whom he desired, and they came to him. And he appointed twelve (whom he also named apostles) so that they might be with him and he might send them out to preach, and to have power to heal sicknesses and to cast out demons. (3:13–15)

41

He called 12 ordinary disciples out of a large group of followers (Matthew 10:1–4; Luke 6:12–16). They were ordinary men from Galilee, chosen, called and appointed by God to do extraordinary work (Mark 3:16–19; John 15:16). Galileans were deemed to be low-class, rural, untrained and uneducated people (Acts 4:13). They were commoners—nobodies. They were ordinary people, like most of us. They were selected from the unworthy and the unqualified. They were used because God worked in them. God prepared, uniquely equipped and empowered them to become the instruments that He wanted them to be.

He chose to give a few of His many disciples a special position of authority. Until then they were disciples, learners or students who sought to learn from Jesus. And then Jesus made them apostles. The Greek word for 'apostle' is translated as 'messenger' and suggests that the Twelve were chosen to be sent forth with a special commission as the fully authorized representatives of Jesus (see Chapter 5). They had a new calling and new roles to fulfil. Carefully note the reasons why He chose and called these 12 into the ministry. The order is very significant:

He called them first of all *so that they might be with Him.*
He called them second *to send them out to preach.*
He called them third *to have power to heal sicknesses and to cast out demons.*

Before they would be sent or ordered to go out to preach and do the works of mercy, they had to learn how to be with him. As I have already explained, everything they did had to come through an intimate fellowship with Him. It is also true for us. Before we can embark on a journey to learn how to invest in the lives of others, we need to learn afresh or rediscover the importance of unbroken fellowship with the Lord Jesus.

Jesus trained and mentored them through His example, conduct, character and relationships (Mark 1:14–15, 38–39; 6:7–13). Being with Him, they were able to listen to His teachings, ask questions and watch how He dealt with people, and enjoy fellowship with Him in every kind of setting.

He gradually released them into ministry through a four-step process:

- He modeled His life and effective ministry and the disciples learned from Him by watching Him.
- He recruited them to work with Him and assist Him in small ministry tasks.
- He gave them assignments and watched what they did and provided instructions.
- He left them on their own.

It was only several months later that He would give them power to work miracles and cast out demons (Mark 6:7–13). The success or failure of their lives and ministry depended on their responses to God's call.

Jesus called, and they came.
They accepted the invitation to be with Him.

Called To Be With Jesus

In reading the Bible, and studying church history, we see that most of the people God called and worked through mightily were ordinary, everyday believers. He called, equipped, enabled and empowered them to work with Him in the world. *God chooses to work through His people to accomplish His eternal purposes.* He wants the world to be saved (John 3:16), not perish (2 Peter 3:9); to get to know His Son more intimately (Philippians 3:10); and to worship and follow Him (Matthew 4:19). When we are saved and born again, it is not the end, but only the beginning of God's purpose for our lives.

Alexander Whyte explains it as follows, 'the victorious Christian life is a series of new beginnings.'[19] We become His children and His people (John 1:12). It is our birthright and privilege. God's ultimate goal for us is 'to be conformed to the image of His Son' (Romans 8:29) and then to use us to expand His kingdom (John 17:18). Their giftedness, abilities or the skills of the people God used were not as important as their relationship with Him. Eternal life began the moment we came to know Jesus Christ as our Savior:

And this is eternal life, that they may know You, the only true God, and Jesus Christ whom You have sent. (John 17:3)

However, to really and truly know Him, we must have an intimate relationship with Him, one that is continuously growing. My wife and I were thrilled when Leoné, our daughter, was born. God filled my heart with love for her from the moment I laid eyes on her. My love for her deepened in the first week after her birth, when we were back at home. My wife was exhausted and needed to sleep, so I had to take care of Leoné throughout that first night. It feels like only yesterday that I held her in my arms and dreamt of the day that she would be able to put her arms around my neck and talk to me. She grew up so quickly. She has now completed her school education, spent a year at Bible School abroad, obtained a law degree at the University of Pretoria, got married and become part of our ministry. She serves as my personal assistant and we are closer to one another than ever before.

When she was born into our family, she received the right through birth to be eternally related to me as her father. However, as we know, birthright relationships do not automatically guarantee an intimate relationship with one another. Intimate relationships with one another must be cultivated. Spending time with one another, talking and listening to one another, was crucial in developing an intimate relationship between me and my daughter. And so is it also with us and the Lord.

God loves us! He wants to be with us, now and for all eternity. He wants to share all He has with us. He is calling ordinary people like us. In order to get to know Jesus more intimately, we need some unhurried time in His presence to understand His heart and agenda. The more 'fellowship' we have with God, the more intimate our relationship will be. The birthright relationship is determined by birth and fellowship is by choice.

We are called to have and enjoy fellowship with the Father, the Son and the Holy Spirit. According to Henry and Norman Blackaby, in their book *Called and Accountable, the essence of God's call is an intimate and life-giving relationship with Him, the Father, that will transform and have an impact on our lives and the world.*[20] He desires fellowship with us. He has called us to enjoy fellowship with Him.

God is faithful, by whom you were called into fellowship of His Son, Jesus Christ our Lord. (1 Corinthians 1:9)

The grace of the Lord Jesus Christ, and the love of God, and the communion of the Holy Spirit be with you all. Amen. (2 Corinthians 13:13)

And they continued steadfastly in the apostles' doctrine and fellowship, in the breaking of bread, and in prayers. (Acts 2:42)

... that which we have seen and heard we declare to you, that you also may have fellowship with us; and truly our fellowship is with the Father and with His Son Jesus Christ. (1 John 1:3)

What does that look like? The Greek word for fellowship is *koinonia*, which suggests partnership, union, communion or having things in common. According to the *Merriam-Webster's Dictionary*, it can be defined as 'Christian fellowship' or 'the body of believers,' 'intimate spiritual communion,' 'participative sharing in a common religious commitment' and 'spiritual community.'[21] In summary, it means:

- Sharing together—this word describes the exchange of thoughts or feelings. Some of the most meaningful of times with our inner circle of friends are when we get into a conversation and share with each other the deepest or most intimate feelings in our hearts (see Romans 9:1; Job 11:7; 1 Corinthians 2:10).
- Partnership—it describes joint participation in a common goal or decisions.
- Mutual association—means a willingness to be seen and associate with one another.
- Communication—to communicate with one another.
- Intimacy—this word sums up all the words above. Intimacy can only be developed by two-way communication.

Just like the disciples, we are called to be with Jesus. It is our privilege and first responsibility. When we respond, we get to spend some time with Jesus and get to know Him better. He would then work within us (Matthew 4:19) and through us to accomplish His purposes (John 17:18). We can choose how close we want to live and be to God but sometimes we get side-tracked and must be made aware of some of the enemies of intimacy.

Enemies of Intimacy

Everyone has a favorite song, quote or Bible verse. Some people's verses have changed their lives—and other people's verses have changed hundreds of lives. Habakkuk 2:4, which goes, 'The just shall live by faith,' not only touched the heart and changed the life of Martin Luther but also ignited Reformation fires that burned across Europe and shaped the history of the church in all the centuries to follow.[22]

God used Scripture verses such as Matthew 4:19 and Jude 24 to call me into full-time ministry. Since then He has led me to many other verses that have had an impact on my life or changed the course of my ministry. The truths of John 15:7, Romans 8:28 and Philippians 3:10 created a real longing and a true hunger for more of God and to become more and more like Jesus. Acts 20:24 and John 17:4 challenged me to finish the race well. These truths not only touched my heart and life but also prompted me to embark on an in-depth study of the life and ministry of Jesus, which led to my writing the discipleship program *Connected—The Jesus Way*. Christlikeness became my goal. I prayed. I fasted. I tried all kinds of methods to 'imitate' the example of Jesus just to recognize a struggle with what I've come to call some 'enemies of intimacy.' I have found it helpful to be aware and identify some of these enemies. I trust that it will help you too.

Drifting

I believe that most people, like myself, in one way or another and at one time or another, find themselves fed up, burned out, frustrated, and out of touch with God. Anyone living in today's society knows the struggle of trying to handle the demands of life. Maybe you are going through a similar struggle in your own life right now. Maybe you have experienced the joy that comes from an intimate relationship with God. Then, through the busyness of life, stress and overload, being pulled in every direction, you lost your focus and started to drift away from God's call for you, His best plan for your life. We are all susceptible to drifting. Paul wrote to the church in Corinth, 'There are, it may be, so many kinds of languages in the world, and none of them is without significance' (1 Corinthians 14:10). We are easily sidetracked and then we start drifting.

We believe that we need more, deserve more, and that if we have more, we will be truly happy. Life gets busy. We face one demand after another on our time and energy levels. We get caught up in the details of everyday life or consumed by its demands, the desire to become successful at what we do, whether it's raising a family, working at a job, running a business or leading a ministry. We might even suffer some setbacks or become distracted and, before we know it, we've gotten out of the habit of spending time with God regularly. We still go to church and give some time or lip service to our relationship with God, but before long He starts to seem distant. *Distance from God is a frightening thing.* He will never adjust His agenda and schedule to fit ours. The moment we start to drift, we are doing things on our own, pursuing our own goals and making decisions based on our self-interest. We become confused between His work and ours, His burden and ours.

In a meeting with a small group of missionaries in China, James Hudson Taylor, founder of the China Inland Mission, reminded them that there are three ways to do God's work:

> One is to make the best plans we can, and to carry them out to the best of our ability ... or, having carefully laid our plans and determined to carry them through, we ask God to help us, and to prosper us in connection with them. Yet another way of working is to begin with God; to ask His plans, and to offer ourselves to Him to carry out His purposes.[23]

We forget we are not called to be successful but to bear fruit (John 15:16). And in order to do so, we must learn to abide in Him (John 15:7). It is when we lose sight of our relationship with God, and neglect making time to spend with Him, reading His Word and praying, that we start to drift away from Him.

Busyness

Jesus Himself faced the danger of becoming extremely busy. Thousands of people with needs followed Him. He was thronged by the crowds. He was busy from early morning to late at night with people. However, we have already seen that He walked away from the crowds to be alone with His Father. In September 2014, Dr. Richard Blackaby, President of Blackaby Ministries International, and I were driving from Bloemfontein to Potchefstroom in South Africa to speak at a revival conference.

During the four-hour drive we talked about the books that we were reading, apart from the Bible, and our preaching and traveling schedules. It dawned on me that I had a schedule that was out of control. I was writing articles, teaching, preaching and traveling extensively, both nationally and internationally. It was an incredibly busy time in the ministry. I wasn't getting much rest or time to have a break between the trips. I was burning the proverbial candle at both ends. Busyness was catching up with me and it was not adding to my spiritual life or longing to be more intimate with God. It was draining me. I had overcommitted myself, was rushing from one place to the next, and was exhausted.

I began to take a deeper look at my schedule, and it is no wonder I was struggling spiritually. My life was overloaded. I had no margin. Dr. Richard Swenson, a Christian family physician from Wisconsin, wrote an insightful book, published quite timely, prompted by the stressed-out, worn out, burnt-out people he kept treating in his surgery. In *Margin: Restoring Emotional, Physical, Financial, and Time Reserves to Overloaded Lives,* he diagnosed the single root of much of the sickness and physical breakdown he was being asked to treat. His diagnosis: too many people living with too little in their lives of something that he called 'margin.' He said:

> Overload is not having time to finish the book you're reading on stress. Margin is having time to read it twice. Overload is fatigue. Margin is energy. Overload is red ink. Margin is black ink. Overload is hurry. Margin is calm.

Overload is anxiety. Margin is security. Margin is the space that once existed between us and our limits.[24]

I had to create space and margin for myself. I had to create the time to read, exercise, rest, and enjoy life, relationships and God. The ministry grew and we were receiving invitations and emails from all over the world. When I received an email on my cell phone it made a distinctive sound, and I could not resist the temptation to look and respond to it, which led to the recipient in turn responding again. I never stopped working, even during my devotional times and vacations. I prayed about this and set boundaries. I had to rethink some core values, which helped me to free up some time to help me with decision-making. I cancelled the emails application on my cell phone. I knew that if there was a real emergency, someone would give me a call. I also removed a great number of other applications from my phone. It created some downtime for me and established margin in my life.

Since then I have developed some routines and determined the values that guide and direct my schedule. I have also revisited my original calling and my identity in ministry to ensure that I am not drawn into something or become involved in activities other than those relating to the call of God on my life. This has helped me to cancel all the responsibilities other than those relating to God's call. It also helped me to refuse all appointments or relationships that would take me away from my first priority—spending time with Jesus or with my assignment and work to accomplish God's purpose. I am happy and proud to report that to this day I have not restored email to my cell phone or downloaded new applications on my phone. I do not need to be available to everyone all the time.

Distractions

What is a distraction? It is something that takes our attention away from what we are supposed to be doing. We might not really be engaged in what is happening around us, but it interferes with our concentration and focus. The meaning of this word in Greek is literally 'to be pulled in every direction.' Henri Nouwen, writer and theologian, once said that while he was driving through Los Angeles, he felt as if he were driving through a giant dictionary— words everywhere, sounds everywhere, signs everywhere, all saying, 'Use me, take me, buy me, drink me, smell me, touch me, kiss me, sleep with me.'[25] The Bible is filled with examples of being distracted. Samson was distracted by a relationship with a Philistine woman (Judges 14:6). Demas was distracted by the culture around him (2 Timothy 4:10). Martha was distracted by household tasks (Luke 10:40). Jesus faced many distractions. And so will you.

The fame of Jesus spread, and people came from all parts of Israel just to be with Him. He was very popular and that became a distraction. People even wanted to make Him the king. Jesus faced the danger of being distracted but He was able to keep His focus on His Father. I can just imagine what it must have felt like to be surrounded all the time by so many people, who had so many ideas. It reminds me of the many times in my life that I have missed an off-ramp on the highway. It happened very often before the invention of the GPS. Distractions can be very dangerous, especially when we are driving along the highway. But not all distractions are dangerous or sinful. Most of us have become distracted in our own homes. While doing something, we are sidetracked into watching something that has come up on the news or by a phone call that we received.

How often have our minds been side-tracked in church? I once preached at a church where they had the custom of allowing questions to be sent in during the service, which were displayed on a screen. I was asked to look at the screen every few minutes, and answer the question that had been sent while the service was taking place. That was a huge distraction that made preaching an almost impossible task. Similarly, many people look on their phones or think during the service about the many things that they need to attend to after church. Some people record parts of the service on their phones and send it to others while the service is still taking place. Helpful tools such as cell phones, iPads, etc. can be a distraction if they are not utilized in the right way. It will help us to take some time out, answer some questions, do a survey of our lives, pray about these issues or even get a mentor or accountability partner to help us process them:

- What are some of the distractions that Jesus faced? How did He handle and overcome them?
- What are some of the distractions you have noticed in your life? In what way have any of them led you away from being connected to God? What is the cause of the disruptions? What are some worldly disruptions that you need to repent of and lay aside?
- How can you overcome them?
- What is the difference between a distraction and a disruption?[26]
- How can a distraction lead to a sin or sinful behaviour (1 John 2:15–17)?

Complacency

The *Merriam-Webster's Dictionary* defines complacency as 'self-satisfaction, especially when accompanied by unawareness of actual dangers or deficiencies.'[27] Jesus was aware of the danger of the crowds, of being popular and successful. They were necessary to spread the news of His message and the miracles, but He knew about the 'hidden dangers.' The disciples wanted to go with the crowds. They were excited and filled with joy and 'satisfaction' about what their Rabbi was doing. They were not aware of the dangers yet. We always run the risk of success dulling our sense of reality because we become blinded by our pride. How many truly successful people do we know who are genuinely humble? Paul stated, 'God forbid that I boast except in the cross of our Lord Jesus Christ'(Galatians 6:14).

Spiritual complacency is a dangerous spiritual condition. It leaves us vulnerable to the dangers around us. It creates a kind of know-it-all, 'been there, done that' attitude. The wonder of God and His mysterious workings dry up and turn into stale familiarity. Surely the root of complacency is pride. We assume we have climbed the mountain and there are no more peaks to conquer. Jesus's answer to such an attitude is, 'You have forsaken your first love. So, because you are lukewarm—neither hot nor cold—I am about to spit you out of my mouth.' God said, 'I hate pride and arrogance.' We see ourselves as more or higher than God has determined to be the case (see Revelations 2:4; 3:16; Proverbs 8:13; Jeremiah 2:2; Matthew 24:12). We think we are OK, but we are not. We can only boast of past successes but have nothing new to say or new experiences to share. David said he had been anointed with fresh oil (Psalm 23). We need to remember that we need to be anointed with fresh oil from the Lord. A few years ago, at the *Heart Cry for Revival Conference*, Nancy DeMoss Wolgemuth spoke about the potential pitfalls for us as leaders. She explained that it usually manifested when:

- We lose the wonder of God, the call of God upon our lives and the wonder of being with Jesus. We take it for granted and it becomes all too familiar to us.
- We start to neglect our own intimate personal devotional life and walk with God.
- We start to proclaim a truth that we are not living.
- We no longer enjoy intimacy with Jesus (Matthew 7:21–23).
- We are no longer part of His purposes (John 15:8).
- We lose our focus on or perspective of the future (John 5:28–30).
- We start to rely on our own natural abilities.
- We become proud and arrogant and leave the path of humility.
- We seek comfort and convenience.[28]

We lose the feeling of 'being content.' *Contentment is to find rest and joy in our walk with God. Complacency can be the cause of our not being in contact or connected with God and His purpose for our lives.*

Busy and Blessed

We have already established that Jesus often walked away from people to be with His Father. We have seen that time alone with the Father was vital to His life and work. It was in these intimate moments when He was revived and restored. It was also during these times of solitude and quietness that wisdom and guidance were imparted to His heart. It became the source and secret of His spiritual power. It became a place of rest. It was the place where

He received the courage and strength to complete His call and mission. Jesus started and ended His day with His Father. Jesus set a good example for us in knowing the importance of a daily 'connecting time' with the Lord.

When we get serious about knowing God more intimately through daily fellowship with Him, we will find that many of our schedules are disrupted and there are many urgent matters to consider and attend to. The enemy of our soul will do his best to make it as difficult as possible to set apart some time to be with the Lord. It will be very difficult to find time to enjoy uninterrupted time in fellowship with God. *Unless we take meeting with Christ personally and privately seriously each day, we will soon end up like Martha: busy but not blessed.*

It is when I get out of my routine of sitting at the feet of Jesus, and spending some time with Him, that things become blurry and chaos ensues. Being with Him has saved me from a lot of self-appointed effort and led me to understanding the difference between His work and mine, and His burdens and mine. God's work can only be done God's way, and if we do not follow His guidelines it can lead to unnecessary trouble and anxiety, which in some cases can lead to our becoming burnt out. Few things are as damaging to the Christian life as trying to work for Christ without taking the time to commune with Christ. I have come to the conclusion that a life of intimacy hinges on my response to the call to settle my life's priorities.

> First, to *abandon, submit and surrender* myself to Jesus. A simple act of surrender to Jesus, not only as Saviour but as Master and Lord, once and for all.
> Second, *to do only* what will please Him regardless of my circumstances.
> Last, *to spend time with Him* in His Word daily (see my book *Connecting Time* for some guidelines on how to spend time with Jesus).

What about You?

Are you on track and happy with the level of intimacy you want to experience with God? Your relationship with Jesus will never become all that God intends it to be unless you set aside time to connect and be with Him.

Ask Him if your time with Him is mere routine and, if it has lost the freshness of an intimate relationship, ask Him what the cause of that might be. Perhaps it is time to ask God which of your activities are really sanctioned by Him, and then have the courage to change your priorities so that intimacy with God remains your first priority.

Ask Him to show you what He desires from you and be willing to adjust your life to be with Him.

It is when we become still or take the time to be with Him that we hear the voice of God speaking to us.

He wants to speak to you.

He is speaking.

Are you listening?

PART TWO
Being Transformed
by Jesus

3

The COMMUNICATION

To hear Him speak

Blessed are the people who know the joyful sound!
They walk, O Lord, in the light of Your countenance.
(Psalm 89:16)

You are used to listening to the buzz of the world, but now
is the time to develop the inner ear that listens to the inner
world. (St. Bartholomew)[1]

My wife and I recently watched the movie *The Art of Racing in the
Rain*. It is based on a novel written by Garth Stein, in which a witty
and philosophical dog named Enzo is the narrator. Through his
bond with his owner, Denny, an aspiring Formula One race car
driver, Enzo gains tremendous insight into the human condition
and understands that the techniques needed on the racetrack can
also be used to successfully navigate the journey of life. Enzo
also believes in the legend that a dog 'who is prepared' will be
reincarnated in his next life as a human. Enzo spends most of his
days watching and learning from television, gleaning what he can
about his owner's greatest passion, race car driving, and relating it
to life.

Enzo is a spectator in all Denny's big moments in life: his
marriage to Eve, the birth of their daughter Zoe, Eve's developing
brain cancer, which he detected through his acute sense of smell.
Enzo eventually plays a key role in Denny's child-custody battle with
his in-laws and distills his observations of the human condition in

the mantra 'that which you manifest is before you.' Enzo helps Denny throughout his life, through his ups and downs, and gets Zoe back to her father. The movie ends with Enzo, now old and fragile, riding with Denny in a Formula One race car.

At some point Enzo wryly observes, 'I never deflect the course of the conversation with a comment of my own. People, if you pay attention to them, change the direction of one another's conversation constantly.' He then gives wise counsel, 'Pretend you are a dog like me and listen to other people rather than steal their stories.'[2]

What struck me about the story was how Enzo focused his attention on the people in his life and how he observed the atmosphere, the emotions or moods of his loved ones. He sat and watched them, and then responded to their needs in whatever way he thought would be helpful. In the story, Enzo adores his owner. He loves just being with him. However, the story of Enzo makes a profound point of how we should observe, watch, pay attention and listen to others. It illustrates an important truth.

What truth is that?

Praying or Listening?

When Jesus taught His disciples how to pray, He began by reminding them, 'Your Father knows the things you have need of before you ask Him.' (Matthew 6:8). Prayer is much more than telling God what we want Him to do for us. It is about living in a growing, intimate, trusting relationship with our heavenly Father and not just about getting what we want. *As we relate more to Him, our prayers will become less of a wish list and more of a conversation.* Therefore, we place ourselves in the presence of God, who knows what we need even before we ask, to receive from Him those things we really and truly need. Therefore, prayer is more about being in His presence and hearing Him speak.

Mother Theresa explained this truth so clearly and with great simplicity several years ago, when former CBS network anchor Dan Rather found himself unprepared for a television interview. He was a little out of his depth. Ron Mehl, in his book *What God Whispers in the Night*,[3] described the newsman's encounter. Somehow all of his standard approaches and formula questions were inadequate for the task, and the little nun from Calcutta, sitting beside him so sweetly and tranquilly, didn't seem inclined to making his task easier.

> "When you pray," asked Rather, "what do you say to God?"
> "I don't say anything," she replied. "I listen."
> Rather tried another tack. "Well, okay … when God speaks to you, then, what does He say?"
> "He doesn't say anything. He listens."
> Rather looked bewildered. For an instant, he didn't know what to say.
> "And if you don't understand that," Mother Theresa added, "I can't explain it to you."

Ron Mehl continued:

> Did this good woman mean that she never said words to God? I don't think so. I would imagine that she prayed rather actively for her work of mercy in the streets and alleys of Calcutta. I think she was trying to make the point to a seasoned television celebrity that prayer is something more than repeating certain phrases or formulas. Prayer is the intimate communication between two hearts … yours and God's. Prayer is letting Him know what's on your heart, and He, in turn, letting you know what's on His.[4]

We have the privilege of speaking to God, but our duty is to learn how to listen to Him. We will hear Him speak when we shut out loud and busy distractions, when we stop talking, and start listening. Margaret J. Wheatley, author and consultant, explains it as follows:

> Listening is such a simple act. It requires us to be present, and that takes practise, but we don't have to do anything else. We don't have to advise, or coach, or sound wise. We just have to be willing to sit there and listen.[5]

We must listen like a child to his father. We must listen expectantly. We must listen with great sensitivity.

God is watching us and wants to talk to us. In fact, He is talking to us every day. We just have a hard time paying attention, listening to Him and hearing Him speak. Charles Swindoll, in his book *Intimacy with the Almighty,* explains that noise and words and hectic schedules dull our senses, shut our ears to His still, small voice and make us numb to His touch. Noise and crowds have a way of siphoning our energy and distracting our attention, making prayer another chore rather than a comforting relief.[6] As in the quote by St. Bartholomew at the start of this chapter, we are so used to listening to the buzz of the world, but now is the time to develop the inner ear that listens to the inner world.

> Are you listening?
> Can you hear Him speak?
> It is time to listen!

Is God Still Speaking?

People everywhere yearn to hear God's voice. They often struggle with these questions:

- Does God really still speak to people today?
- Will He speak to me personally?
- If I listen, will He speak in such a manner that even I can understand?
- Is it possible to hear His voice?
- How are we to listen?
- How do I know if it is God speaking to me or some other voice?
- I've asked the Lord to give me insights and direction, but it is as if I hear two voices. How do I know if God is the one I hear or if Satan is involved? Or am I just talking to myself?

The Bible contains many instances of where God spoke to His chosen ones and revealed His purposes. God speaks in ordinary and extraordinary ways, in a variety of circumstances and to different people. We see that He spoke in the morning, at night, during mealtimes, in a crowd, on a boat, in the homes of people and through miracles and so on. He spoke to both believers and unbelievers. He also talked to those who tried to avoid Him, like Jonah, who ran from Him. He even answered Job in a storm.

Just as Jesus spoke throughout the New Testament in the Bible, He is still speaking today. Jesus talks to anyone: a child, a parent, people who are leaders, or people who are followers. He talks to the faithful and the faithless. He talks to the helpless and the hopeless. He speaks both gently to those who are humble and sternly to those who need to be humbled before Him. He talks to those who are depending on and desperate for His help. He spoke to His disciples.

According to Henry and Richard Blackaby, in their book *When God Speaks,* the way God speaks to people has several characteristics.[7] They explain it in this way:

- Though God used many ways to speak to His people, the key was that God spoke, not how He spoke. Those to whom God had spoken focused on God's message, not the means by which He spoke.
- Whenever God spoke, the person spoken to had known it was God.
- Whenever God spoke, the person knew what God said. Usually, our problem is not knowing what God is saying, but in hearing Him speak, understanding His message and having the willingness to obey what He wants us to do.
- When God spoke, the person knew what to do in response.
- The person who received a word from God could not always prove to others that God had spoken. He or she could only obey and allow the results to testify to God's word and work.

It is not how God speaks that is important, but that He speaks. How He chooses to get our attention will vary from person to person, and from assignment to assignment.

Bottom line? God still speaks, and He will speak to us too. Can you hear Him speak?

What is God saying to you?

Called To Hear Him Speak

And he went up on the mountain and called to him those whom he desired, and they came to him. And he appointed twelve (whom he also named apostles) so that they might be with him and he might send them out to preach. (Mark 3:13–14 *KJV*)

Let's look at the background of this section of Scripture. We have already seen that Jesus was summoned by the Father to spend some time in His presence. Jesus 'went out to the mountain to pray and continued all night in prayer to God' (Luke 6:12). He spent the night in prayer and listened to His Father as He, one by one, revealed the names of those He wanted His Son to invest in. They were to be discipled, mentored and prepared to preach. We read, 'And when it was day, He called His disciples to Himself; and from them He chose twelve, whom He also named "apostles"'(Luke 6:13), so that they might be with Him.

The disciples were, first of all, called to be with Jesus. They were to be with Him, to watch and learn from Him before they could be sent out to preach and to minister to others. In being with Jesus they discovered the wellsprings, the sources, from which His life, ministry and evangelism flowed. Second, the Lord spoke to them. He called them by their names. He called them personally and knew them intimately. God is not calling us to follow a theory but a Person. His life was the example, an illustration, of what He wants all of us to become. He is calling all of us for *Himself.* Just like the disciples. We must pay attention to Him and learn to listen to His voice.

We may wonder how many times God has spoken to us without our even realizing it. I wonder how many times He had something specific to say that we needed to hear, but we were too preoccupied or too busy to pay attention.

I believe one of the most valuable lessons we can learn is how to listen to God. In the midst of our complex and hectic lives, nothing is more urgent, nothing more necessary, nothing more rewarding than hearing what God has to say. One can almost feel the heartbeat of God as He pleads through His Prophet Jeremiah, 'Please, obey the voice of the Lord which I speak to you. So, it shall be well with you, and your souls shall live' (Jeremiah 38:20). His voice waits to be heard and, having heard it, we are launched into the greatest, most rewarding adventure we could ever imagine. But it takes time to learn how to listen and understand what God is saying to us.

It is God's plan for us to get to know Him intimately. Jesus said in John 17:3: 'And this is eternal life, that they may know You, the only true God, and Jesus Christ whom You have sent.' He is constantly speaking and calling, 'Behold, I stand at the door and knock; if anyone hears My voice and opens the door, I will come in to him and will dine with him, and he with Me' (Revelation 3:20). God will speak to you as He wants to speak to you, but you must take the time to learn how to listen. The disciples were called to be with Jesus, and while they were with Him, they were learning:

- Why is God speaking?
- When does He speak to us?
- Why do so many people struggle to hear Him speak?
- How does He speak to us?
- How can I hear His voice?

Why Is God Speaking?

God wants each of us to hear and know His voice for ourselves. But oftentimes we do not know what to listen for. God nevertheless makes it clear that He has confidence in our ability to hear Him!

Whether you turn to the right or to the left, your ears will hear a voice behind you, saying, "This is the way; walk in it." (Isaiah 30:21)

My sheep listen to my voice; I know them, and they follow me. (John 10:27)

God believes you'll know His voice when He calls out to you. If God has this much confidence in us to hear His voice, it's time that we gain that same confidence. When Jesus called the disciples, He told them why they were called. They were to become fishers of men, preach, cast out demons and do works of mercy. Why did He speak to them? He wanted them to get to know Him more intimately and indicate that He understood the reason of their call. I believe it is for the same reason God spoke to His Son and why He will speak to us too. Why is God speaking?[8]

First and foremost, He *loves us* with an everlasting love. The greatest verse concerning God's love for you is one you probably know by heart. We read in the Gospel of John 3:16, 'For God so loved the world that He gave His only begotten Son, that whoever believes in Him should not perish but have everlasting life.' The Lord made a conscious decision to come to earth to demonstrate His love for you by living as a man and identifying with your every need. But His love did not stop there. He died for our sins. He did what you and I could not do for ourselves. He wants you to be saved and have eternal life.

Jesus said 'I Love you' by giving His life. He died at the cross for all of us. He did it to give us hope for our messy lives. Jesus says, 'I love you' by inviting us to be with Him forever. Jesus says 'I love you' by caring for us. Jesus watches over us day and night. When one of us gets lost, He finds us and brings us back to Himself. Jesus says 'I love you' by spending time with us. Jesus spent time with sinners and those who were sick. Jesus says 'I love you' by changing our hearts. Jesus promised His disciples that they would not be alone when He left. Life is full of sorrow and Jesus came to give us hope because God loves us.

The second reason God speaks is for us to enjoy *fellowship with Him*. Fellowship consists of a two-way conversation. He wants to talk to you and wants you to talk to Him. He enjoys being with you. He finds delight in those who love and honor Him and rejoices over them (Isaiah 62:5). The disciples were called, 'that they might be with Him' and hear Him speak to them.

The third reason God speaks is because He knows that *we need love, acceptance, reassurance, affirmation and confidence*. We all experience difficult times, face problems and challenges and sometimes find ourselves with our backs against the wall. During those times God knows that we need comfort. God likes to let us know that we are on the right track. When Jesus was baptized by John the Baptist, as a sign that Jesus was entering into His public ministry, God spoke from heaven to confirm who He, Jesus, was! 'A voice came from heaven: "You are my Son, whom I love; with you I am well pleased"' (Mark 1:11). Jesus knew that the disciples would face hardships and challenges; that they would need His encouragement and comfort. And, so do we! God's voice can come in the form of confirmation while you're on your journey.

The fourth reason is *guidance and direction*. We need counsel for effective decision-making. Since God wants us to make the right choices, He is responsible for leading and guiding us, which happens when He talks to us. Have you ever had the experience of an idea popping into your head and you knew there was no way you could have had that thought by yourself? God guides our lives through small promptings like that. Jonah knew that He was hearing God's voice but going to a town called Nineveh to preach to people was not exactly on his agenda. So, he ran away from God's instructions and he was swallowed by a giant fish for his trouble. Many of us do not act on what we hear from God because we are afraid. We are afraid we might have heard God incorrectly or we are afraid to act on it. But don't worry, because God is a God of second chances. 'Then the word of the Lord came to Jonah a second time, "Go to the great city of Nineveh and proclaim to it the message I give you"' (Jonah 3:1–2). Jonah went to Nineveh this time, and many people experienced God's love and mercy.

The fifth reason for God speaking is that He *reveals our destiny* to us. When God called Moses to free the Israelites from slavery in Egypt, Moses was an outcast among to his people. But God had not forgotten him. Moses was gaining personal knowledge of every trail, well, and mountain in the desert of Midian and Sinai—experiences he would need later to lead the Israelites to the Promised Land. God said, 'So now, go. I am sending you to Pharaoh to bring my people the Israelites out of Egypt' (Exodus 3:10).

Through Moses, God revealed Himself as the 'I AM THAT I AM' and used him to bring the people from slavery to freedom.

Last, in speaking to us, God *reveals more and more of Himself*, His plans and purposes for our lives, our families, churches and His ways of working in and through us. God's ways are not our ways. Oftentimes, we miss what God is saying or doing in our lives because we do not understand *why* He is doing it.

> For My thoughts are not your thoughts, nor are your ways
> My ways, says the Lord. For as the heavens are higher than
> the earth, so are My ways higher than your ways, and My
> thoughts than your thoughts. (Isaiah 55:8–9)

We often miss what God is saying or doing because we are more concerned with *what* God is doing or saying than obeying Him. God said that Israel saw the acts of God, but Moses came to understand the way God was working (Psalm 103:7). Likewise, David knew some truths about God but longed for even more of God in his life. He pleaded with God to show and reveal His ways.

> Show me Your ways, O Lord; teach me Your paths. Who is
> the man that fears the Lord? Him shall He teach in the way
> He chooses. (Psalm 25:4, 12)

God has a plan for your life. *When God looks at your life or mine, He sees only potential.* You can make a decision right now to live the rest of your life doing what God wants you to do and enjoy His blessings. Or you can resist Him, chase your own dreams, and more likely fall short of your God-given potential.

> For I know the thoughts that I think toward you, says the
> Lord, thoughts of peace and not of evil, to give you a
> future and hope. (Jeremiah 29:11)

> David chose to listen.
> Mary chose to listen.
> The disciples chose to listen.
> God wants you to listen.

If you are not hearing God's voice, ask Him to show you if you have moved away from Him.

When Does He Speak To Us?

The first time I heard God's voice it came as a total surprise. I remember exactly where I was and what I was doing. I was driving in Sunnyside, Pretoria, looking for a parking spot, when God spoke to me.

Until that moment, I was like most Christians. I was taught that prayer was a time when we poured out our concerns before God. I did not really understand that God actually wanted to speak to me too. Usually we are so busy talking to God about our problems that we fail to listen to all the riches He has for us. And, because I didn't expect God to speak to me, I never really learned how to listen to Him or tried to hear His voice. Even before I was saved, I knew that God was speaking to me and calling me. Just like Samuel, God used several 'Elis' to teach, mentor and coach me on hearing the voice of God on this journey (1 Samuel 3:1–4).

Looking back in my life, God drew my attention to the title of a book in a bookshop, and inspired my reading of that book to make me realize that I needed Him. Then God used a friend who invited me to go with her to a youth meeting to learn more of Him. God used the preaching of a sermon, and a verse of Scripture to convict me of my sinfulness, which led me to accept Jesus as my Savior. Since that day, it has been a wonderful journey getting to know Jesus more and learning to recognize His voice. I have learned how to become quiet in order to prepare my heart to hear God speak in His many ways.

And so, I set my heart on a course to know God more intimately and be all that I can be for Him. It was during my quiet and devotional times that I learned how God revealed Himself to me. These times have made a deep impact on my life. They have affected me irrevocably. Bobby Moore, in his book *Your Personal Devotional Life,* wrote that Dr. Henry Blackaby, author of *Experiencing God,* once said, 'My quiet time is not for a devotional thought, but for a deeper relationship with my heavenly Father. It alerts me to what God wants to do in my life the rest of the day.'[9] God wants to speak to us, reveal Himself to us, but we must learn to listen. True communication comprises talking and listening. *Prayer is not so much about speaking as it is about listening to God and then responding to Him in prayer.* Being close to God means communicating with Him, telling Him what is on our hearts in prayer and then listening to what He is saying to us. It is this second half of the conversation with God that is so important but also so difficult for many people to do.

We are called to hear Him speak to us. God can speak at any time. He can speak early in the morning, during the day or in the night. He can speak to individuals or crowds. A casual reading through Scriptures reveals that those who heard the voice of God were at the *right place* and *had a listening and understanding heart.*

Right Place

Abraham, the friend of God, was a giant in the spiritual realm of prayer. He interceded for the cities of the plain in ways that are incomparable (Genesis 18:23–33). What made him such a giant? I believe it was his habit of meeting with God as he went 'out early in the morning to the place where he had stood before the Lord' (Genesis 19:27). When he listened to God (Genesis 12:1; 13:14–18), and followed His ways, he became a blessing to the nations and became known as the friend of God.[10]

Moses spent 40 years serving as a shepherd in the Midian wilderness. One day, as he was working, he came to Horeb, the mountain of God. There it was the angel of the Lord who caused the commotion of the burning bush. It got Moses' attention. God spoke to Moses because he had stopped, noticed and turned aside. 'When the Lord saw that he turned aside to see, God called to him out of the bush' (Exodus 3:4). God commissioned Moses to go back to Egypt and lead the people of Israel out of Egypt (Exodus 3:12). Moses learned that one of the basic disciplines of a leader was the ability to withdraw from the responsibilities and busyness of life and ministry to listen and pray for the wisdom that he needed. On the journey back to Egypt, God spoke to Moses through his encounters with Pharaoh and the plagues. He even gave him Aaron, his brother, to speak on his behalf. When they arrived in the wilderness, God invited Moses to meet with Him on the mountain (Exodus 24), and again later on after the people had sinned against God by making the golden calf (Exodus 32).

It was on the mountain that God revealed to Moses His design for a Holy Place where He could meet with His people.[11] God told Moses that He would meet with him and speak to him from the mercy seat (Exodus 25:22). Every time that Moses entered the Tabernacle in the wilderness,[12] he heard God's voice speaking to him from the mercy seat.[13] Moses heard the voice of God because he was at the right place and had a heart that was able to listen.

Even *Jesus* Himself lived in this way, by simply taking the time to be with His Father, listening to Him and obeying what He heard. Jesus said, 'For I have not spoken on My own authority; but the Father who sent Me gave Me a command, what I should say and what I should speak' (John 12:49).

Mary of Bethany appears in the Gospels three times, and on each occasion, she is in the same place: at the feet of Jesus. As I have explained already in the previous chapter, she sat at His feet and listened to His Word, fell at His feet and shared her woe, and came to His feet and poured out her worship. Jesus commended her because she had 'chosen the good part and it would not be taken away from her.' She was at the right place, her priorities, focus and attention were upon Jesus, and she had a heart that was willing to listen.

The Gospel of Mark, chapter 5:21–34, records the miracle of *the sick woman* who was healed from her illness. In the story we see God's willingness to give us help. I believe it teaches us how and when to ask and receive. How shall we ask? When I look at the sick woman, the answer to this question is simple. We need to ask in His presence. We need to get close to Jesus and touch Him. It was when she came so close to Jesus that she was healed. She was in His presence. She was at the right place, with a longing and expectation to receive from Him. She knew that He was the answer. He was her only answer. He is our only answer too.

Peter, one of the apostles, had been engaged in an itinerant ministry (Acts 8:25) when he found himself called to Joppa. The apostles, as indicated in the book of Acts, were a praying people. They often met together and waited upon God in prayer as they anticipated the coming of the Holy Spirit. It was during a time of prayer that Peter heard the voice of the Spirit directing him to go to Caesarea (Acts 10:9–19).

John wrote the book of Revelation about A.D. 95, during the reign of the Roman emperor Titus Flavius Domitian. This emperor had demanded to be worshiped as 'lord and god,' and the refusal of the Christians to obey his edict led to severe persecution. It was during this time that John was sent to the isle of Patmos, a Roman penal colony off the coast of Asia Minor. On the Lord's Day, he heard a voice behind him (Revelation 1:9–18). According to tradition, John regularly visited a cave where he prayed. It was at this place and at the time of prayer when Jesus spoke to him and revealed to him things that were yet to come. He heard the sweet voice of Jesus because he was at the right place and had a willingness to hear. The Twelve, when called to be with Jesus, were at the right place.

What did they all have in common?

They were in His presence.

They were all in close contact with the One who had all the answers to their problems.

We will hear His voice when we are in His presence, and when we are closely connected to Him. If we really want to hear from God or receive His guidance, we must put ourselves in the place where He can communicate with us and encounter a heart in us that is able to listen and understand.

We must be at the right place but we must also have a *listening and understanding heart.*

A Listening and Understanding Heart

What would you ask for if you were absolutely certain God would give you anything you wanted? Would you ask for a long life? Riches? A great marriage? A successful career? A fruitful ministry? King Solomon was given such a promise.

Now the king went to Gibeon to sacrifice there, for that was the great high place: Solomon offered a thousand burnt offerings on that altar. At Gibeon the Lord appeared to Solomon in a dream by night; and God said, 'Ask! What shall I give you?' (1 Kings 3:4–5)

Solomon was King David's son and heir. In response to the young king's extravagant sacrifices—a thousand burnt offerings—the Lord responded with an incredible offer: 'Ask! What shall I give you?' His answer was quite surprising.

> Therefore, give to Your servant an understanding heart to judge Your people, that I may discern between good and evil. For who is able to judge this great people of Yours?" (1 Kings 3:9)

Instead of asking for more power or greater wealth, Solomon asked for a blessing that would bless God's people. Why would he ask for that? Could it be that his assignment as king and the building project of the temple was overwhelming? His responsibilities could easily become a distraction. He was not asking for something for himself. He asked for a blessing to be a blessing to others. He asked for an understanding heart so that he would be able to make good decisions. He asked for the Lord's help so that he could serve God's people more effectively. He asked for a heart that could clearly hear the Lord's direction and guidance.

Leb Shama

The Hebrew word for 'understanding heart' is *leb shama*. *Shama* literally means to 'hear, listen to and obey.'[14] *Leb* refers to 'the inner man, mind, will, heart, or understanding.' An understanding heart is thus a heart that is surrendered to the will of the Father and willing to obey any instruction that comes from Him. Solomon wanted to hear and understand the Lord's instructions and had a deep desire to implement what He said. The Lord took notice that he didn't ask something for himself but that he was rather concerned with the welfare of God's own people. God responded by giving him an understanding heart and also blessed him with blessings beyond his request (vv. 10–13).

According to Lois Tverberg, in her book *Walking in the Dust of Rabbi Jesus,* we usually translate the word *shema*, which is similar to *shama*, as 'to hear.'[15] It, however, has a much *wider* and *deeper meaning* than 'to perceive sound.' It encompasses a whole spectrum of ideas that include listening, taking heed, and responding with action to what one has heard. Tverberg furthermore explains that the deeper meaning of the word *shema* helps us to understand why Jesus often concluded his teachings with the words, 'Whoever has ears to hear, let them hear' (Mark 4:9). He wants us to be doers of the Word, and not hearers only (James 1:22). Jesus was in fact saying, *You have heard my teaching, now take it to heart and obey it!*

It is clear from studying the life and ministry of Jesus that He had a *shema heart,* a heart that was able to hear, understand and obey His Father, even to the point of dying on the cross. The Prophet Isaiah, in referring to Jesus, whose mind and heart were submitted to doing the will of God, said:

> The Lord God has given Me the tongue of the learned, that I should know how to speak a word in season to him who is weary. He awakens Me morning by morning. He awakens My ear to hear as the learned. The Lord God has opened My ear; and I was not rebellious, nor did I turn away. I gave My back to those who struck Me, and My cheeks to those who plucked out the beard; I did not hide My face from shame and spitting. (Isaiah 50:4–6)

What God taught the Servant Jesus, the Servant shared with those who needed encouragement and help.

> Come to Me, all you who labor and are heavy laden, and I will give you rest. Take My yoke upon you and learn from Me, for I am gentle and lowly in heart, and you will find rest for your souls. For My yoke is easy and My burden is light. (Matthew 11:28–30)

The Servant had a listening heart. When asked what the greatest commandment was, Jesus answered:

> Then one of the scribes came, and having heard them reasoning together, perceiving that He had answered them well, asked Him, "Which is the first commandment of all?" Jesus answered him, "The first of all the commandments is: 'Hear, O Israel, the Lord our God, the Lord is one. And you shall love the Lord your God with all your heart, with all your soul, with all your mind,

71

and with all your strength.'" This is the first commandment.
(Mark 12:28–30)

Why is this Important?

The Apostle Paul found himself in Corinth when he wrote to the church in Rome. The sins listed in Romans 1:19–32 were everyday sins committed on the streets of Corinth. It was very difficult to be a Christian in that time. In his letter Paul explained, 'There are, it may be, so many kinds of languages in the world, and none of them is without understanding' (1 Corinthians 14:10). There are many voices, sounds and languages that are crying out for our attention. Every day we as Christians are exposed to the voices of man, the world, the flesh, the voice of deception from the evil one and the voice of God. We are safe as long as we stay closely connected to God, true to our calling, and tuned in to understanding His voice. *The essence of the meaning of the word is to listen to His voice, to learn from Him, hear and understand what He is saying and then to obey it.*

We must learn how to listen and obey.

Do you have a listening heart?

Why Do So Many People Struggle To Hear Him Speak?

To many believers prayer often feels like a burden. It feels like a senseless activity of talking to the ceiling rather than actually communicating with a loving and caring Father and God. We might even try to listen, as we strain our ears and hearts to hear, but we are never sure if God is truly talking back to us. People have a difficult time discerning God's voice. Didn't Jesus say that we will be able to hear His voice, 'My sheep hear My voice, and I know them, and they follow Me' (John 10:27). At the same time, He refers constantly to people who have ears but do not hear or understand.[16] God intends to make us channels of His blessings so that we can bless others in His name. But we must be able to hear from Him in order to be a blessing to others.

Why do so few people hear Him speak? It can be for a number of reasons. The most important reason is that some people are not truly born again. Samuel needed help to realize that God was speaking to him. 'Now Samuel did not yet know the Lord, nor was the Word of the Lord yet revealed to him' (1 Samuel 3:7). It is only when we have accepted Jesus Christ as our Savior (John 1:12) and have received the Holy Spirit, who testifies that we are born again and a child of God, that we will be able to truly hear and understand His voice (Romans 8:16).

Paul wrote to the church in Corinth that 'the natural man does not receive the things of the Spirit of God, for they are foolishness to him; nor can he know them, because they are spiritually discerned' (1 Corinthians 2:14). Our spiritual eyes must be opened first, to be able to hear the voice of God. The Prophet Isaiah was able to hear the voice of God, after the seraphim touched his mouth with a coal from the altar, and his sin was purged (Isaiah 6:6–8).

Peter Lord, in his book *Hearing God,* explains that there are six main reasons why we do not hear God's voice:[17]

Reason 1—We are too *distracted* to pay attention to His voice. Jesus informed Martha that she was worried because her priorities were wrong. She was too distracted to pay attention to the words of Jesus. If we are going to learn how to hear from God, we can't allow ourselves to become distracted by the demands of everyday life.

Reason 2—We are in a *hurry.* When Jesus was busy with His earthly ministry, He was never in a hurry. He did not go from place to place to get as much done as possible. Jesus was not in a hurry because He operated on God's schedule and made every moment count as He was instructed by the Father. We must resist the temptation to be busy and in a hurry.[18]

Reason 3—We do not know how to *listen.* Jesus told Martha that the one thing that was important was to sit at His feet and listen to His voice. We cannot have a genuine conversation with someone without listening to the other person. Listening is not only a part of prayer. It is probably *the* most important part of prayer. Jesus modeled a life that was in tune with the Father. He taught, 'He who has ears, let him hear' (Matthew 11:15). We need to learn how to listen with our spiritual ears, because God is always speaking to us. The Prophet Isaiah encourages us to 'give ear and hear my voice, listen and hear my speech' (Isaiah 28:23).

Reason 4—We do not *respond* to His words. Whenever God speaks to us, it's important to put into expression what we have heard in some tangible way. If we ignore it, we will become hardened to it (Hebrews 3:15). If we respond to it, we will become sensitive to His voice in the future. If we respond with an appropriate action, such as obedience, He can trust us with more the next time He wants to talk to us. So, remember to act on His instructions the next time the Lord speaks to you.

> So shall My word be that goes forth from My mouth; it shall not return to Me void. But it shall accomplish what I please, and it shall prosper in the thing for which I sent it. (Isaiah 55:11)

Reason 5—Our *view of God is distorted.* Some people view God as bad. They do not see Him as a loving Father or as the Good Shepherd (John 10:14). Their relationship with God or perhaps their personal opinion is tainted by their own perspective. Why would you listen to or even want to get to know someone you do not like or trust?

Reason 6—*Pride* turns God away. James wrote, 'God is opposed to the proud but gives grace to the humble' (James 4:6). Pride manifests in a variety of ways, such as vanity, gloating, looking down on others or bragging about accomplishments. It is when we humble ourselves and submit to God that He will help us.[19]

> Submit therefore to God. Resist the devil and he will flee from you. Draw near to God and He will draw to you. (James 4:7)

A Few More Reasons

We like the idea of God communicating with us. We feel strongly, as we also believe, that God must communicate with us in a way that suits us. However, we want God to communicate with us in a way that requires minimal input from our side. We want Him to impart His wisdom and guidance to us, but we do not want to work on our relationship with God.

Also, we are interested in what God can give us or do for us and not for Who He is. We have become people who seek God's hand instead of His face. We are more concerned about the acts of God than the ways of God.

Then, we are also too impatient to follow God's plan. We desire immediate answers and results instead of living and following God's agenda and timetable.

We only approach God when we need His help and wisdom. We do not cultivate a relationship with God but only reach out to Him when we have a decision to make or when we face challenges.

Another reason is that we have become lazy and passive. We are not willing to trust and seek God for His instruction; we just want God to show us His ways. We do not want to actively participate in the things of the Lord. We want God to use extraordinary ways to turn our eyes to see what He wants us to see. But we forget that God does not work like that. He longs to have an interactive relationship with us, and He will not succumb to our lower levels of commitment to Him. His standard of relationship is set and only those who are willing to seek God will have communion with Him. God does not hide Himself (Deuteronomy 30:14). He does not play games with us or give us the silent treatment. He speaks. He is active and wants to speak to us.

We must take the time to learn how to listen.
So how does He speak to us?

How Does He Speak To Us?

My experience in walking with God has shown me that God does speak to His people. He gives clear, personal instructions which enable us to fully understand and experience His power, presence and love. In a casual reading though the Bible we see that God has spoken in different ways throughout the Old and New Testaments and continues to speak today in many of those same ways. God is not limited to one form of communication. He is all-powerful, He is omnipresent, and He is sovereign. On numerous occasions the Bible records that God's voice was heard, but the exact way in which His voice was heard is not described. For example, 'now the Lord had said to Abraham' (Genesis 12:1); 'and the Lord said to Abraham' (Genesis 13:14).

Let me give you a short overview of the primary and secondary ways God speaks to us through the Holy Spirit. It is by no means complete and my intention is not for you to gain more intellectual knowledge but for you to gain some insight into how God can speak to you. I hope it will create a longing in your heart to study the many ways God wants to speak to you. My hope is that you will genuinely experience God speaking to you, have the joy of listening to God and understanding His ways. Marilyn Hontz, author of *Listening for God,* said:

> When we really learn to hear God's voice, we allow him to share his plans with us and actually involve us in his work! We never know what truth God will show us or how he will impact others through us, but one thing is sure: Life becomes an adventure.[20]

So, we must learn how to listen when God communicates with us. If we do, we are in for an incredible journey, and you will soon have your own stories to tell of divine appointments.

How did God Speak in the Days of the Old and New Testaments?

What does God's voice sound like? The Prophet Elijah described God's voice as a still, small voice or a 'gentle whisper' (1 Kings 19:12). Habakkuk, the prophet, learned to recognize the audible voice of God. 'Then the Lord said to me, "Write my answer plainly on tablets"' (Habakkuk 2:2). It is when we take the time to listen and pay attention that we see what God is doing or hear what He is saying. The Bible teaches us that God had spoken to His people since the beginning of the earth, when He walked with Adam and Eve in the garden. We can learn and discover more of His ways, purposes and methods by reviewing how He revealed Himself in the days of the Old and New Testaments. Henry and Richard Blackaby, in *When God Speaks,* give us a list of means through which God used to speak to people in the Bible.[21]

- Angels (Luke 1:26)
- Visions (Genesis 15:1)
- Dreams (Job 33:14–18; Matthew 2:12–13)
- Prophets (Acts 21:10–11)

- Symbolic actions (Jeremiah 18:1–10)
- Preaching (Jonah 3:4)
- A still, small voice (1 Kings 19:12)
- Miraculous signs (Exodus 8:20–25; Judges 6:36; 1 Kings 18:37–39; Daniel 5:5)
- A burning bush (Exodus 3:2)
- A donkey (Numbers 22:28)
- Prayer (Acts 22:17–18)
- A trumpet (Exodus 19:16, 19)
- Fire (1 Kings 18:37–39)
- Fleece (Judges 6:36)
- Writing on the wall (Daniel 5:5)
- Casting lots (Acts 1:23–26)

Some more examples are:

- Direct revelations (Genesis 12:1–3)
- Physical appearances (Exodus 3:2)
- The written Word (Psalm 119:105)
- Audibly (Acts 9:4)
- Circumstances
- Holy Spirit (Acts13:2; 16:6–7; Romans 8:16)
- Jesus Christ (Hebrews 1:2)

How does God Speak to Us Today?

While we marvel at the many ways and methods God used to speak to His servants in the Old and New Testament times, we also long to engage in meaningful communication with God in this day and age. We want to be able to hear Him today. We want to hear Him for ourselves, 'Now we believe, not because of what you said, for we ourselves have heard Him and we know that this is indeed the Christ, the Savior of the world' (John 4:42).

As I was praying one morning, I began to feel that the Lord had something very specific to say to me. I was reading through and reflecting on John chapter five. I noticed the words, 'Jesus went up to Jerusalem' (v. 1). I had never thought about going to Israel until that moment. It seemed as if the words 'went up to Jerusalem' jumped out from the page and into my heart. The Holy Spirit began to stir my heart with an intense desire to visit Jerusalem and walk in the footsteps of Jesus. I just knew that God wanted me to go to Israel. My heart was at ease and I had perfect peace. I had a word from the Lord but felt a bit hesitant on how to proceed. I was excited but still unsure about the next step. It felt as if there was a veil that kept me from knowing and understanding the unknown.

Over the next few weeks God sent two people across my way who, on two separate occasions, confirmed His desire for me to go to Israel. There was only one problem, though. I had no money to pay for a trip like that and I had no desire to take out a loan from the bank and be in debt for a trip to Israel. I felt certain that God wanted me to go and that the answer was close but that I had to wait upon Him to reveal the next step. Around that time I had a speaking engagement at a local church. While I was away, someone phoned our home, looking for me. The call was from a travel agency taking pastors who were willing to be trained as future tour leaders on a ten-day pilgrimage to Israel. The trip was offered at a much reduced cost. The agent said she wanted me to join them. My wife gladly accepted on my behalf. But I still needed to pay the fee, reduced as it was. When I returned to the office the following Monday, I was told that my employer had given me a bonus for my hard work. The bonus I received was exactly the amount of the reduced tour fee. God changed my circumstances (no money) and He removed all the uncertainties and obstacles that were in my way. It became clear to me that God wanted me to go to Israel. Since then I have been able to travel to Israel many times.

I am so thankful that He still speaks and wants to speak to us.

The Five Principles

God employed five principles, which I call primary ways of speaking, when He spoke to me about going to Israel. All the other methods act as secondary ways or confirmations of what He had said to me.

God desires to make known the unknown to us as His children. *God desires to reveal to us His plans and purposes. Yet, so often we are satisfied with not knowing.*

Principle 1: The Example of Jesus Christ

God spoke to me through the example of Jesus who 'went up to Jerusalem.' God's primary way of speaking to us today is through His Son. He revealed Himself through His Son (Hebrews 1:1–2). We need to view the life of Jesus from that perspective. When Jesus was on the earth, God spoke to people through Him, and when Jesus returned to the Father, the Holy Spirit was sent to lead us into all truth as our 'communicator,' who comes from God.[22]

If you are a believer, the Holy Spirit dwells within you, but it is still necessary to nurture your relationship with Jesus in order to learn how to be attentive to His voice—and we do so by spending time with Him. As you grow in faith and mature as a believer, you will learn to hear God speak. Jesus said, 'My sheep hear my voice, and I know them, and they follow me' (John 10:27).

The key, according to Dallas Willard, in his book *Hearing God*, is not so much to focus on individual actions and decisions as on building our personal relationship with God.[23] How are we to live our daily lives and glorify Him? We do so by constantly looking at the life of Jesus, especially His words, commands, example, ministry, message, miracles and relationship with His Father. When we follow in the footsteps of Jesus, we are actually walking in the footsteps of the Father. When we enjoy fellowship with Jesus, we have fellowship with God. What did I learn from looking at His relationship with His Father and from His life and example?

Personal *relationship* with His Father

First of all, Jesus said that each moment of the day He was utterly *dependent* on His Father: 'the Son can do nothing of Himself.' How did Jesus live out His life during those years in which He walked here on the earth? He lived it in utter dependence on God. 'The words that I speak to you I do not speak on my own authority; but the Father who dwells in Me does the works' (John 14:10). Whatever He did, was in the name and power of the Father. Jesus, the Son of God, felt the need to maintain the life of fellowship with God in prayer. His life was a continual waiting on the Father for all He was to do.

Could it be that Jesus was teaching the disciples to be dependent upon Him, just as He was dependent on His Father? Their spiritual life and effectiveness depended on the renewal of the joy of daily fellowship with Him, Who is the life and light of this world. We not only need Him as an object of trust, but we must have His power working in and through us. Maybe Jesus was thinking about this when he said, 'for without Me you can do nothing' (John 15:5). Do you live your life in your own strength? Bill Stafford, revivalist, once told me he experienced a personal revival when Manley Beasley was preaching in his church in America. He said, 'God convicted me of having a ministry of trying instead of having a ministry of trusting.'

Second, Jesus only sought to *imitate* His Father, 'but what He sees the Father do; for whatever He does, the Son also does in like manner' in all that He does (John 5:19). The Greek word *blepo*[24] means to look at, behold, contemplate, to perceive and to know.[25] The Son not only does what the Father does but He does it exactly like His Father does it. God called Moses into His presence and gave him the tables of stone on which He had written the Ten Commandments (Exodus 19:20). He remained on the mountain for 40 days and 40 nights and during that time God gave him the plans for the Tabernacle (Exodus 25:9, 40). God designed the plan and warned Moses to make everything according to the pattern that He had revealed to him on the mountain (Exodus 25:40; Hebrews 8:5). The Tabernacle was an imitation of the Heavenlies. God also had a perfect plan for His Son. Jesus had to live in such a way that the world would be able to see the Father (John 14:9). Maybe that was on His mind when He said:

> For I have given you an example, that you should do as I have done to you. (John 13:15)

> As You send Me into the world, I have also sent them into the world. (John 17:18)

> As the Father has sent Me, I also send you. (John 20:21)

Maybe Peter was also thinking about imitating Jesus when he wrote:

> For to this you were called, because Christ also suffered for us, leaving us an example, that you should follow in His footsteps. (1 Peter 2:21)

Imitating Christ was also on Paul's mind:

> ... for we are His workmanship, created in Chris Jesus for good works, which God prepared beforehand that we should walk in them. (Ephesians 2:10

> ... imitate me, just as I also imitate Christ.
> (1 Corinthians 11:11)

Third, Jesus responded in *obedience* to do only what the Father showed Him ... *for whatever He does, the Son also does in like manner* and to speak only what His Father taught Him ... *but as My Father taught Me, I speak these things* ... and to speak only what His Father commanded Him to say, *gave Me a command, what I should say and what I should speak.*

He did not receive God's commandments as a whole, but one step at a time and day by day as He taught and worked. He lived in continual communication with His Father and only received His instructions as He needed them (John 8:16; 14:10). It is only when we walk with God and hear His voice that we can really respond to Him in obedience. Our obedience to God is dependent on a moment-by-moment fellowship with Him.

Last, we then clearly see the level of *intimacy* to which the Father commits Himself. He is willing to make the unknown known to us, 'For the Father loves the Son and shows Him all things that He Himself does; and He will show Him greater works than these, that you may marvel' (John 5:20). The Father had a glorious plan for His Son, that in and through Him eternal salvation would take place for all mankind. And we are part of that plan.

Personal *life* and *example*

The life, ministry, and leadership of Jesus impacted people and the whole known world of His time. The more we learn about and from Him, the closer we walk with Him, the more we will be like Him, and the more He will reveal Himself in and through us.[26]

> Then Jesus answered and said to them, "Most assuredly, I say to you, the Son can do nothing of Himself, but what He sees the Father do; for whatever He does, the Son also does in like manner. For the Father loves the Son and shows Him all things that He Himself does; and He will show Him greater works than these, that you may marvel. (John 5:19–20)

> Then Jesus said to them, "When you lift up the Son of Man, then you will know that I am He, and that I do nothing of Myself; but as My Father taught Me, I speak these things." (John 8:28)

> For I have not spoken on My own authority; but the Father who sent Me gave Me a command, what I should say and what I should speak. (John 12:49)

Why was Jesus so successful? Why was He so effective? What was His secret? Jesus found Himself at the place where God wanted Him to be and had a heart that was tuned in to the Father, to listen to the Father. It is clear from these Scriptures that His life and heart were set upon His Father.

Principle 2: The Word

God spoke to me through His Word when He called me to go to Jerusalem. God speaks to us through the Bible. Jesus loved the Scriptures. Whether He was praying to the Father or speaking to men, He did so by the Word of God. Jesus allowed the Scriptures to shape and guide His life and ministry. He said, 'Man shall not live by bread alone, but by every word that proceeds from the mouth of God'.[27] The Bible is one of God's provisions to equip us to do His will.[28] God's Word is alive, and it is active in our lives. The Bible is an absolute and essential part of our walk with God. We must not neglect His Word. It is one of the ways in which God will speak to us personally. We must read, meditate on and memorize the Word.[29]

By His Holy Spirit, who dwells in each believer, God will focus your attention on specific verses or passages of Scripture (John 14:26). They will have special application to your life because of decisions you are facing, character goals you are working on, questions you have, or pressures you are experiencing. As you meditate on those verses to which the Spirit of God leads you, God will guide you in 'paths of righteousness for his name's sake' (Psalm 23:3). Not only are we to have a growing relationship with the Lord through His Word, but we should also be ready to give an answer to others whenever necessary (1 Peter 3:15–16).

When the devil tempted Jesus in the wilderness, Jesus responded to the devil's temptations by quoting the truth from God's Word (Matthew 4:1–11). We must learn the truth, which is found in the Word of God as it is identified as the 'sword of the Spirit.' With the sword of the Spirit, we can defeat the enemy of our souls, and as we 'put on the whole armor of God,' we can 'stand against the wiles of the devil' (Ephesians 6:11).

Honoring and obeying God's Word is the key to hearing God's voice. Through obedience, we demonstrate our love for God. Through failure to obey, we demonstrate traits of a rebellious heart. If we resist His Word, our fellowship with God will be limited. Jesus said:

> He who has My commandments and keeps them, it is he who loves Me. And he who loves Me will be loved by My Father, and I will love him and manifest Myself to him. Judas (not Iscariot) said to Him, "Lord, how is it that You will manifest Yourself to us, and not to the world?" Jesus answered and said to him, "If anyone loves Me, he will keep My word; and My Father will love him, and We will come to him and make Our home with him. He who does not love Me does not keep My words; and the word which you hear is not Mine but the Father who sent Me. (John 14:21–24)

Principle 3: The Holy Spirit

The Holy Spirit removed all the uncertainty and filled my heart with peace when I received the call to go to Jerusalem. A third method God uses to speak to us today is through the Holy Spirit. Jesus spoke through the Holy Spirit. Today, God still speaks to our spirits through His Spirit, Who now lives within us. He usually speaks to us as an inner witness, an assurance, a voice (a still, small voice), peace, uneasiness or images.[30] The Inner witness can also be defined as having joy and peace when we do God's will. It is also in having a lack of peace when we are doing or thinking of doing something which is not God's will. God's peace should rule in our hearts (Colossians 3:15). The word *rule* doesn't simply mean merely to exist. It means to reign or to be a deciding factor. If we don't have peace about a decision, then it isn't from the Lord. Don't move forward unless you have His peace.

Principle 4: Circumstances

God also speaks to us today through circumstances. God first spoke to Jonah, but Jonah didn't heed His voice. So, God spoke to Jonah through circumstances. First, he was swallowed by a great fish, and second the Lord grew a vine to provide shade for Jonah, and then the vine withered (Jonah 1–4). Circumstances can take many forms. Sometimes it is a failure. Sometimes it is a tragedy, but God uses all circumstances in life to speak to us. We need to examine our circumstances and ask if we are hearing the Lord through these circumstances.

Ask yourself two questions: What's happening in my life right now? What is the Lord telling me through these circumstances? You must be diligent to seek God and to be attentive to His work in every facet of your life, because another way that God speaks to us is through our circumstances. As you focus on the Lord, especially during difficult or painful circumstances, God can show you His perspective of your circumstances. Rather than try to figure out everything, with our limited knowledge and understanding, we can acknowledge the Lord in all of our ways and rely on His love for us, His sovereignty, and His plan for our good.[31] He is totally trustworthy. I needed money to pay for the trip to Israel, and God opened the door so that I could travel to Jerusalem at a reduced cost and I also received a bonus to be able to pay for it. He removed all the obstacles and changed the circumstances.

Principle 5: Other people

God speaks to us today through people. The Bible records many instances in which God has used an individual to deliver His message to another individual.[32] God may speak to you through another individual—a friend, a parent, a pastor, your spouse or even a stranger. You would be wise to confirm what you hear God saying by seeking affirmation from wise and godly people. One of the best places to find individuals who can give you godly counsel is at your local church. Even if your fellow church members do not give you counsel directly, God can use their words to reveal or confirm His will, as the Holy Spirit works in your life. Also, as a member of a local church, you can observe what God is saying to the entire church.

Other Ways In Which God Speaks

God also speaks to us when we pray. Unfortunately, many of us have the mistaken idea that the purpose of prayer is to change God's mind. We think, 'If I can just plead with God long enough and hard enough, He'll give me what I'm asking for.' Prayer is not a way to twist God's arm. Prayer is God's means of getting through to us, so that we can do things for Him! As we pray, God takes our focus off our needs and puts our focus on His love and His power. Through prayer, God changes our perspective to conform to His purposes; He establishes His priorities for our lives; He leads us into all truth.

God can speak to us through *dreams and visions*. This pattern is shown in the lives of Joseph, Solomon, Jacob, Peter, John, and Paul. This method is also available to us today.[33]

God can speak through our *thoughts and thinking*. The Prophet Amos explains that God makes known His ways to us through our thoughts (Amos 4:13). God spoke to Joseph in a dream and while he thought about these things, God revealed to him what to do next (Matthew 1:1–21). We need to be careful here because not every thought in our minds come from the Lord. Thoughts can also be placed in our minds by the devil. And we can simply think about things that come from our own hearts. So, every time we get a thought, we need to judge if it is from God. Does it align with the Scriptures? Does it in any way contradict the character of God? Does the Holy Spirit confirm it with peace in your heart?

God can also speak through *natural manifestations* and makes Himself known through *nature* (Romans 1:18–20). The voice of God can be revealed through mountains, water, trees, meadows, landscapes, and any other object He deems fit. God has spoken from heaven, and when He had done so, some people who stood nearby thought that they heard thunder. Sometimes if we hear thunder, see floods, hurricanes, high winds or volcanoes, it may actually be the voice of God. God spoke to Moses through a burning bush. He spoke to Gideon through a fleece (Judges 6:37–40). He spoke to Saul on the Damascus road through a bright light (Acts 9:1–5). He even spoke to Balaam through a donkey (Numbers 22:1–35).

God often speaks in a *still, small voice*. When the Prophet Elijah was discouraged and depressed, God spoke to him through a whisper:

> Then He said, "Go out, and stand on the mountain before the Lord." And behold, the Lord passed by, and a great and strong wind tore into the mountains and broke the rocks in pieces before the Lord, *but* the Lord was not in the wind; and after the wind an earthquake, *but* the Lord was not in the earthquake; and after the earthquake a fire, *but* the Lord *was* not in the fire; and after the fire a still small voice. So it was, when Elijah heard *it,* that he wrapped his face in his mantle and went out and stood in the entrance of the cave. Suddenly a voice *came* to him, and said, "What are you doing here, Elijah?" (1 Kings 19:11–13)

Sometimes God will speak through 'the wind or an earthquake or a fire,' but most often He speaks in a still, small voice. Be attentive! When we pray, God will hear, and He will answer us with 'yes,' 'no,' or 'wait.' Hearing God's clear answers to our petitions is essential.

As you spend time with your heavenly Father through prayer, and as you learn to know Him through His Word, you will hear His voice, you will learn to view the circumstances of your life with discernment and perceive God's answers to your prayers.

God always answers our prayers but, unfortunately, we do not always recognize His answers. That takes practise.

> We need to tune in to the frequency of heaven and hear the voice of God.

I love the promise given by Paul, 'So then faith comes by hearing, and hearing by the Word of God' (Romans 10:17). If you've ever met a person of great faith, then you've met a person of great hearing, who knows how to listen to the Word of God. We need to truly listen to God. Once we hear from Him, then we need to act in faith. Have you heard from God and truly listened to His voice? Then good, now is the time to obey with confidence.

God Speaks through Journaling

What is a journal? The *Merriam-Webster's Dictionary* defines the word journal as 'a record of experiences, ideas, or reflections kept regularly for private use.'[34]

Moses had to keep a record of what God was saying to him, 'Then the Lord said to Moses, "Write these words, for according to the tenor of these words I have made a covenant with you and with Israel"' (Exodus 34:27 KJV). Recalling the mighty acts of God was essential in reminding the people of God's goodness, greatness and power that had brought them out of slavery in Egypt.

Habakkuk had to write down the vision that he received, 'Then the Lord answered me and said: "Write the vision and make it plain on tablets, that he may run who reads it. For the vision is yet for an appointed time; but at the end it will speak, and it will not lie"' (Habakkuk 2:2–3).

Throughout history, great Christian leaders have kept personal devotional journals as an aid to their spiritual life and growth. They recorded God-given insights and expressions of their victories, and personal struggles. I love to read and reread the biographies and autobiographies of George Mueller, Hudson Taylor, James O. Fraser and others. They speak to me about believing God for the impossible, vision-trusting God in and for ministry, about how an effective prayer life can change ministry, and so forth. These *mentors* stay with me today and continue to encourage me on my journey, whispering applications of their principles as they apply to me today.

Charles Swindoll, in his book *So You Want to Be Like Jesus*, explained that a journal is not merely a record of how you're spending time, it's actually a record of your spiritual journey. A journal isn't to be confused with your calendar, your organizer, or even a diary.[35] He recommends not to write in it every day, to prevent it from becoming shallow.

Some years ago, I began journaling. I stopped for a while and as I was developing the material for this book, God spoke to me about journaling and I started to journal once again. When going back to what I had written, I saw how God worked in and through my life. I also discovered that when I wrote down and responded to the Scriptures, impressions, and thoughts, it made them more memorable. I could clearly see a pattern of how God directed my path and ministry, paying attention, watching and observing. 'Blessed is the man that heareth me, watching daily at my gates, waiting at the posts of my doors' (Proverbs 8:34). There are many benefits to keeping a personal devotional journal. *Keeping a journal is a constant reminder of how God has met my needs, and how is He at work in my life.*

Where do I Start?

If you have never had a journal, you may wonder where to start. You need a pen, writing pad or a notebook. You open the book and write down the first thought that comes to mind. You are not writing for someone else; it is your journal. You are not writing and recording your journey in the hope that you will become famous or popular and that it will be published someday.

What do I Write in my Journal?

Gordon MacDonald, in his book *Ordering Your Private World*, reveals the following:

> I write in my journal almost every day, but I am not overly disturbed if an occasional day passes without an entry. And what is in there? An account, of things that I accomplished in the preceding day [yesterday], people I met, things I

learned, feelings I experienced, and impressions I believe God wanted me to have. I include prayers, insights that come from the reading the Bible and other spiritual literature, and concerns I have about my own personal behavior. All of this is part of listening to God. As I write, I am aware that what I am writing may actually be what God wants to tell me.[36]

I begin my own journaling by simply writing down the key Scripture verse or verses which I have underlined in my Bible reading for the day. It helps to impress the Scriptures on my mind and to recall them later during the day. I would also write them down in different translations, the *Amplified Bible* or the *Living Translation*. I then proceed to write down some insights that I have gained or felt that God has spoken to me about. I ask and reflect on some questions, such as:

- What does this passage teach me about God?
- What did I learn about God, Jesus or the Holy Spirit?
- What does this passage teach me about the ways and purposes of God?
- Is there a warning or a sin that I need to be aware of?
- Is there an example to follow?
- Is there a command to obey?
- Is there an invitation to respond to?
- What is God asking me to do right now?
- What person or concern has God given to me to pray for?
- What struggles do I have at the moment?

In closing, I write down a response or a conversational prayer. Sometimes, I start with writing a prayer before writing down what I sense or feel. Sometimes I simply write down my struggles and where I am emotionally at the moment. Don't quit if you have missed a day or more. It is not a duty or contest. Just continue the next day. The length is not important; the idea is key. You may write a sentence or a couple of pages. Looking back and rereading your own thoughts, you will not just see what God is doing, but the content will also speak to you again.

So, let's start where you are. What is the primary thing God is saying to you right now? What does God want you to do? We all have to begin somewhere, so begin where you are. Write down what God is telling you.

How Can I Hear His Voice?

There is no shortcut in learning to recognize God's voice, just as there is no shortcut to mature from infancy to adulthood— it takes time. I make myself available and accessible to God to communicate with me.

First, ask God for a *heart* that is willing to hear. When Solomon was given the opportunity to ask for whatever he wanted, he asked God for 'an understanding heart.'

Second, set aside a *daily time and place to meet* with God. We have already seen how Mary gave priority to be with Jesus. Just as Jesus was waiting to speak to Mary, we can be assured that He is waiting to speak to us.

Third, have a *Bible-reading plan*. Since all of Scripture is given through the inspiration of God, and since it is the means by which God speaks to us, we should have a plan to read through the Bible on a regular basis. During this time of reading, we should pay attention and listen to how the Holy Spirit reveals truths that hold special meaning or significance for us.

Fourth, *meditate on and try to memorize* Scriptures. Manley Beasley once said, 'Truth is not to be learned but to be lived.'[37] We must meditate on Scriptures to which the Holy Spirit draw our attention and apply them to our lives. Didn't Jesus promise, 'If you abide in Me, and My words abide in you, you will ask what you desire, and it shall be done for you' (John 15:7)?

Fifth, make yourself accessible in the many *opportunities* that are available for God to speak to you. He can use the weekly Bible study, or men's or women's groups, conferences, reading of books or whatever. We must be careful not to limit God to just one way of speaking to us.

Sixth, *cultivate* your relationship with Christ. The more you get to know Him, the easier it will be to recognize His voice.

In the final instance, make yourself available to God through *obedience.*

God is speaking.

He wants you to hear His voice. And there is nothing in this world that will put you in a better position to hear what He's saying than deciding to set aside some time to be with Him.

Do you want to hear God's voice?

Ask the Lord to give you an understanding and listening heart. Ask the Lord to help you reprioritize your schedule, agenda and schedule a daily meeting time. Make an appointment with Him, when you sit and listen to Him speak.

> The more time we spend with Him ... the more we will be able to listen and hear Him speak.
> The more we hear Him speak ... the more we will be able to recognize His voice.
> The more we recognize His voice ... the more we will be able to understand His intentions.
> The more we understand His intentions ... the more we will be able to be faithful to His agenda and accomplish His purposes.

If you decide to embark on this journey, you will not be disappointed. You will be blessed beyond any possible human expectation.

He is speaking. Are you listening?

4

The CHANGE

To understand and realize His intentions

Being confident of this very thing, that He who has begun
a good work in you will complete it until the day of Jesus
Christ. (Philippians 1:6)

When God raises up a man for special service, He first
works in that man the principles which later on are, through
his labors and influence, to be the means of widespread
blessing to the Church and the world. (D.E. Hoste)[1]

Several years ago, during a preaching tour in Cornwall, England,
I had two experiences that radically touched my heart and set
my life on a course to seek and experience more of Jesus in my
life. I stayed in the coastal town of Penzance, from where the
small islands of Mount's Bay are clearly visible. The nearest small
island, St Michael's Mount, is one of 43 unbridged tidal islands
that you can walk to from mainland Britain. A man-made granite
causeway provides access to the island when the tide is out. If
you are caught on the island at high tide, the only way to get back
to the mainland is by boat. During low tide the sea completely
withdraws from the bay, leaving the sandy seashore exposed. All
the boats in the little harbor become stranded during low tide
and the vast sea life in the little harbor is limited to the small
organisms, crabs and small fish remaining in a few shallow pools
of water. When high tide returns, the boats float and the sea life
is back.

One afternoon, as I walked along the beach at low tide, I sensed that the Lord was saying, 'the lives of many Christians and churches are like this ... at low tide ... there are signs of life, but it is not visible.'

At Tuckingmill, a small village near Redruth, I was thrilled to be at the place where God had sent a mighty revival in the early 19th century. I addressed the congregation of the local church and on my way back to my overnight accommodation, I walked past a small grocery store. It was deserted except for a young lady behind the counter. I went in to buy a snack and water. I handed her some money but she did not look up. She just took the money and continued to browse through her magazine. When I looked at the magazine, I saw that it was an x-rated magazine. I was shocked to see someone reading such a vulgar magazine in an open public space. I thought to myself she could at least hide it or stop reading it when customers come in, but she did not. She was not in the least concerned about what others might think or say of her behavior.

The Lord reminded me about the story in the Old Testament of a woman and her husband who had built a 'prophet's chamber' on the roof of their house and furnished it with lamp, bed, table and chair. (2 Kings 4:8–11). This woman noticed that Elisha often passed through Shunem on his way north for his ministry. She discerned that he was a man of God—only by looking at him—and she wanted to serve the Lord by serving His prophet. So, they built a place where Elisha and his servant could stay when they passed through her town.

This brought to mind John Wesley, founder of the Methodist Church, who had had a similar experience in his day. He used to travel by horseback from London to preach in Gwennap Pit and surrounding areas in Cornwall. One day a lady saw him riding through Trewinth, a small village near Launceston. She had read, that same morning during her devotions, the story of Elisha and the prophet's chamber (2 Kings 4:8–11) and told her husband that she saw a holy man passing through their village on horseback. They built a small room next to their house, and put in a bed, table, chair and a lamp. This became the overnight accommodation for Wesley on his Cornwall ministry trips.

I once read that, during his ministry, he passed through Trewinth 17 times. The little room the couple had built for Wesley became known as the smallest Methodist chapel in the world.

The lady in Shunem saw a man of God passing through. The lady in Trewinth saw a holy man of God passing through. What saddened me was that the young lady looked at me—and did not see that I was any different from all the other customers at the grocery store.

> When people look at us, what do they see?
> Do they see that we are different?
> Do they see Jesus Christ in and through us?
> The night Peter denied Jesus he was 'convicted' of being a follower of Jesus.

The little servant girl looked at Peter and told him that he had been with Jesus because his speech betrayed him (Matthew 26:69–73). He talked like Jesus. Later on Peter and John, although uneducated and untrained, were recognized as people who had been with Jesus (Acts 4:13).

Why is it that we often start out strong in our Christian walk, and then later discover that we are struggling to continue steadfastly in our faith? And before we even realize it, we experience a spiritual setback or a moral decline of some kind. Charles F. Stanley, in his book *Living in the Power of the Holy Spirit,* gives us three reasons for that. First, is that we *drift away* from the very principles that we learned at the beginning of our relationship with Christ. Second, we *become so familiar* with the Word of God and the messages that we hear preached that we no longer take the truth of God's Word to heart as diligently and as eagerly as we once did. Third, we *stop relying* on the Holy Spirit to lead us, and guide us, to give us the spiritual power we need to withstand temptation, and to give us the spiritual wisdom we need to recognize and avoid error.[2]

We all face that.

Warren Wiersbe, in his book *God Isn't In A Hurry*, highlights the importance of knowing and allowing the truths of God's Word to penetrate our inner person:

> There is a subtle danger in cramming ourselves full of Bible knowledge that never really gets into our inner person. We start equating knowledge with spirituality, and activity with ministry; and then we start living on substitutes. Knowing Bible truths is not the same as receiving Bible truths and making them a vital part of our inner person.[3]

It takes time to be holy and grow. Too many of us are caught up in a religious rat race, and we do not take the time to digest the Word of God. As we become familiar with the things of God, we might stop abiding in Jesus and start to rely more on our own understanding. If we do not rely on the Holy Spirit as a reality in our daily lives, we will end up far away from God or deeply engrossed in sin. *A decline in our spiritual lives because of sin, disobedience, or a lack of quiet time with God.* Our lives will be 'low tide' lives. We will have life but it will not be visible.

What made the difference in the lives of the apostles?

Being with Jesus laid the foundation for them to be changed and transformed into His likeness. They were empowered, enlightened and energized by the Holy Spirit. The Christian life is meant to be increasingly dependent on His power working within us.

Who is the Holy Spirit?

The Holy Spirit is a person. Jesus describes the Holy Spirit as 'another Jesus' (John 14:16). The Greek word for Holy Spirit literally means 'another who is exactly the same.' He is the same as Jesus—but without a body. Jesus, the Son of God, came in the flesh and lived out His life as a physical being to do the will of God. Jesus completed His work on the cross. He had accomplished what God sent Him to do. His work on earth was finished. God sent the Holy Spirit to continue His work on earth through the hearts of people. Since then, God has chosen to work through the person and power of the Holy Spirit. It is the Holy Spirit who guides us onto the right path and convicts us of sin if we stray from that path. It is the Holy Spirit who reminds us of the truth of what Jesus said, and teaches us how to apply it in our daily lives.

But, most importantly, it is the Holy Spirit who works within us to change, transform, and conform us into the image of Jesus, and who works through us to minister the presence and power of Jesus to others. We need to keep in step with the Spirit (Galatians 5:16, 25), be led by the Spirit (v. 18) and live in the Spirit (v. 25). Once the Holy Spirit has full control, He has accomplished the second purpose: to equip you for ministry (baptize) and empower you with Himself.

The ongoing lesson we must all learn and understand is that the Holy Spirit is working out God's purposes in our lives. No matter where you are on your journey with the Lord, this is essential for you to become like Jesus. Be with Jesus and allow the Holy Spirit to change and transform us into the image and likeness of Jesus Christ to enable Him to empower us to be witnesses for Him.

Called For A Purpose

Would you like to know Jesus more intimately and also know that you are in the center of His will and plan for your life? Would you like to become more like Him? Would you like to have a positive impact and be a blessing to other people? If you are a believer, the answer is more than likely yes. You read your Bible, go to church, and give your tithe. You may also be sure that He loves you and has a plan for your life because He promised it in Jeremiah 29:11–13:

> For I know the thoughts that I think toward you, says the Lord, thoughts of peace and not of evil, to give you a future and a hope. Then you will call upon Me and go and pray to Me, and I will listen to you. And you will seek Me and find Me, when you search for Me with all your heart.

You may even understand right from wrong, but you might know very little about the ways and purposes of God. It is not until you get to know Him, His purposes and ways that you will have the knowledge and understanding of why God wants you to live in a certain way. Once you start to understand the way God thinks and works, you will understand Him better. When your knowledge of God deepens your desire to be with Him, and to be like Him and please Him will also increase. God wants to know you personally and be known by you. We have the opportunity to be a part of God's global initiatives to draw people closer to Himself.

Many Christian people believe that only certain people are called by God to accomplish specific tasks on this earth. The Bible tells us, however, that all believers are called according to God's purpose (Romans 8:28).

> Did God intend for all believers to be with Him? Absolutely.
> Does God want to change, transform and conform us? Absolutely.
> Does God want our lives to bear fruit? Absolutely.
> Does God want to use us? Absolutely.

We are all called for a purpose. His purpose. The disciples were called to *become fishers of men and to preach, cast out demons, heal the sick and later on to become witnesses and make disciples of all nations.*

And so are we.

In Matthew 4:17–22 we read of the moment God called Peter, Andrew, James and John. They were men who had already met Jesus and trusted Him (John 1:29–42). They had returned to their fishing but then Jesus came and called them to give up their work and follow Him (see also Mark 1:16–20 and Luke 5:1–11). He told them, *Follow Me, and I will make you fishers of men* (Matthew 4:19). Just like the disciples, the Lord comes to us and invites us to join Him and work with Him. This initial call comprises three key elements.

> First, we are called to *follow.*
> Second, we are called to *change and be transformed.*
> Third, we are called to be *sent.*

Follow Me

Before Jesus called the disciples to join Him, He announced that He came to preach the gospel of the kingdom of God (Mark 1:14). People were to 'repent and believe in the gospel' (Mark 1:16). *Repentance means a change of mind and heart that ultimately leads to a new way of life.* In essence Jesus was saying that people needed to change their view of things and their way of life. Repentance is the first step to allowing Jesus to change and transform our lives. Jesus then called people to believe the 'good news of the gospel.' The good news was His message about the kingdom of God, which refers to the reign of God in people's hearts, and His demonstration of God's reign in and through their lives. The word for 'believe' places emphasis on trusting a person more than merely believing an idea. Most people believe that there is 'a god,' but fewer people are willing to trust God the Father enough to open their hearts and lives and live as He commands us to live. In order for us to become followers of Jesus, He requires that we trust Him and not just believe facts about Him.

Jesus's favorite invitation was simply, 'Follow Me.'

He used these words 24 times in the gospels. Jesus called Peter, Andrew, James and John to follow Him, and they left everything behind to do so. He spoke these words to Matthew, the hated tax collector, and Matthew left everything to follow Jesus (Mark 2:14). The same invitation was extended to Philip from Bethsaida, and he followed Jesus (John 1:43). He spoke these words to casual observers who praised Him with their words but were unwilling to change their lifestyles (Luke 9:59–62). He even used that invitation with a wealthy young ruler who chose to hold on to his riches rather than to follow Jesus (Mark 10:21–22). Jesus is inviting everyone to follow Him.

The first major change in our lives will take place when *we decide to respond to His call* and accept the invitation when Jesus says, 'Follow Me' it is a call to believe in Him and trust in Him. When we answer the call and accept Jesus as our Savior, we are *born again, saved, converted.* We have recognized Jesus as the true Lamb of God and Lord of all.' Repent and embrace Him by faith (see Matthew

4:17; Acts 2:36–41; Ephesians 2:8–9). We are saved by putting our faith and trust in Him. Then, in reality, we spend the rest of our lives becoming what He has called us to be. Willingly, we devote ourselves to Him and His cause.

The second part of the call to follow is to *be with Jesus and learn from Him*. Once you and I have confesed our trust in the Lord Jesus as our Savior, we have the opportunity to learn the spiritual principles by which we are to live the Christian life. We have so much to learn and Jesus has much to teach us. Just as He explained to the disciples, 'I still have many things to say to you' (John 16:12), He comes to each and every one of us and extends the invitation to learn from Him.

The disciples believed in Jesus and were saved. He confirmed that, 'Nevertheless do not rejoice in this, that the spirits are subject to you, but rather rejoice because your names are written in heaven' (Luke 10:20). John MacArthur, in his book *Twelve Ordinary Men*, explained that the calling of the disciples took place in a few phases.[4] First was the call to *conversion*. Later on the disciples received the call to follow Jesus in *ministry* (Luke 5), when Jesus said, 'Do not be afraid. From now on you will catch men' (Luke 5:10). The call to follow led them into *apostleship* (Matthew 10:1–4; Mark 3:13–15; Luke 6:12–16) and eventually into *martyrdom as witnesses* for Christ (Acts 1:6–8). The Lord does not guarantee us a long, prosperous life on earth; a life without pain, sorrow, or the burden of paying taxes. However, He promises that we will have a life of victory and abundance (John 10:1–11). The abundance the Lord promises will satisfy our deepest longings, but we Christians should know that it is not on our terms and conditions. We must come to Him with openness for Him to work in us, for there is no real life apart from life in Jesus Christ. And we must be willing to exchange our old life for a life changed, crafted and directed by God. Some people believe that once they had accepted Jesus, He would fulfill all of their wishes and their plans for their lives. It is not true. It is not about us or our happiness. It is all about Him and His purpose and His goal.

Jesus guides and leads.
He equips and grows us.
We follow.

If you are a believer, abundant life is yours. The question that needs to be answered is, 'Are you living abundantly and victoriously?' It has only one requirement: you and I must be willing to exchange our old life for a new life. It is not something we can claim. It is something we receive from Jesus Christ when we are willing to submit ourselves to Him and follow Him.

And I Will Make You ...

The second major change is not just a once-off event but rather a *continuing process of change and transformation.* Jesus invited the disciples to follow Him and said that He would make them fishers of men. The Greek word *poieo* means 'and I will make you,' which implies endowing a person with certain qualities; producing and bringing forth of something which, when produced, has an independent existence of its own.

When we read the Gospels and study the lives of the disciples, we find that they often acted in ways that were selfish, rude, clueless, and immature. They were not spiritual giants, they were just regular guys like us, with the same struggles and fears we all have today. Jesus did not choose them because they were special. He chose them because He knew what they could become. *Christianity is not what we know but what we become.* He was going to 'unmake' them and 'remake' them into His image. Moses, like all of us, was a human being with faults and frailties. He was sometimes disobedient and weak, but he became the greatest leader of God's people in all of the history of Israel. God took him into the desert for 40 years and 'took Egypt out of him.' He changed and transformed him into a humble and meek person (Numbers 12:3), who walked with God in selfless dedication. He knew God face to face (Deuteronomy 34:10) and reflected the glory of God (2 Corinthians 3:18). Likewise, Jesus saw the potential in the fishermen, but He knew that it would take a process to develop them. He wanted them to get to know Him more intimately. He wanted them to live, act and minister, not from the viewpoint of what they know, but rather from what they have become. Over the next two years, He would begin to develop them. He was going to change them into something new. *They were transformed from converts into spiritually mature followers who would become effective and efficient laborers in the harvest and eventually leaders.* The disciples had to learn many things from Jesus that would later form the foundation of their own ministries. What did they learn?

First of all, they learned about *conviction.* The Holy Spirit works through the lives of people by bringing forth certain convictions in their hearts and minds. We read in John 16:7–11:

> Nevertheless, I tell you the truth. It is to your advantage that I go away; for if I do not go away, the Helper will not come to you; but if I depart, I will send Him to you. And when He has come, He will convict the world of sin, and of righteousness, and of judgment: of sin, because they do not believe in Me; of righteousness, because I go to My Father and you see Me no more; of judgment, because the ruler of this world is judged.

The key word here is reprove. It is a legal word that means 'to bring to light, to expose, refute, to convict and convince.' The Holy Spirit will convict the world of the sin of unbelief so that they may believe and trust in Jesus. That conviction can only come to the 'world' when the Holy Spirit, in His fullness, dwells in us as believers. He will convict the world of righteousness by revealing Christ in the lives of believers. He will convict the world of judgment as He prepares us for His second coming. When the Holy Spirit came at Pentecost, He empowered Peter to preach, and his preaching brought conviction to those who heard the message.

When the Holy Spirit comes to us, He enables and empowers us so that, through our lives, words, testimony and prayers, we are able to witness to others. He will, both by our lips and lives, convince others. In doing so, He will purge and cleanse our conscience to serve the living God. He gives us a new perspective, a fresh conviction for our lives. Jesus wants to set us apart from the world, not so that we can judge others but so that we can promote the salvation of the lost. Jesus is also interested in giving us guidance so that we can live extraordinary, victorious and abundant lives while we strive to become more and more like Jesus.

Second, they learned about *consistency* in their Christian life. Ron Dunn, in his book *Extraordinary Victory for Ordinary Christians,* wrote that Stuart Briscoe compares the life of an average Christian to an old iron bedstead, 'firm on both ends but sagging in the middle!' He said that the statement intrigued him, not because it is catchy but because it described perfectly his own Christian life. He knew that he had been saved. He knew that he would go to heaven when he died. He was firm on both ends but sagging in the middle.[5] It certainly described my state at one stage in my life. I knew that I was born again and saved. I knew that I was going to heaven but I constantly experienced defeat in my life. I became aware of a coldness, a lack of devotion and prayer, and a lack of consistency in my spiritual life. I longed for God to be a greater reality in my life and to be aware of His power in my life. I longed for more victories and fewer failures in my life. I needed to be more consistent. According to the *Cambridge Dictionary,* consistency means 'the quality of behaving or performing in a similar way.'[6] Most of us today are living subnormal Christian lives. *God desires for every believer to experience a life of abundance and victory.* We as Christians can experience that but only when the indwelling Christ is the source and power behind every thought and action in the heart and life of a believer.

Third, they learned how to be *conformed* to God's will. What is God's will for our lives? He wants to change and transform us into the image and likeness of Jesus Christ and use us for His eternal purposes. When we surrender ourselves, our possessions, agendas, and plans, and release our grip on things, we are conformed to God's will as we continue to be aligned with His will for our lives.

Fourth, they learned about having *compassion* for the needy and lost. God experiences a deep anguish when people die without Him as their Savior, when they enter into a Christless eternity. He loves us so much that He was willing to send His Son (John 3:16) so that all people may have eternal life and not perish. As the Apostle Peter put it, 'The Lord is not slack concerning His promise, as some count slackness, but is longsuffering toward us, not willing that any should perish but that all should come to repentance' (2 Peter 3:9). Jesus was profoundly moved with pity for all the stressed and aimless people wandering the face of the earth. Jesus had compassion for the needy and lost. 'But when He saw the multitudes, He was moved with compassion for them, because they were weary and scattered, like sheep having no shepherd' (Matthew 9:36). Read also Matthew 14:14; 15:32 and 20:34, where Jesus had compassion for the crowds, the sick, the hungry and two blind men. In all these passages the Greek word *splagchnizomai* describes the force of Jesus' feeling for lost and needy people. It is this deep compassion for mankind that motivated Jesus to go from town to town and share the gospel and the same would become the driving force of the disciples to travel to the ends of the earth with the same message as Jesus.

Fifth, they learned about the importance of *Christlikeness* or *becoming like Christ*. There is no question that nonbelievers evaluate the claims of Jesus Christ by the lives and character of those who profess to follow Him. The world needs Christ. God's will for us to become like Him becomes our goal when we have Christ. Some people seem to think that becoming like Christ means that we should strive to be perfect—like Jesus. They think if we follow a set of rules and disciplines, we will be more like Him.

I once had a coaching session with a pastor who longed to have greater intimacy with God. He thought that if he prayed for two hours every day that he would enjoy greater intimacy with Him. His intentions were pure, but his method was wrong. It is not when we pray that we experience more intimacy but when we are sitting at His feet and listening to His voice that we grow deeper in our walk with Christ. *Christlikeness is not gaining more knowledge, but it is about getting to know Jesus as a person and allowing Him to change us.* We must focus and study the life of Christ and compare ourselves to Him:

> ...looking unto Jesus, the author and finisher of our faith, who for the joy that was set before Him endured the cross, despising the shame, and has sat down at the right hand of

the throne of God. For consider Him who endured such hostility from sinners against Himself, lest you become weary and discouraged in your souls. (Hebrews 12:2–3)

So, you want to be like Christ? Me too. Fix your attention exclusively on Christ for the sake of understanding and measuring yourself against His life and example. Keep Him as your standard. Remember, Christlikeness is not mere profession but possession: the possession of the Lord Jesus dwelling in the heart of a Christian.

Last, they learned and developed *commitment to Jesus and His cause.* At the beginning of their walk with Jesus, when they had just accepted the call to follow Him, they still lacked commitment. In the beginning of Jesus' ministry, it was easy for the disciples to feel special and pleased to be a part of His inner circle, when they saw the crowds cheering at their Rabbi doing miracles. They were popular and loved. But as soon as the soldiers came to arrest Jesus, they all forsook Jesus; they ran away (Mark 14:50). Peter, the leader, denied Jesus, by swearing that he didn't even know the man. However, their relatively brief time with Jesus bore fruit. Soon after the ascension of Jesus, the Holy Spirit came, infused them with power to be witnesses, and enabled them to do what Jesus had trained them to do. Due to the persecution that broke out in Jerusalem, the apostles and disciples of Jesus were scattered over the whole world, and they preached the gospel everywhere they went. They were faithful and committed to the very end, even in the midst of persecution and hardship.

It was not an easy process for the disciples to go through. Why was their training and learning process so difficult? According to John MacArthur, in his book *Twelve Ordinary Men,*[7] there are several reasons for this. They lacked *spiritual understanding.* They were slow to hear and slow to understand. They lacked *humility.* They were self-absorbed, self-centered, self-promoting, and proud. They spent an enormous amount of time arguing about who would be the greatest among them (Matthew 20:20–28; Mark 9:33–37; Luke 9:46). They lacked *faith, commitment* and *power.*

Jesus knew about their weaknesses and struggles. He graciously encouraged them, lovingly corrected them, and patiently instructed them. He developed them into the people that He wanted them to be. And He is still doing so with us today! What did He do? How did He do it?

What Did He Do?

First, He changed their *hearts and lives*. The disciples were changed because they encountered Jesus in a deep and meaningful way. The disciples believed in Jesus and were saved. Their names were written in the book of life (Luke 10:20). Just like the disciples, nobody inherits a relationship with Jesus from their parents. Nobody becomes a follower by attending church, doing good things, and avoiding bad things. The disciples had to make a decision to accept and follow Jesus, just like us, and as a result of that decision received a new heart: a heart filled with forgiveness and love. A heart filled with the Holy Spirit that testified that He had entered into their hearts and lives (Romans 8:16–18) and continued to renew their minds and lives (Romans 12:1–2). Their changed hearts led to their changed lives.

Bill Wohl

I once read the story of Bill Wohl, which illustrates how a new heart can lead to a new way of life. But it starts with a stuntman for Universal Studios, Michael Brady, who specialized in skydiving. During filming in Benson, Arizona, Michael was ready for his stunt that day. He parachuted from a plane and landed on the top of a moving train, when he slipped and fell from a great height. He struck his head on impact and died instantly. However, that is not the end of his story. Michael's body was taken to the University Medical Center in Tucson, where his heart was removed and transplanted into the body of another man, Bill Wohl, who had suffered heart failure more than five months earlier. Six months and one day after receiving his new heart, Bill Wohl opened a letter from Michael Brady's family, which included a picture of Michael and some background information. Bill was shocked to learn that he had been given the heart of a 36-year-old Hollywood stuntman.

'I looked at this picture,' Bill said, 'at this incredibly good-looking, super-fit, super-athletic guy. And I thought: Are you kidding me? That's whose heart I've got?' That moment proved to be a life-altering moment in Bill Wohl's life. Before his heart transplant, Bill Wohl had been a Type A, overweight, money-obsessed businessman pursuing a jet-setter lifestyle. Today, he works part-time, and spends most of his new-found energy winning performance medals in swimming, cycling, and tracking.

When interviewed by a reporter at his Scottsdale condo, Bill Wohl spoke passionately about the blessing he'd received, 'Every day, all day, I thank God for Michael Brady.' Glancing at his many medals, won in athletic competitions, Wohl added, 'When I ride, when I work out—the biggest thing is to honor him.'[8] Bill Wohl had become painstakingly aware of the value of his new heart and the second chance to life he had received. His life was dramatically changed, totally transformed, by the gift of a new heart.

The same should be said of Christians who receive Jesus as their Lord and Savior. The reality of our new lives in Christ should be so profound that we leave any evidence of our old lives behind and embrace our new life and identity in Christ with wholehearted devotion. The initial change takes place in our hearts when we accept Jesus Christ and then continually allow Him as our Savior to change our hearts in accordance with His will. When Christ's heart beats in your chest, you will want to live and honor Him each day and you will want to share His passion to take the gospel to the world.

Second, He changed the *character and conduct* of the disciples. Jesus Christ Himself is the epitome of a true follower and a leader. He was perfect in all the attributes that make up the character of a disciple, effective laborer and leader. Obviously, the great and ultimate goal and objective is to bring people to a place of Christlikeness. That is why Jesus lived and modeled His character, conduct and inborn Christlikeness to the disciples. He wanted them to walk like He walked (1 John 2:6) and do what He did (John 14:12). He wanted them to develop godly character in their own lives. According to *Merriam-Webster's Dictionary,* the meaning of character is 'qualities or features that make you distinct from other people.'[9] It is the single most distinguishing aspect of a person's life.

God cares more about our character than our skills, personality, or intelligence. He chose and called people He could mold through various circumstances, tests, trials and tribulations, so He could use them for His eternal purposes. It is our character that determines our next and bigger assignment, or impact on people. During school and college, the hearts and minds of students are greatly influenced, one way or the other, by the quality and caliber of their teachers. There are teachers who, by their unique personality, profound knowledge and unusual form of instruction not only grip the attention of students but also leave a lasting impression on them.

Jesus is our standard, the One by whom all others are measured. He invites us to 'come' and 'learn' from Him (Matthew 11:28–29). He described himself as 'gentle and lowly in heart' (Matthew 11:29). The Greek word for gentle can also be translated as humble. It means 'one who is lowly of heart.' Jesus not only taught humility as a kingdom virtue (Luke 14:11) but also practised it. Paul, in his letter to the Philippians, encourages us to do 'nothing through selfish ambition or deceit, but in lowliness of mind' (Philippians 2:3) submitting to the plans of God over our own plans. Jesus humbled all He was to the will of the Father, which included death on a cross (Philippians 2:8). Peter continues to exhort us, 'Therefore humble yourselves under the mighty hand of God, that He might exalt you in due time' (1 Peter 5:6).

So, what are the qualities that set Jesus apart from all other people? He expressed ultimate love and joy. He exemplified peace and patience in all circumstances. He modeled kindness to the forgotten, goodness to the wayward, faithfulness to the faltering, and gentleness and self-control even in the worst of situations. Jesus is our primary example of how to develop a godly character in the lives of others.

Third, He changed their *competencies.* God has gifted each person with a set of skills, knowledge and life experiences. It helps us to discern more specifically how we can serve God. What a great realization it is to know that God has created, in advance, a great plan and purpose for our lives. What we 'do for a living' may be a part of how we serve, but we are so much more than our jobs. Jesus was going to develop and give the disciples a new set of skills and competencies. Although they were trained as skilled fishermen, they would also become trained as skilled 'fishers of men.' Fishing implies learned skills, experience as well as knowledge. Competence is a set of characteristics and skills that enable and improve the efficiency of or performance in a job.

According to the *Merriam-Webster's Dictionary*, competencies are 'the ability to do something successfully or efficiently.'[10] There is a certain baseline of knowledge and a set of skills the disciples would need to master. Jesus was not interested in giving them more information and knowledge but rather to train them in a new way of living. He wanted them to be like Him and carry on with His work. They needed to learn a new set of skills of how to live under God's rule and to be effective laborers in the harvest.

In the New Testament, the Greek word for disciple occurs 264 times. In its original ancient Greek context, it meant someone who was either an apprentice in a trade or the pupil of a teacher. Bobby Harrington and Alex Absalom, in their book *Discipleship That Fits,* explained it takes time and practise to become a mature disciple, yet the only way you truly grow is by trying out the lifestyle you are observing. Apprenticeship allows us to gain experience and knowledge conveyed to us in the context of a long-term, deeply committed relationship.[11]

A better image of a disciple is an apprentice, someone who is learning from a master craftsman. An apprentice is with someone in order to be like him or her or learn a skill from that person. Dallas Willard, author of *The Divine Conspiracy,* explains, 'I am Jesus' disciple ... that means I am with Him to learn from Him how to be like Him.'[12]

What did the disciples learn from Jesus? How important were the lessons they learned from the life, the example and teaching of Jesus? Imagine how His wisdom must have strengthened their belief in Him as the Messiah! How their faith was confirmed by the miracles He performed! How His character and conduct contributed to the formation of their own faith! They discovered that all His words were wise and truthful. They learned about the divine kingdom of God. They watched Him pray and learned about the privilege, power and importance of prayer. They often heard Him quote the Scriptures and saw how He applied it to all circumstances of life. They learned about their need to be sensitive to the Holy Spirit. They learned about humility, self-control and sacrifice. They learned to look for a man of peace on their missionary journeys. They learned to live by faith and trust the Lord for all their needs.

How Did Jesus Do That?

Jesus' method of teaching, training and developing people was what we call the 'Follow Me' method. He knew that to make the disciples to be like Himself, they would have to learn from His way of doing. He also knew that explanations or sermons would never be enough. So, what did Jesus do? When we observe His life, we see that Jesus not only called His disciples, He taught them, exposed them, modeled to them, encouraged and empowered them to live as 'fishers of men.' When the disciples left their nets and followed Jesus, they entered His school of development. He changed their hearts, and those changed hearts resulted in a new way of life and ministry.

First, Jesus called them to *follow Him*. He met the men on their level, where they lived and worked. He called them to follow Him, to learn a new way of living and to join Him on mission to reach the world. God revealed Himself through Jesus to the disciples, and to us so that we can adjust our lives and join Him on His mission. Where He takes us is not for us to decide but His decision. We do not get to choose our assignment. He does. He wants to reveal Himself to a dark and needy world through us.

Second, Jesus *taught and trained* them. They gained knowledge by listening to and watching Jesus. They learned new skills— becoming competent as they received 'on-the-job' training.

Third, Jesus *exposed* them. He exposed them to many life experiences, issues, conflicts, persecution, and rejection. Jesus wanted to prepare the disciples because He knew that they would experience the same things He did during their lives and future ministry. He called them, in Mark 3:13–15, before they were sent on their first missionary journey, as captured in Mark 6:7–13. When they traveled with Jesus and watched Him minister and interact with people, they faced a number of challenges. Jesus exposed the disciples to:

- Conflict with and persecution by religious leaders (Mark 3:20–30)
- Crowds (Mark 3:20–30)
- Conflict and family issues (Mark 3:31–35)
- Daily life and circumstances (Mark 4:1–41)
- Conflict with evil (Mark 5:1–20)
- Sickness and death (Mark 5:21–43)
- Rejection (Mark 6:1–6).

Fourth, Jesus gave them an *example* to follow. S.D. Gordon, in his book *Quiet Talks on Prayer,* tells us that there are two ways of receiving instruction: one is by being told, and the other is by watching someone else. How better can we learn to pray than by watching how Jesus prayed, and then to try to imitate Him.[13] How better can we learn how to the live the 'Christian life' than by watching how Jesus lived and taught, and then to try to imitate Him. He modeled what He taught. The way Jesus taught was first to do and then to teach. Luke declared in the book of Acts, 'I wrote about all that Jesus began both to do and to teach' (Acts 1:1).

Jesus ministered first and then explained what He had done. He fed the 5,000, then called Himself the bread of life (John 6). He washed the feet of the disciples, then He talked about servanthood (John 13). He prayed for many days before the disciples asked Him to teach them how to pray (Luke 11:1). They were not only watching and listening to the teachings and ministry of Jesus but also watching how He modeled His life and relationship with the Father, displaying by example His conduct, behavior and character in all that He said and did (1 John 3:18). He was actually imparting a new way of living to them. By watching Him, they not only gained knowledge and information about themselves and how to live and love but also learnt the skills how to do it.

Last, Jesus encouraged them to *grow.* He gave them small ministry tasks and challenges as part of their transformation and training. First the assignments were small tasks, which they were already capable of doing, like providing hospitality. But as they developed in their confidence and skill, He began to use them to confirm others in the faith. To see how the disciples were coming along, He would check on them, ask them questions, respond to their queries, establish in them a sense of accountability. It was on-the-job training all the way. Their encounters with life circumstances and situations enabled Jesus to deal with issues as they came up, which gave the assurance of authenticity. Jesus was molding and shaping their hearts, lives and characters to come in alignment with His. *He constantly kept them moving towards the goal of discipling the nations for the glory of God.* He kept them growing and going.

What about Us?

What about us? Words are cheap. No one is fooled today when a person says one thing but his or her actions tell another story. What have you done to model what you teach others? Do your words match your actions and behavior?

Getting to know Jesus more intimately includes walking with Him through life's challenges and darkest valleys. He uses these times to mold and shape us to become the people we were meant to be. God Himself describes, in Deuteronomy 32:10–12, the process that He uses to develop faith and character in His children, so that they can carry out His purposes.

> He found him in a desert land and in the wasteland, a howling wilderness; He encircled him, He instructed him, He kept him as the apple of His eye. As an eagle stirs up its nest, hovers over its young, spreading out its wings, taking them up, carrying them on its wings, So the Lord alone led him, and there was no foreign god with him.

> He found him out in the wilderness, in an empty, windswept wasteland. He threw his arms around him, lavished attention on him, guarding him as the apple of his eye. He was like an eagle hovering over its nest, overshadowing its young, then spreading its wings, lifting them into the air, teaching them to fly. God alone led him; there was not a foreign god in sight (MSG).

Charles Swindoll, in his book *Moses,* explains that the Lord, who set you down in the desert land, knows precisely what experience you and I need. He knows the very place where the distractions of life will be silenced, and where you will hear His voice.[14] He knows exactly what our motives and the condition of our hearts are. Each person's 'howling wilderness' or 'empty, windswept wasteland' may look different but God is teaching us the same lessons. He understands what it will take to strip us of our excuses, which keep us from doing His will. Moses tried and failed and had to flee for his life (Exodus 2). God knows the noise that keeps us from hearing His words of love and from understanding His ways and purposes. It is in the midst of our howling wilderness that God works.

> First, He *encircles us* and throws His arms around us (v. 10).
> Second, He *instructs* us with care and lavishes attention on us (v. 10).
> Third, He *guards* us as the apple of His eye (v. 10).

They were the 'apple of his eye,' referring to the pupil of the eye (Psalm 17:8; Proverbs 7:2; Zechariah 2:8). Isn't that beautiful? Your eye, and mine, is the most protected part of the body. We safeguard it from dust and the sun. When the tiniest speck of dust enters your eye, you will take great care to remove it. Likewise, God says that He will take the utmost care with us.

Last, He alone *guides* and leads us towards maturity and His goals (v. 12). At a certain age in the lives of the young eagle, the parents stir and destroy the nest and force the young to fly. To make sure the young don't fall, the adult birds stay close to the young as they 'try their wings,' by flying beneath them and even carrying them in their strong claws. 'He teaches them to fly and then to soar.' It is a beautiful picture of the difficult process of achieving maturity that God put all of us through, just as He did with the nation of Israel. God took Israel on the same journey. He exposed them to the plagues in Egypt; the challenge of crossing the Red Sea; the bitter water; the bread from heaven; the victory over the Amalekites, to name only a few. In their book *Learning to Soar,* Avery and Matt Willis explain that God often 'stirs our nests' through uncomfortable circumstances to nudge us toward growth in spiritual maturity.[15] He uses hardships to align our hearts with His and get us off our own agenda and onto His purpose. And, as a result 'soar' in our relationship with Him.

Jesus took the disciples on the same journey. He is taking us on the same journey. He uses the same pattern to grow, develop and mature us. It is with the same care, detail and commitment that God uses various tests, checks, hardships, challenges, trails, frustrations, and difficulties to transition us from where we are to align our hearts and lives with His purpose.[16] Even pain can be an instrument of spiritual growth—if we're trained by it. It can push us closer to God and deeper into the Word (Psalm 119:71; 1 Peter 4:1–3). Affliction, and pain, is a means by which He graciously shapes and molds us to be like His Son. He is making more of us—something much better—than you and I can ever imagine.

Helen Roseveare

Dr. Helen Roseveare spent several years doing medical missionary work in Africa, giving herself to others, until one day she fell into the hands of rebel soldiers. She was mercilessly beaten with a rubber truncheon and cruelly kicked, losing some of her teeth, her mouth and nose were gashed and her ribs bruised. When one of the rebels pressed a gun to her forehead, she prayed that he would pull the trigger. Alone, she was at the mercy of her attackers, knowing that worse pain and humiliation lay ahead.

She had been a Christian only for a short time when she was privileged to come under the ministry of Dr. Graham Scroggie. He wrote in her Bible the verse Philippians 3:10, 'That I may know Him'—and he added 'You have come there; and I pray that you will go on to know "the power of His resurrection."' He paused, and then, looking her straight in the face, he added, 'And one day you may be privileged to know something of "the fellowship of his sufferings."' This statement proved prophetic, for 20 years later, Dr. Helen Roseveare was the first missionary to be taken during the rebellion of 1964 in the Congo. She cried out to God that she could bear no more, when suddenly she was reminded that 20 years before she had told Him she would accept the privilege of fellowship with His suffering. Her fears were stilled, and she knew God was there, love enveloped her, and an incredible peace flowed through her.[17]

Then the Lord breathed into her troubled mind the word privilege. She said then:

> For twenty years, anything I had needed, I had asked of God and he had provided. Now, this night, the Almighty had stopped to ask of me something that he condescended to appear to need, and he offered me the privilege of responding. He wanted my body in which to live, and through which to love these very rebel soldiers in the height of their wickedness … He offered me the inestimable privilege of sharing with him in some little measure, at least, on the edge of the fellowship of his sufferings. And it was all a privilege.[18]

God does not hurry in His process to change and develop us. According to Miles Stanford, in his book *Principles of Spiritual Growth,* since the Christian life matures and becomes fruitful by the principle of growth (2 Peter 3:18), much time is involved. In that the husbandman's method for true spiritual growth involves pain as well as joy, suffering as well as happiness, failure as well as success, inactivity as well as service, death as well as life, the temptation to take a shortcut is especially strong unless we see the value of, and submit to, the necessity of the element of time. In simple trust we must rest in His hands, 'being confident of this very thing, that he which hath begun a good work in you will perform it until the day of Jesus Christ' (Philippians 1:6). But since God is working for eternity, why should we be concerned about the time involved.[19] Graham Scroggie affirmed:

> Spiritual renewal is a gradual process. All growth is progressive, and the finer the organism, the longer the process. It is from measure to measure; thirtyfold, sixtyfold, and hundredfold. It is from stage to stage, 'first the blade, then the ear, and after that, the full corn in the ear. And it is from day to day. How varied these are! There are great days, days of decisive battles,

days of crisis in spiritual history, days of triumph in Christian service, days of God's hand upon us. But there are also idle days, days apparently useless, when prayer and holy service seem a burden. Are we, in any sense, renewed in these days? Yes, for any experience which makes us more aware of our need of God must contribute to spiritual progress, unless we deny the Lord who bought us.[20]

It is interesting to note how often in Scripture there is a delay between the moment of God's call to follow, an experience of God's presence, a blessing or a vision that seems to come from God about the future, and when these things actually come to pass.

Consider Abraham, who was told in Genesis 12 that God would make him 'a great nation,' and in Genesis 22 that his descendants would be 'as numerous as the stars of heaven.' He was 75 when he first heard God's call and promises. But it was only nine chapters later, when he was 100 years old, that Isaac was finally born. He had to wait 25 years.

Consider Joseph, Abraham's great-grandson who, at the age of 17, had visions of greatness he could not understand and did not handle well. It was only after he had been sold as a slave that Joseph became Pharaoh's right-hand man at the age of 30, and it was another 7 years before he was vindicated, and the visions fulfilled.

Consider Moses, who spent 40 years in the wilderness minding goats before God finally called him back to demand the release of the Israelites. David was anointed by Samuel to be the next king of Israel, but he went through 25 years and a whole lot of trouble before he finally assumed the throne.

Consider Jesus, who at the age of 12 knew He had a unique relationship with God, but there would be 18 years of waiting before He was baptized and ready to begin His three-year public ministry.

And *consider Paul*, who trained for 14 years in the wilderness and obscurity before ministering for 10 years.

Throughout the Bible and history, God exposed people to being tested so they would follow Him wholeheartedly. All of us face challenges in our lives, times when God takes us or allows us to go through a wilderness experience to develop us or draw us closer unto Himself. Often this means that God needs to push us out of our comfort zones. As we go through various life experiences with God, we start to understand the sufficiency of God in every circumstance and situation. We get to know God more intimately. It leads to a life that models godliness.

When the Holy Spirit changes and transforms a life into the image of Christ, the characteristics of love, joy, peace, longsuffering, gentleness, goodness, faith, meekness and temperance give credibility to that person being consistent in their inward and outward walk with God. Furthermore, gifted power is clear testimony of divine intervention in our lives and ministries as it is demonstrated in and through us.

Shelley Trebesch, in her book *Isolation,* explains that a person who responds to God in processing these deeper experiences and encounters is a different person afterwards as these experiences transform their inner life, spiritual life and ministry. They live life more maturely and minister out of the spiritual overflow of what they have become.[21] As a result, we 'soar' in our relationship with Him.

No Brick—No Book

Samuel Logan Brengle (1 June 1860–19 May 1936) was a Commissioner in the Salvation Army, and a leading author, teacher and preacher on the doctrine of holiness. His books include *The Soul Winner's Secret, Helps to Holiness* and *Heart Talks on Holiness.*[22]

Brengle was once holding a street meeting in Boston when a drunk man came along and threw a brick at him. It hit him squarely in the head and so seriously injured him that he hovered between life and death for many weeks. Slowly he began to recover, but for 18 months he was unable to preach or travel. During those months Brengle wrote several articles on holiness. They were published and began to sell all over the world. Later, he collected them into a book, titled *Helps to Holiness,* and it too had phenomenal sales. It has been translated into many languages all over the world. The book is still being used today to bring believers into a deeper experience with the Holy Spirit. Brengle's wife got hold of the brick that had hit her husband and painted Genesis 50:20 on it: *…ye thought evil against me; but God meant it unto good.* She placed it on their mantle. When people would thank Brengle for his book, he would smile and say, 'Well, thank God for the brick because if there had been no brick there would have been no book.'[23]

I departed on 11 March 2020 for the USA on my annual preaching and teaching tour in North America. I arrived in Charlotte, NC, when COVID-19 had just hit the world, and I had no idea what to expect. I spoke at a conference on that Friday and Saturday, and preached Sunday morning and evening. As I was returning to my accommodation, I received the message that the South African government was going to close the borders. I had to return to South Africa immediately. I left on Monday 16 March 2020 on the last flight from Atlanta to Johannesburg. On my arrival in South Africa, I found myself in quarantine for two weeks, just to enter another three weeks of nation-wide lockdown that eventually lasted for several months. My local and international programs were cancelled for the remainder of the year. My home became my office and my study my pulpit, from where I had to teach, preach, disciple, coach and write. It reminded me of Paul, who was in 'lockdown' in Rome for two years.

Just as Paul wrote some of his letters to the church, I was able to write articles and finish the book that you are reading right now. I can truly say, to echo S.L. Brengle, *Well, thank God for the lockdown because without it there would have been no time to write and there would have been no book.*

In these circumstances I learned to be patient, to wait upon God and to exercise faith while God was working out His plan for my life. I have also come to know Jesus as the Source in our lives. We were forced to stop trying to do things for Him, and instead allow Him to work through us. We have to believe, trust and lean with our full weight upon God until we fulfill our God-given potential as we 'soar to new heights.' Just as many others have experienced this before, now it is our time to say, 'Lord, I am here by your appointment. This is no accident. I am waiting upon you. I am trusting that you will work it out within me.' *Why not ask God what the new circumstances, challenges or opportunities you are facing have to do with His purpose for your life right now?* He is at work. He is working out His promise, 'I will make you …'

Fishers Of Men

The third major change that will take place in our lives and ministry is to *accomplish His goal.* God's intention is to make us 'fishers of men' as we reflect the glory of Jesus in a dark and needy world.

Their entire lives Peter, Andrew, John and James were 'fishers of fish.' Fishing was all they knew. They knew how to throw the net into the water, wait for the right time, and then haul out fish to sell at the market. Jesus changed all of that when He said to them, 'Come, follow me' (Matthew 4:19). They did so for several years as Jesus trained them to do what the rest of His call stated, 'And I will make you fishers of men.' It indicated a response or an action, something that would affect their lives forever.

It is the same for us. God's intention is to change our lives in a way that glorifies Him. During our day-to-day lives we represent God more than we do ourselves. It can be an overwhelming thought to know that all we think, say and do should continually be transformed into our God-given identity. Do you have a desire today to follow God more closely and steadfastly and to experience greater intimacy with God? Do you desire today to experience more of God's power flowing in you and through you to others? Do you want to reach your full potential of faith and devotion? According to Charles F. Stanley, in his book *Living in the Power of the Holy Spirit,* we are wise to ask God daily:

- What do You want me to do?
- How do You want me to act?
- When do You want me to act?
- How can I best represent You today?[24]

No longer were these men going to settle for just fishing; now they were going to fish for people. Jesus took the disciples on six 'fishing trips' to teach, train and model to them how to fish for people (See Luke 4:31–37; 4:38–44; 5:1–11; 5:12–16; 5:17–26; 5:27–31). For the first part of the training, Jesus provided them with the opportunity to be with Him and learn from Him. Then

He shifted the focus and gave them opportunities to practise what He had taught them by letting them preach, heal the sick and cast out demons. Later on, as Jesus prepared to return to heaven, He gave them the Great Commission and the responsibility to carry it out. From that point forward they were going to be captivated by a greater vision of making, duplicating and multiplying disciples, and taking the message of Jesus to all the corners of the globe. He gave them a new purpose: to bring people to salvation in Jesus Christ. They were tasked with saving the world.

What a task! They planted churches, taught people about the Bible and traveled as missionaries. In doing so, we read how they took care of the widows and orphans and how they did wonders and signs among the people (Acts 6:1, 8). You and I, too, are at the place where God is extending the responsibility to reach the world to include us.

I am Sending You to Bear Fruit

Several years ago, I had the privilege to spend some time with Dr. Dennis Kinlaw in Wilmore, Kentucky. He served as the president of Asbury College twice and was the principal there during the Asbury College Revival in 1972. Before I left, I looked forward to talking to him and learning more about that *'One Divine Moment'* when God sent revival to the campus and how it spread to neighboring colleges.[25]

However, the Lord had much more in mind for me. The conversation soon turned to several words and pictures describing Jesus in the Old and New Testaments. We talked about the fact that Jesus calls us His friends. We read in John 15: 13–16:

> Greater love has no one than this, than to lay down one's life for his friends. You are My friends if you do whatever I command you. No longer do I call you servants, for a servant does not know what his master is doing; but I have called you friends, for all things that I heard from My Father I have made known to you. You did not choose Me, but I chose you and appointed you that you should go and bear fruit,

and that your fruit should remain, that whatever you ask the
Father in My name He may give you.

Dr. Kinlaw then shared with me how God had transformed
his relationship with his wife Elsie over the years, from being in
love when they were dating, to loving and caring for one another
in marriage, and later as parents and grandparents, to the point
where they enjoyed nothing more than to go for a walk and hang
out together as friends. The main reason why they liked to do that
was because they liked one another. We usually spend more time
with those we like than those people we do not like. We share more
intimate moments with those who are close to us. He related it to his
own relationship with God and mentioned that, over the years, he
has grown fonder and fonder of God. He said that God was more
real to him than any person in his life. I am sure that you love Jesus
and are thankful that He has died for you on the Cross.

But do you like Him?
Do you like to hang out with Him, maybe even go for a
walk with Him?

Jesus said that He loved us, and He was willing to lay down His
life for us. He did so voluntarily for the good of those He loves.
Jesus did not choose the rich or famous, clever or influential,
educated people or those with high standing to save from eternal
condemnation. He chose all of us. He chose you. Jesus chose the
disciples, called them out of this world, and ordained them to do
His will. The Greek word for ordained is *etheka,* which means to be
placed, sent or appointed. It speaks of the act of setting someone
apart for special service. Some of the disciples would become
famous authors and others would remain obscure. But they were
all to go out and bear fruit.

Just before I left, Dr. Kinlaw prayed with me and he quoted a
verse of Scripture. He asked me to think, pray and live with John
20:21 in my mind, and heart for at least 14 days. It had a profound
impact on my heart and my thinking:

So, Jesus said to them again, "Peace to you! As the Father has
sent Me, I also send you."

When Jesus spoke these words to the disciples, He brought them back to the realization of the great responsibility that rested upon them. He told them that they were to be His messengers and representatives in the world. He had called them to become fishers of men. He had uniquely prepared them and gave them His authority so that they would be able to carry out their commission, which would later become the Great Commission. It is significant that Jesus did not use the same verb to describe how He was sent by the Father as He did to describe how He sent the disciples.

The two Greek words for sent are used about six times in John 20, and forty times in the Gospel of John. The word sent that is used in relation to Jesus is *apostello* and the word sent that is used in relation to the disciples is *pempo*. The word *apostello* means 'a delegated authority.' It is where the word apostle comes from, which marks the setting apart of someone.

Jesus was set apart for us and came to earth so that He could set people aside for Himself. He was 'sent of God.' Jesus was aware of His 'being set apart' status and that was how He related to His Father and to the world. On the other hand, *pempo* never refers to a delegated authority. It stands for a dispatch under authority. God delegates all authority to Jesus. Jesus retains it and we, as His apostles, or messengers, are to run errands under His authority. We are people who are 'under orders.' *The Father sent Jesus into the world. Jesus sent the disciples into the world, and, likewise, Jesus sends those of us who are willing into the world.*

What does that mean? Jesus spells out the Christians' commission in the world. He came to redeem the world. Having finished the earthly part of that commission, He sends us as His co-workers out to complete the task. According to Dennis Kinlaw, in his book *Preaching In The Spirit,* every person has the right to choose whether to become a Christian or not. But once a person has chosen to follow Jesus, they inevitably sign up to be discipled and developed as they accept the task to continue with the ministry Jesus began on earth. Our business is now to finish the ministry which Jesus began.[26]

Not every person is called to be a preacher, pastor, missionary, evangelist or Bible teacher. Some are called to be businessmen, doctors, mothers, fathers, or plumbers. God calls people to fill every niche of society with His presence. Not every person is going to have a radio or television program or be a successful author. That's why God places His people in every sector of society and in every type of circumstance or situation.

Every believer is called by God to be a witness for Jesus Christ in the world in which God has placed him or her. Believers can speak the name of Jesus in the marketplace, the hospital, the courtroom, the classroom, the family kitchen, the construction site, the factory floor, the sports arena, or any other place they might be. He speaks through us and through our lives, words, actions and behavior to people we don't even know we are influencing for Jesus Christ.

We are to the world something of what Jesus is to us. His method of reaching the world through us is the same as the Father used to reach us through His Son. Whatever Jesus Christ is to you, you must be in this world. That ultimately means that we need to become like Jesus and 'be Jesus.' I must be Jesus for my spouse, neighbor and acquaintances. Jesus is sending us out to bear fruit. That is the intention of the Father.

In Closing

Every once in a while, I pick up a biography of someone who had or has the same interests as me. I do this because it is important for me as a person to grow in myself and be exposed to other like-minded people who love the Lord. I want to reach my full potential for God. I want to live an extraordinary life as a normal, ordinary Christian. I want to become all that God has in mind for me. I want to be a victorious, Christlike Christian. I want to be a fisher of people. I want to be a blessing to others. In order for me to become all of these, I need to continuously push myself to greater heights. That is my prayer. Even Jesus prayed that, 'And for their sakes I sanctify Myself, that they also may be sanctified by the truth' (John 17:19).

Do you have a desire to follow God more closely and steadfastly? To experience more intimacy with God and reach greater effectiveness for Him? Ask the Holy Spirit to help you reach your full potential. I have found it helpful to follow some steps.

The first step is to be *available*. You must make yourself available for a personal, loving, intimate relationship with Jesus Christ.

The second step is to have a *desire to please God*. If your desire is to please the Lord, He will make sure that you are in the center of His will. If you draw near to Him with an open heart and desire to make decisions based on what He wants, He will show you the way.

The third step is to *listen* to and *obey* only Him. He might reveal some things in your life or sinful behavior that you must confess and repent of. He might ask of you to do things that you have never done before. He might ask you to step out in faith and trust Him for a miracle, and you must obey.

The last step is to *embrace* change and *transformation*. You must allow Him to change and transform your heart, thoughts, perspective, conduct and life to become the person that He wants you to be. According to Ruth Haley Barton, in her book *Strengthening The Soul of Your Leadership*, said, the best any of us have to bring to leadership is our own transforming selves.[27] Jesus called the disciples to *follow* Him. His intention was to *transform them* and *send* them out. The disciples were now ready to be sent out on their first missionary journey. They had been with Jesus for almost a year. During this time, they knew that they were being prepared to be sent out by Jesus to do His work. They had been observing Him and listening to His every word. They had seen the manifestation of His power. They had seen the wonderful ease with which He had healed physical infirmities, the authority with which He cast out demons and the graciousness with which He forgave sinners.

They were not the same as when they had met Jesus for the first time. They had undergone tremendous change. He changed them and they would change even more in the years to come. But the hour had arrived for them to be sent out as His representatives and messengers to say the things He Himself had been saying and to do the things He Himself had been doing. They were ready to take the next step in becoming 'fishers of men.' They were ready to bear fruit. They were ready to work for Jesus.

They were ready to be *commissioned* to go on their first missionary trip.

So, He called them again …

God, who called you to become his child,
will do all this for you, just as he promised.
(1 Thessalonians 5:24 *The Living Bible*)

PART THREE
Being Sent for Jesus

5

The COMMISSION

To receive His enabling and empowerment

And He called the twelve to Himself, and began to send them out two by two, and gave them power over unclean spirits. He commanded them to take nothing for the journey except a staff—no bag, no bread, no copper in their money belts— but to wear sandals, and not to put on two tunics. (Mark 6:7–9)

We must get to know God in secret – alone in the desert. It does seem to me that true spirituality lies in this – utter dependence on God for everything ... We shall dread to ... do anything in our wisdom ... If a man can only get down before God and get His plan of work for him, individually, that is what will make him irresistible. (D.E. Hoste)[1]

Some time ago I traveled from Johannesburg to Poland to speak at a revival conference in Warsaw, and at some local church meetings in Poznan. I was excited about the invitation, not only to speak at the conference but in hoping that I will be able to visit the area known as the Warsaw Ghetto. The days before I left my home had been hectic and I did not pay attention to the news. On my arrival in Poland, it transpired that there had been two major incidents.

First, the president of Poland, Lech Kaczynski, his wife Maria, along with several dignitaries, 18 members of the Polish parliament and others had died in a plane crash near the Russian city Smolensk, on 10 April 2010. All 96 people, who were on route from Warsaw to attend the commemoration of the 70th anniversary of the Katyn Forest Massacre near Smolensk were killed in the crash.[2] The area near the president's house was filled with news media vehicles and reporters from all over the world, interviewing people and reporting on what was happening. Thousands of people had filled the area and were wandering through the streets. Hundreds were waiting in a line to convey their condolences to the families. The country was in mourning. Shock, unbelief, sadness and even despair were visible everywhere. People were asking questions:

What happened?
What was the cause of the crash?
Who was responsible?
Why is this happening?
Why has God allowed this to happen?

Tough questions … no easy or any answers.

Second, the volcano Eyjafjallajökull in Iceland had erupted, and although relatively small as volcanic eruptions go, this one caused enormous disruption to air travel across Western and Northern Europe for six days in April 2010. Ash covered large areas of Northern Europe. About 20 countries closed their airspace to commercial air traffic and this affected approximately 10 million travelers.[3] The airport in Warsaw was also closed. I remember thinking, 'How long will this last? When will we be able to fly again? How will I get home?'

Some circumstances are beyond our control.

In the story of the Red Sea, the Israelites followed the pillar of cloud and fire as carefully as possible, thrilled with their new freedom and full of excitement about the future. However, God deliberately led them into a cul-de-sac among hostile hills, to the edge of a sea too deep and too wide to cross. God then told them to *turn and camp* (Exodus 14:2). They were in exactly the place where He wanted them to be. The Lord occasionally does the same with us. He leads us into hardship, tests our faith, molds our characters, teaches us wisdom and then reveals His glory and provision. Our first reaction is usually to panic. We experience a sense of alarm, but we must learn to wait on the Lord, pray, consult Scriptures for guidance and get His perspective on what is happening, and why.

I was stranded in Poland, but I was exactly where God wanted me to be. I had no hope of returning to South Africa in time for my next appointment. He allowed me to be there for reasons known only to Himself. It is only when we look back that we understand what really took place. Soren Kierkegaard, a well-known Danish philosopher, once said, 'We live life forward but understand it backwards.'⁴ God had brought me to Poland and allowed the air traffic to be shut down. He was the one who would take me out. So, I asked God for guidance and direction. The day's reading was 1 Samuel 30. I felt as though the Lord Himself were speaking to me, directing my thoughts and my understanding. David returned with his 600 men to Ziklag, to find that their city had been burned down, their wealth had been confiscated, and their wives and children had been kidnapped. The men wore themselves out weeping, and David was 'greatly distressed.' He was in a tight corner. People react in different ways to the same circumstances. Some of his men wanted to stone David. And David knew that the encouragement he needed could only come from the Lord. He ordered Abiathar, the priest, to bring the ephod and together they sought the will of the Lord. So, David inquired of the Lord, asking, 'Shall I overtake them?' And He answered him, 'Pursue, for you shall surely overtake them and without fail recover all' (1 Samuel 30:7–8).

As I prayed through 1 Samuel 30, the Lord reminded me of all the moments that David had found himself in a tight spot and each time he had taken the time to strengthen himself in the Lord, inquiring of Him what to do next.⁵ David's multiple inquiries of the Lord reveal that he was a man of prayer, who was always intent on knowing His will. This was the main reason he was called a man after *God's own heart*. God says, 'I have found David, the son of Jesse, a man after My own heart, who will do all My will' (Acts 13: 22). And David did! He followed God step by step. In my situation, I sensed that God wanted me to pray and trust Him step by step, just like David. He sees and knows the bigger picture.

I read about an incident in the life of South African pastor Andrew Murray, who once faced a terrible crisis. Gathering himself in his study, he sat a long while ... quietly, prayerfully, thoughtfully. He picked up his pen, and wrote:

> First, He brought me here, it is by His will that I am in this strait place: in that fact I will rest.
>
> Next, He will keep me here in His love, and give me grace to behave as His child.
>
> Then He will make the trial a blessing, teaching me the lessons He intends me to learn, and work in me the grace He means to bestow. Last, in His good time He can bring me out again – how and when He knows.

Let me say I am here:

- By God's appointment;
- In His keeping;
- Under His training;
- For His time.[6]

Even in the midst of seemingly impossible situations, God promises to make a way for us. His loving guidance will protect us through danger, illness, marital strife, financial problems ... even when stranded in Poland ... because He sees and knows the bigger picture.

During my stay in Poland, I was able to speak on a local radio station about the crisis in Poland, and record an interview about revival with a team from Prague in the Czech Republic. My last meeting took place on a Tuesday night and I was able to fly home the next day, Wednesday, the first day that the airports were open again ... the exact date and time printed on my plane ticket.

My book on *Revival! The Glory of God* was translated into the Polish language and a copy sent to each church in Poland. It was also translated into the Czech language and is used today as a supplementary book in theological studies. Since this occasion I have returned to Poland several more times. Looking back at that time, I realize that God's agenda and purpose is so different from mine.

God Is Searching

When we are on vacation, we like to play board and card games together as a family. I do not exactly enjoy building puzzles, but my family can get quite excited about building a new puzzle. As I have watched my family build puzzles over the years, I have oftentimes been reminded of the similarity between our lives and puzzles. Sometimes life and ministry can feel like doing a ten thousand-piece jigsaw puzzle. Although we know what the puzzle should look like at the end, it still remains a challenge to complete.

The same happens in life: we know certain truths about God and His will for our lives, but we do not always know how God's design for our lives will unfold. With a puzzle one first needs to sort out the pieces, the straight-edged pieces here, the red ones there and the blue ones somewhere else and so on. It is best to start by assembling the edged pieces so that the size and proportion of the puzzle becomes clear. Once that is finished, it is a good time to start assembling the rest of the pieces. Soon parts of the picture become clear and the more pieces are put in, the clearer the picture as the bigger picture becomes visible. It is the picture on the box that provides the perspective, the future vision of what is being built. The picture is a map that shows you where to build next. *Like every piece of the puzzle fits into the puzzle, we need to know that every aspect of our lives fits into the bigger picture and purpose that God has in mind for us.*

A few years ago, I had the opportunity to go up in in a hot air balloon in Turkey. Hot air balloon rides are one of the most popular activities in Cappadocia. These balloons typically lift off at sunrise and the rides in the air last about an hour as the balloons literally go wherever the windstreams may blow them through the Goreme Valley. The atmosphere fills with excitement as spectators gather round to enjoy the beautiful sight of several dozen balloons taking flight each day. A balloon ride provides beautiful landscape views from the air. Cameras flash as happy travelers take pictures of the region, small villages and towns below. Those who enjoy the ride can see far into the distance as nothing obstructs their 360-degree panoramic view at 3,000 ft. in the air.

What a magnificent sight!

I thought about God looking down from heaven. The Bible says that God is *looking down from heaven*. His eyes are searching for them who fear Him.

> The Lord *looks from heaven*; He sees all the sons of men. From the place of His dwelling He *looks* on all the inhabitants of the earth; He fashions their hearts individually; He considers all their works. No king *is* saved by the multitude of an army; A mighty man is not delivered by great strength. A horse *is* a vain hope for safety; Neither shall it deliver *any* by its great strength. Behold, the eye of the Lord is on those who fear Him, on those who hope in His mercy, to deliver their soul from death, and to keep them alive in famine. (Psalm 33:13–18 *KJV*)

> For the eyes of the Lord run to and fro throughout the whole earth. (2 Chronicles 16:9)

God is engaged in a search. God is not searching the earth to find men and women of remarkable faith and stature. He is not looking for someone with multiple talents, qualifications and degrees. He revealed where his true interest lay when he sent the Prophet Samuel to anoint the future king of Israel. He said, 'Do not look at his appearance or at his physical stature ... For the Lord does not see as man sees ... but the Lord looks at the heart' (1 Samuel 16:7). What made David so special was his heart and that had not changed yet. He was a man after God's own heart, 'The Lord has sought for Himself a man after His own heart' (1 Samuel 13:14) and 'I have found David, the son of Jesse, a man after My own heart, who will do all My will' (Acts 13:22). He is looking to find someone who is available and willing to do His work. He is looking for a man or a woman whose heart is loyal, wholly and completely focused on Him. He wants a person through whom He can reveal Himself to the world. He desires to pour out an abundance of blessings into that person's life and to bless others through that person.

Jesus saw through the outward shows of religion and affirmed the importance of a right heart when he condemned the hypocrisy of the Pharisees (Luke 16:15). God sees behind the outward behavior of a person and understands their deepest motives (1 Chronicles 28:9). He looks into the heart, and there he finds the real person.

What is God Searching For?

He is searching for a heart that is in harmony with His heart, agenda and purposes.

> He is looking for someone *after His own heart who will do all His will.*
> God searches our hearts to see if you and I might be that person.
> Every believer in Jesus could be 'that someone.'

God only asks for our devotion, through which He wants to work His marvelous plan. God is available to all of us but how much we experience of Him depends on us.

Will you make yourself available so that God can use your life as a channel of blessing and hope?

How Do We Make Ourselves Available to God?

First, we need to understand that God has a *plan* and *purpose* that can be trusted, whether or not we can visibly see His hand in it.

Second, we need to realize that God sees *the bigger picture*. He has a clear perspective on all things. He knows what needs to be done, takes the initiative to do those things, and determines the next step. God's sovereignty operates in conjunction with man's responsibility. When we change our perspective to His perspective, it helps us to understand, adjust our lives, and respond to Him accordingly. It is vital that we establish the understanding that God sees the bigger picture because it helps us to know that He is actively involved in the events and activities of our lives. He is constantly at work. Many don't realize that truth. We spend our time utterly unaware of it. When we understand that He sees and is at work—in the bigger picture—and we look back over our lives and experiences, we can see how this truth has unfolded in our lives.

Third, once we see and understand God's plan unfolding before us, we can actually see how *God is moving in the hearts of people, continuously directing circumstances, people, and activities to work out His plan and purpose.* The good news is that while He is at work, He has blessed us with the opportunity to be a part of it. Thankfully God does not wait until we are in perfect condition, or fully trained, before using us to carry out His plan. He enables and empowers us to accomplish His purpose in the place where we are in life. That is why we need to realize that He directs our lives.

Last, we must be willing *to adjust and submit* ourselves to Him to do His will.

May the Lord give us grace to emulate David's example and to cultivate the habit of always inquiring of the Lord and waiting for His answer. The more we seek direction from God in prayer and the more we desire to know His will, the more He is honored and the more we are blessed. May we cultivate David's spirit more and more, for it is written, 'In all your ways acknowledge Him, and He shall direct your paths' (Proverbs 3:6).

Jesus On Mission With God

We have already established that God wants us to be like Jesus, who always obeyed Him. Jesus indicated through His life that He was joining the Father on His mission. He announced that He had come not to do His own will, but the will of the Father, who had sent Him.[7] To know the Father's will, Jesus listened to the Father and whatever He heard the Father say, those were the things that He would say (John 14:10–11). Jesus also said He watched to see what the Father was doing. Then Jesus joined Him in that work, 'I tell you the truth, the Son can do nothing by himself; he can do only what he sees his Father doing, because whatever the Father does the Son also does' (John 5:17,19). Jesus did not take the initiative but depended on the Father to reveal Himself and what He was doing (John 17:6–8). And He bore witness to the Father, and the Father worked through Him (John 14:10).

The Father loved the Son and took the initiative to come to Him and reveal what He (the Father) was doing or what He was about to do. Jesus kept on looking around Him for the Father's actions, so that He could unite His life with His Father's mission. One of the assignments from the Father was to invest His time and life into the training of the Twelve, through whom He wanted to reveal Himself to the world and live out His purposes.

Sending Of The Twelve

Jesus finished two preaching tours of Galilee. He was accompanied on the first tour by four disciples and on the second tour by all twelve. They had been traveling with Him everywhere—to small, isolated villages—and He concentrated on preaching, teaching and training the disciples. He had just returned from Nazareth, where they had rejected Him. There was still a whole country and the world to be reached. He would do so by starting to send out the Twelve to reach the entire country with the good news. It was time for them to represent Him on another tour ... but this time without Him. At the end of the second tour Jesus called them and gave them power over unclean spirits (Mark 6:7). He also gave them detailed instructions for their mission trip, their outreach. We read:

> And He called the twelve to *Himself,* and began to send them out two *by* two, and gave them power over unclean spirits. He commanded them to take nothing for the journey except a staff—no bag, no bread, no copper in *their* money belts—but to wear sandals, and not to put on two tunics. Also, He said to them, "In whatever place you enter a house, stay there till you depart from that place. And whoever will not receive you nor hear you, when you depart from there, shake off the dust under your feet as a testimony against them. Assuredly, I say to you, it will be more tolerable for Sodom and Gomorrah in the day of judgment than for that city!" So, they went out and preached that *people* should repent. And they cast out many demons, and anointed with oil many who were sick, and healed *them.* (Mark 6:7–13. See also Matthew 10; Luke 6, 9)

Why Did Jesus Send Them Out?

The twelve disciples had been called and ordained some months before (Matthew 10; Mark 3:13–15; Luke 6:13–16) and had been traveling with Jesus as His helpers. When Jesus originally called them, His purpose was to teach and train them so that they could assist Him and eventually to be able to take His place when He returned to the Father (Matthew 28:18–20, Acts 1:1–8). They had been with Him on two tours but now it was time for their first mission trip on their own. This was the beginning of their own ministry, without Jesus. What did they have to do?

Called to Preach

First, they were called to preach that people should repent. The Greek word *kerusso* means preaching, proclaiming or heralding. Later on they would preach the Gospel, which included preaching about Jesus' death and resurrection, repentance, the forgiveness of sins and the coming of the Holy Spirit (Luke 24:46–48). But now they were to preach on what they had seen and learned from Jesus as well as heal sicknesses and cast out demons.

Learning while Ministering

Second, ministry opportunities would help them grow spiritually, grow their skills and competencies, and shape their characters. Being with Jesus was the best possible 'seminary training' ever. They were able to watch Jesus, listen to Him teach, ask questions, and enjoy intimate fellowship with Him as they learned. They were learning while watching and ministering with Jesus, but now they would be learning while ministering together in teams and be on their own without Jesus being with them.

What Did They Have To Do?

We have already established that the Twelve were called to preach, heal the sick and cast out demons. They had received valuable training when they followed Jesus. But what did they have to do apart from growing in their walk of faith? They also had to learn how to speak, act and live on His behalf and share what they had seen and heard (1 John 1:1–4). First, they were called to be disciples. Second, they were sent out to be His witnesses (Matthew 11:1; Luke 9:1) and, finally, to represent Him.

Disciple

First, they were called as *disciples*. What is a disciple? The Hebrew word for disciple is *talmidim,* which is derived from the root word for 'to learn.' In the Old Testament there were schools for prophets, to 'seal the law among my disciples' (Isaiah 8:16)[8] and schools for musicians, who were trained for service in the temple (1 Chronicles 25:8). In Jesus' culture religious leaders, called rabbis, would gather a group of adherents who would follow in their footsteps, learn from them and heed their teachings. In the Gospels you see different kinds of disciples. There were the disciples of Moses (John 9:28), the disciples of the Pharisees (Matthew 22:16; Mark 2:18; Luke 5:33), the disciples of John the Baptist (Matthew 9:14; Mark 2:18; Luke 5:33), and the disciples of Jesus (Matthew 28:18–20). The term 'disciple' that Jesus used in Matthew 28:19 is the Greek word *mathetes,* which means 'to learn.' The term 'disciple' originally meant a pupil (of a teacher) or an apprentice (to a master craftsman). So, a disciple was a person who was close to a master and followed that master to become like him and carry on his work.

What does it mean to be a disciple? The term disciple is the primary term used to describe a follower of Jesus. It is used 264 times in the Gospels and the book of Acts.[9] To put it simply, a disciple of Jesus is someone who has chosen to follow Jesus. In the New Testament, the term 'disciple' becomes synonymous with 'believer' in Jesus Christ.[10] Later on they would be called 'Christians' (Acts 11:26) and in the Epistles they are called 'brother,' 'sister,' 'saint,' 'believer' or 'Christian.' A disciple is someone who has chosen to follow and learn from his master and is determined to become like him and carry out his work.[11]

Witness

Second, they were called to *witness*. What is a witness? The word witness is used 29 times in the book of Acts. The Greek words *martus* and *martur* could be explained as someone who bears testimony, witnesses, declares facts, even to the point of death. They are not to judge people but to be a witness to Jesus Christ and tell lost people and sinners how to be saved. *Witnessing is not something we do for the Lord; it is something that He does through us.* There is a difference between me trying to be and do something for the Lord and His doing it through me.

When Moses tried, he failed, but when God worked through him, it was a success. Peter became a follower of Jesus because of his brother Andrew. Andrew listened to Jesus, witnessed to Peter and brought him to Jesus (John 1:40–42). It is true that not all people have a calling to evangelize (Ephesians 4:11), although all of us, God's people, are expected to be witnesses and tell others about Jesus, and what He had done for us.

A witness simply tells what they have seen and heard (Acts 4:19–20).

Apostle

Third, Jesus appointed the disciples as *apostles.* What is an apostle? As mentioned in the previous chapter, the Greek word *apostello* could be explained as meaning 'to be sent.' An 'apostle' is an important early Christian teacher or pioneer missionary with the commission to represent someone or Jesus. He is also a vigorous believer, advocate or supporter of a particular policy, idea, or cause. The ancient word refers to being commissioned for official service. Jesus gave the disciples His 'official commission' to speak His words and do His work on His behalf. Jesus gave His disciples the full authority, power and divine ability to do the job in hand. They were truly ambassadors of Jesus. Not only were they sent by Him, but also went before Him to prepare the way for His coming.

Jesus taught the disciples that to receive Him was to receive the Father, and to receive the Father was to receive Him, Jesus (John 13:20). Jesus also taught them that if they had seen Jesus, they had seen the Father (John 14:9). Now Jesus was sending out the disciples, not only to represent Jesus and the Father but to 'be them' to a lost world.

Where Did Jesus Send Them?

Where did Jesus send them? It must have been a startling moment when Jesus gave them their marching orders. I can imagine the excitement when they were appointed as apostles and ordered to go on their first mission trip without Jesus. Some of them had traveled with Jesus on two separate occasions. But now they would be *sent out on their own* (Mark. 6:7). But as they were getting ready to leave, it might have occurred to them that they did not know where to go or what to do next. Jesus told them not to go into the cities of the Samaritans or the way of the gentiles (Matthew 10:5) but go to the lost sheep of Israel. They were to visit the towns and cities in Galilee (Luke 9:6). What did they have to do when they got there?

Find a Person of Peace

Jesus was always on the move (Matthew 9:35, 11:1; Luke 10:1–11). He continuously met new people and visited new places. He sent His disciples into villages, towns and cities, where they would seek out people who had been prepared by the Holy Spirit to receive the message. Jesus told them to look for a man of peace (Psalm 37:37) or a household of peace (Matthew 10:12–13). David Watson explains, in his book *Contagious Disciple Making,* that the person of peace is the one God has prepared to receive the gospel in a community for the first time.[12] Some persons are people of peace by nature, and some become men and women of peace as a result of God's direct influence in their lives, families or communities. Cornelius and Lydia are representatives of the 'person of peace' by nature. The Philippian jailer and Samaritan woman at the well are examples of those who become 'persons of peace' through God's direct intervention in their lives. A person of peace has usually been prepared by the Holy Spirit to be receptive to the messengers and the message they bring. They usually also have some form of standing in society, some influence, a network or relationships with people who would follow their directive. For example, Matthew the tax collector prepared a banquet for

Jesus and invited all of his friends. Likewise, the disciples had to look for a person who had been prepared by God.

Being Prepared

God was at work around Jesus all His life (John 5:16–17). Jesus said that the Father showed Him everything He did (John 5:20). Even before the world was created, the Father invited Jesus to be involved in His work (John 1:1–3). His life was filled with examples of His Father at work.

On one occasion when Jesus was passing through Jericho, He looked up into a tree and saw Zacchaeus (Luke 19:1–10). He knew that the Father was at work because no one comes to know Christ without the Father's prompting (John 6:44). Jesus knew that something was happening in the tax collector's life; something which had made him climb that tree. Accordingly, Jesus adjusted His plans and had lunch with him. Jesus traveled from place to place, as His Father directed Him (John 5:19, John 8:28). People saw how Jesus was baptized (Mark 1:5) and they were exposed to Him as He taught and preached in their cities and synagogues (Matthew 9:35). It was to those same places that Jesus sent the Twelve. He sent them to people who and places that had already been exposed to the life, message and ministry of Jesus, and would be receptive to hearing more about Jesus. His agenda was set through prayer as He heard from His Father.

When was the last time you checked your schedule to see if it fits the heavenly agenda for your day? Have you been missing out on 'Divine appointments' due to working according to your own plan and agenda? *We need to follow Jesus' example and let our time in prayer set the agenda for our day and our lives.* It might be that we will meet a person of peace, which will lead to spreading of the gospel's message.

The Law of the Second Witness

As we have seen, we are never the first witness in the hearer's life. According to Dr. Dennis Kinlaw, in his book *Preaching in the Spirit,* the preacher is never God's first witness in the hearer's life. God himself is already there, before the preacher. The Holy Spirit is at work in every person's life long before a believer speaks a word of truth to that person. Dr. Kinlaw explains, 'I have come to realize that we are never first, and we are never alone in witnessing. We never arrive in someone's life before the Holy Spirit. We never touch someone before God touches him. When God leads us to somebody, He has been there before us. We never preach to someone in whose life God has not already been at work. That prior work of the Spirit of grace makes the effectiveness of our witness possible. I call this 'The Law of the Second Witness.'[13]

Where did they go? Jesus sent them to people and places where His Father was already at work. *It gives great comfort to know that when God is asking something from us or sending us, He is already at work.*

What about Us?

If Jesus commissioned us to go—where will we go, or where do we start? In 7 *Truths From Experiencing God,* Henry and Richard Blackaby explained that God is at work around you. To live a God-centered life, you must focus your life on God's purposes and not your own plans. You must seek God's perspective in your circumstances rather than your own distorted human outlook. When God starts to do something in the world, He takes the initiative to reveal His will to people.[14]

We have already seen that the Father took the initiative and called His Son to spend some time with Him. It was in those moments that He revealed to Jesus the names of the disciples (Mark 3:13–15). Jesus, obediently and faithfully, finished the work that He was given by His Father (John 17:4) and delivered His Word to them (v. 8). Jesus confirmed once again that they were coming from His Father when He prayed in John 17:6, 'I have manifested Your name to the men whom You have given to Me out of the world. They were Yours; You gave them to Me, and they have kept Your word.'

What can we do? W. Oscar Thompson, in his classic book *Concentric Circles of Concern,* concludes that effective ministry starts close to home. Today's evangelistic emphasis is often on preaching to strangers, anonymous crowds or in foreign countries. He gives specific details of how best to share Christ's love, which is by meeting the spiritual needs of immediate family first, followed by friends, and then all others, moving outward in concentric circles.[15] God created us for relationships. We are called into a relationship with God through Jesus (1 Corinthians 1:9) and the Holy Spirit (2 Corinthians 13:13). When we accepted Jesus, He placed us in the body of Christ because we need each other. We can and should 'stimulate one another to love and do good deeds' (Hebrew 10:24). I believe relationship is the greatest tool in reaching out to those whom God has uniquely brought into our lives or to use in our communities to make a difference.

God wants to work through your life to make disciples of those in your world—in your concentric circles. Do a survey of all the people in your life, starting with yourself. Then write the names of your immediate and extended family members, neighbors, friends, business associates and colleagues at work. Continue to write down any acquaintances or people whom God has brought into your life and follow the seven stages of discipleship.[16]

So how do we do that? Thompson highlights seven stages for making disciples:[17]

Stage 1: Get Right—*Get right with God, self, and others.* The starting place for everything is a right relationship with God. First you must come to God on his conditions for forgiveness and salvation. If you have not been in a right and obedient relationship with God since your salvation, you need to repent and get back into that relationship with Him so His Spirit can flow through your life. Second, you also need a proper view of yourself. A right relationship with Jesus Christ can bring balance in your life that will not only make life more meaningful and fulfilling for you, but it will also be far more effective in revealing the character of Christ to others. Third, once you have the right vertical relationship with God and a balanced view of self, God will move you to the correct relationships with others. You cannot be right with God and still have broken relationships with others.

Stage 2: Survey—*Survey your relationships.* We don't stop to think about all the people whom God brings into our lives or into our circles of influence. First, look at those closest to you in your immediate family and circle of relatives. Then identify your friends, neighbors, business or school associates, and your acquaintances. This survey will become a prayer list for you to begin praying for those whom God has brought into your concentric circles of concern.

Stage 3: Pray—*Work with God through prayer.* God invites us to pray so that when He answers, we will know He did it. You will pray about the people in your survey and watch to see where God is working in their lives. When you become aware of any needs— that will be your invitation to join God and show love to the needy person.

Stage 4: Build bridges—*Build relationship bridges to people.* You can build relationship bridges to people in a variety of ways. You can show interest in them during special times of joy or times of stress.

Stage 5: Show love—*Show God's love by meeting people.* God works in your heart to motivate you to love a person who may not be very loveable. God also provides the resources to meet the needs of others through you. As He loves that person through you, by meeting his or her needs, He will begin to draw that person to his Son. As God engineers circumstances in the lives of those you are praying for, He will create opportunities for the person to experience His love through your life. They will know that they have been loved by the heavenly Father.

Stage 6: Make disciples—*Make disciples and help them grow.* After people turn to Christ, or respond to Him, they need to grow as His disciples. You will help them develop their personal relationship with Jesus through prayer and the Word of God.

Stage 7: Begin again—*Help new Christians make disciples.* Making disciples is only the beginning. Helping others to grow into fully devoted followers of Jesus Christ is also a part of the church's assignment to make disciples. The cycle of making disciples doesn't end when a person becomes a Christian. For that person, the cycle has just begun.

I would suggest that you spend time in prayer. It was while Jesus spent time in prayer that the Father revealed the names of those Jesus had to pay attention to. We must take the time to pray. Then allow the Holy Spirit to reveal the answer to the following questions in our hearts. Who are those people God has uniquely brought into my life? Who are those people God has sent to me? What doors have God opened for me to minister or reach out to others? Jesus said, 'Most assuredly, I say to you, he who receives whomever I send receives Me; and he who receives Me receives Him who sent Me' (John 13:20). Next, respond obediently and faithfully to those people; open doors, or do the assignment that you received from Him. Jesus promised, 'Well done, good and faithful servant; you have been faithful over a few things, I will make you ruler over many things' (Matthew 25:23).

When Did They Go?

The Twelve saw how Jesus healed a demon-possessed man (Mark 5:1–20), restored a young girl to life (Mark 5:21–43) and healed a woman who had been struggling with a blood illness for 12 years (Mark 5:25–34). They saw Jesus do all that and now He wanted them to do the same. The disciples must have wondered if they would be able to handle persecution and rejection, do the works of mercy, heal sick people, and even cast out unclean spirits. They must have felt weak and probably needed special empowerment. But Jesus gave them divine authority and entrusted them with the power to do His work and speak His words. They also had his example to imitate.

The Example of Jesus

The Holy Spirit came upon Jesus when He was baptized, assuring Him as He began His ministry that the Spirit's power would always be with Him (John 3:34). Jesus, led by the Spirit, went into the wilderness, returned and ministered in the power of the Holy Spirit. With authority and in power He proclaimed that the Kingdom was at hand and that all had to repent. They saw the power of the Holy Spirit at work in the life of Jesus.

Authority and Power

Jesus has absolute authority in heaven and on earth. He said in Matthew 28:18, 'All power is given unto me in heaven and earth.' The word 'power' here is the Greek word *exousia*, which refers to authority or delegated power along with the right to use it. There was authority in Jesus' teaching (Matthew 7:29). He exercised authority in healing (Matthew 8:1–13) and in the forgiving of sins (Matthew 9:6). He had authority over Satan. When Jesus sent out His disciples, He delegated that authority to them (Matthew 10:1; Mark 6:7; Luke 9:1). He gave them the ability (*exousia*) and the power (*dunamis*) to go out and complete their mission. Power is the ability to accomplish a task, and authority is the right to do it, and Jesus gave them both. Their ability to heal was a special gift that confirmed and authenticated their position with the people (Romans 15:18–19; 2 Corinthians 12:12; Hebrews 2:1–4). The miracles were the evidence that Jesus had sent them (Mark 16:20).

Disciples and the Holy Spirit

Later on Jesus explained to them that they would receive the Holy Spirit, Who would empower them (John 14:16–18, 26; 15:26–27; 16:7–15). It would be a special anointing of power from God so that they would be able to serve Him and accomplish their assignment. They would also soon discover that they had to live in step with the Holy Spirit as they faced new opportunities, obstacles and challenges (Acts 2:4; 4:8, 31; 9:17; 13:9).

However, the example of Jesus's earthly ministry was such a powerful testimony to them that they trusted God for their every need. God always enables us when He gives a command (2 Corinthians 3:5–6). He has given us the presence and power of the Holy Spirit.

What about Us?

We also need power and a special 'anointing' or 'enabling' to do His work and speak His Word. The Lord Jesus promised in Acts 1:8, 'But you shall receive power when the Holy Spirit has come upon you; and you shall be witnesses to Me in Jerusalem, and in all Judea and Samaria, and to the end of the earth.' The Greek word *dunamis*, power, can be translated as permission, authority, right, liberty and the power to do anything. It is an inherent power that causes something to happen or releases external power. When the woman with the blood illness touched the hem of His garment, spiritual virtue left Jesus and healed her from her sickness (Mark 5:25–34).

We need to realize that the person God uses, and will continue to use, is one who works in the power and anointing of the Holy Spirit. When we read the biographies of God's men, we discover that each one sought and obtained the power from on High. It reminds us of some of the last words of Jesus, '... but tarry in the city of Jerusalem until you are endued with power from on high' (Luke 24:49) and 'but you shall receive power when the Holy Spirit has come upon you; and you shall be witnesses to Me' (Acts 1:8). They tarried as Jesus commanded while the thought of preaching and witnessing without that power never entered their minds. Dr. Dennis Kinlaw explains in his book *Preaching in the Spirit,* 'A preacher is looking for something that human energy alone cannot provide. For that reason, a preacher must be immersed in the Holy Spirit.'[18]

What about You?

Are you ministering in His power or out of your own strength and energy? One sermon preached in His power is worth far more than a hundred sermons preached out of the energy of the flesh.

How Were They to Go?

How did they go? Jesus commanded them to take nothing for the journey except a staff—no bag, no bread, no copper (coins) in their money belts—to wear sandals, but not to put on two tunics. He wanted them to be adequately supplied, but He also wanted them to trust Him as they stepped out to live by faith. They must have wondered to themselves:

> How will we do this?
> What will we eat, drink and wear if we have no food, no clothes and no money to buy it with?
> Where are we going to stay?
> Who will help us?

Jesus had already told His disciples that they were dependent on Him, just as the Son was dependent on the Father. Now it was time for their practical test. They had to go out, believing and trusting that He would provide for them (Matthew 6: 25–34).

Don't do it Alone

Jesus sent them out in pairs of two. He knew the value of friendship and partnership in doing His work. Jesus matched them according to their strengths, weaknesses, abilities and faith. Solomon had understood the value of people traveling together:

> Two *are* better than one. Because, they have a good reward for their labor. For, if they fall, one will lift up his companion. But woe to him *who* is alone when he falls, for *he has* no one to help him up. Again, if two lie down together, they will keep warm; But how can one be warm *alone?* Though one may be overpowered by another, two can withstand him. And a threefold cord is not quickly broken. (Ecclesiastes 4:9–12)

Working together made the disciples more effective and ensured that they accomplished what they had to (v. 9). When they worked together, they were able to help one another where necessary (v. 10). When they were traveling, they could keep one another warm, and they would have company (v. 11). When they faced a situation where they were overpowered, two of them could defend themselves better than one could (v. 12). They could also support one another's testimony (Deuteronomy 17:6). If this only applies to our physical walk, just imagine of how much more value a friend could be to us in our spiritual life should we stumble or fall. We all need a friend who can help us walk in God's ways and hold us accountable.

Even today God does not intend to leave us to live on our own. I noticed something in the Old Testament. Attached to every great Bible character is the phrase 'God was with him' or 'The Lord was with him.' They were all successful because they did not do it alone but with God. This is a theme that continues in the New Testament. We read in Matthew 1:23, 'Behold, the virgin shall be with child, and bear a Son, and they shall call His name Immanuel,' which is translated, 'God with us.' What does that mean? Immanuel, 'God with us,' refers to a heightened experience of the manifest presence of God in our lives. This presence helps us to be in step with God and to move in the sphere of His activity.

> Jesus also promised that if we gather in His name that He will be in their midst, "Again, I say to you that if two of you agree on earth concerning anything that they ask, it will be done for them by My Father in heaven. For where two or three are gathered together in My name, I am there in the midst of them. (Matthew 18:19–20)

Jesus also promised to send us the Holy Spirit as our companion to be with us and walk beside us.

> And I will pray the Father, and He will give you another Helper, that He may abide with you forever—the Spirit of truth, whom the world cannot receive, because it neither sees Him nor knows Him; but you know Him, for He dwells with you and will be in you. I will not leave you orphans; I will come to you. (John 14:16–18)

You are not alone. If you are married, it would be helpful to get your spouse involved in your life and ministry as much as they are willing and able to be. If you are single, pull in some friends or disciples who can team up with you. And remember, God the Father, the Son and the Holy Spirit are with you.

By Faith

Jesus told them to *take nothing for the journey except a staff—no bag, no bread, no copper in their money belts—but to wear sandals, and not to put on two tunics.* It must have been a scary thought for them to go without Jesus, while not knowing what will happen to them or how their needs would be met. He wanted them to have everything they needed but not to the point where they would cease to believe and trust in Him for all their needs. When they traveled with Jesus, He provided for them in all their needs, by trusting His Father. Jesus and the Twelve received ongoing support from individuals wherever they went.

> Now it came to pass, afterward, that He went through every city and village, preaching and bringing the glad tidings of the kingdom of God. And the twelve were with Him, and certain women who had been healed of evil spirits and infirmities—Mary called Magdalene, out of whom had come seven demons, and Joanna the wife of Chuza, Herod's steward, and Susanna, and many others who provided for Him from their substance. (Luke 8:1–3)

Jesus went everywhere, proclaiming 'the glad tidings of the Kingdom of God' (Luke 8:1). Jesus depended on the freewill offerings of His friends to sustain His livelihood. He had the means to spread a banquet in the wilderness, command stones to be turned into bread and change water into wine, yet He lived from the goodwill of others. He was a carpenter but had given up His profession to minister full-time. He was not rich at all. The disciples looked to Him for their needs and Jesus looked to the Father to provide. Jesus modeled His reliance upon God and to provide, through those around Him, what they needed. God provided people who took care of their needs. The word provided, or contributing in the original language, implies continuous action, repeated over and over. It is a tremendous lesson for us. Scott Morton, in his book *Funding Your Ministry,* explains, 'If it were wrong to be supported by the personal gifts of others, Jesus would not have allowed it in His own ministry. If Jesus became vulnerable enough to be supported by others, you and I must be willing as well.'[19]

Jesus modeled to the Twelve how He wanted them to raise their support and undertake their ministry. They were not to ask for money. They were not to stand on street corners with a hungry look on their faces and ask for funds. No, they had to work hard as they represented the Savior, while He would take care of their needs. Everything that Jesus did was in part so that His disciples could see and learn how to live His life. He knew that people would provide for them and take care of them. They had not yet experienced it, but they knew that His word was true.

I once found myself in a similar position as the disciples on a preaching tour to Penzance and Tuckingmill in Cornwall, South West England. After paying for my plane ticket from South Africa and purchasing a return train ticket from London, I only had 20 pounds left in my pocket. That was all I had for the next 14 days. Within the first few days, God laid it upon my heart to give 10 pounds to the family where I was staying. I did so, knowing that 10 pounds would not be enough to provide for me for the rest of my journey. The very next day, as I was preaching, an elderly lady put a small envelope in my Bible. When I opened it later, I found 10 pounds in it along with a letter. God honored my obedience to His prompting and continued to provide all that I needed for the duration of that preaching tour.

So, the disciples stepped out in faith, believing that they would be provided for, just as Jesus promised. And so it was. In every place someone would be waiting for them, glad for the opportunity to extend hospitality to them. It was a system that developed the faith of the Twelve and provided the opportunity for people to enjoy fellowship with them.

In my ministry over the years, I have stayed in guest houses, hotels and the homes of many people. I have slept on a rock, park benches, vehicles, campers, overnight buses, planes, taxis, and even once in a telephone booth. One of the sweetest times I ever had with Jesus was when I preached in Ireland and was staying in the home of a Roma family. I knew right away that I was sharing my bed with their big dog. Although he did not actually sleep in the bed with me, I could tell that it was where he slept when there were no visitors. I can be a little fastidious sometimes and decided to sleep on top of the bed, fully dressed, every night. One night, after settling down in the room, I knelt at the bedside and prayed. The Holy Spirit reminded me about Jesus and how He had no place to lay His head (Matthew 8:20). In that moment that little room became like heaven to me because I knew that Jesus was with me.

Expect Rejection

Jesus explained to them that not all the people would accept them and that some would reject them, just as He had been rejected in Nazareth (Mark 6:1–6). Not all would receive them with open arms. Where they were not welcome, they were to leave.

Also, He said to them, "In whatever place you enter a house, stay there till you depart from that place. And whoever will not receive you nor hear you, when you depart from there, shake off the dust under your feet as a testimony against them. Assuredly, I say to you, it will be more tolerable for Sodom and Gomorrah in the day of judgment than for that city!" (Mark 6:11)

I remember walking on the boardwalk along the shore of Brighton, England, a few years ago. I was invited to speak at a conference and had some free time between the meetings and decided to go for a walk. I had some gospel tracts in my pocket, which the Lord had prompted me to take with me. While I was walking, I had the opportunity to talk to some people and I gave them tracts. Some took it and put it in their pockets to read later. Some, however, looked at it with disgust and cussed as they threw it on the ground. I simply picked it up and continued to walk. I realized that they were not rejecting me but the good news of Jesus and Jesus Himself. Did He not say in Luke 10:16, 'He who hears you hears Me, he who rejects you rejects Me, and he who rejects Me rejects Him who sent Me'?

When Jesus sent out the Twelve and later on the Seventy, in Luke 10, He warned them about rejection by saying, 'Go your way; behold, I send you out as lambs among wolves' (Luke 10:3). They were to go and search for a hospitable person. Once they had found that 'man of peace,' who would provide them with room and board, their 'peace would rest on him.'

So, they went out and preached that people should repent. And they cast out many demons, and anointed with oil many who were sick, and healed them. (Mark 6:12–13)

The disciples' mission was a success. They found that it was exactly as Jesus had said it would be. Looking back, they were happy that they believed in and trusted Jesus, and that they had obeyed Him.

In Closing

While you and I may not understand all the twists and turns of life, you can be sure of the following: First, God exists and actively governs His creation (Psalm 111:10), Second, God sees the bigger picture. Third, God loves you and has been actively involved in your life and mine from the day we were born—and even before that. Last, God has a plan and a purpose for you, and this plan includes blessings greater than your ability to imagine. You can live each day with a sense of hope and assurance that whatever comes your way has passed through God's omnipotent, loving hands.

Even a casual reading of the Bible shows that God's ways and plans are completely different from the ways in which people accomplish their goals. God said, 'My thoughts are not your thoughts, neither are your ways my ways' (Isaiah 55:8). Learning to follow God's ways may be more important than any sincere attempt to do His will. God is eager to reveal His ways to us because they are the only way to accomplish His purposes. God wants to complete His work through you. He also has an awesome plan and strategy for your future. He sees the bigger picture. He opens exciting doors of opportunity, although He sometimes also closes doors. He knows where we need to go. He knows what we need to accomplish. He sees the potential; He knows what might happen but He also knows that it is up to us to accept the *commission*.

He can only bless us and use us if we adjust our life to Him. He is waiting on our response!

6

The COMMITMENT

His concern, our response and obedience

He who has My commandments and keeps them, it is he
who loves Me. And he who loves Me will be loved by My
Father, and I will love him and manifest Myself to him.
(John 14:21)

If Jesus Christ be God and died for me, then no sacrifice
can be too great for me to make for Him. (C.T. Studd)[1]

I had the privilege to preach in Barvas, a small town on the Isle of
Lewis, one of a group of islands known as the Hebrides, just off
the West Coast of Scotland. In November 1949, the fire of God
fell on the Isle of Lewis and a mighty revival broke out in those
parts of the United Kingdom. I traveled to various parts on the
Isle of Lewis to capture the stories of those who were impacted
by the revival and to visit the places connected with the revival. It
is one of the personal highlights of my life to have been to and
prayed at the places where it all started. God used many people
to pray and prepare for that revival. Duncan Campbell was the
preacher God used as an instrument in the revival.

It is interesting to note that before the revival, Duncan Campbell
was struggling in his walk with God. God used Duncan Campbell,
a Pilgrim in the Faith Mission, mightily as he saw revival in Ireland
and the Highlands of Scotland. Following the revival, he served as
a church minister for 24 years. During that time, he lost the fullness
of the Holy Spirit, which he had treasured so, and felt like a failure.

He went through a time when prayer was a burden and the Word of God just a book to read. But God was at work in the shadows to bring him back to His glory and fullness.

In his book *Catch the Wind*,[2] Brad Allen shares how God met with Duncan again. Duncan was sitting in his upstairs study on 15 November 1947, preparing a message he was to preach at the Keswick Convention in Edinburgh. It was 05:00 a.m. in the morning and he had heard singing coming from the parlor downstairs. He sat back and listened. It was his 16-year-old daughter Sheena who was singing. She sang, 'Coming, coming, yes, they are, Coming, coming from afar; From the Indies and the Ganges, Steady flows that living stream, To love's ocean, to His fullness, Calvary, their wondering theme.'

He made his way downstairs, slipped into the parlor and sat down. As Sheena sang, something stirred in Duncan's heart. When she had finished singing this song, she came over, sat on his lap and said, 'Daddy, I would like to talk to you.' Duncan replied, 'Sheena, I would be happy to talk to you, but first, what is it that is moving you this morning?' Sheena replied: 'Oh, Daddy, isn't Jesus wonderful?' Duncan asked her, 'Sheena, what is it that makes Jesus so wonderful to you at 05:00 a.m. in the morning?' Sheena said, 'Daddy, I have just spent an hour with Jesus, and He is so wonderful.' Then she said, 'Daddy, for several days I have been battling about asking you a question, but I must do it. Daddy, when you were a young Pilgrim with the Faith Mission, you saw revival. Daddy, why is it not with you now, as it once was? Daddy, how is it that you are not seeing revival now?' Then Sheena hit Duncan with a crushing question, 'Daddy, you have a large congregation, and many are joining the church, but when did you last kneel beside a poor sinner and lead him to Jesus?'

He went to the Keswick Convention with a heavy heart, and delivered his message, which he later admitted to being glad it was over. God was to use his daughter's question and the testimony of Dr. Tom Fitch to convict him. As he walked home, he decided that unless God did something in his heart, unless God gave him back what he had lost, he would resign from the ministry and go into business. After reaching his home, he did not eat supper but sought the face of God in his study. He prayed and told the Lord, 'I will not come out to eat or to drink until I am right with You.' He said:

> As I sat listening to Dr. Fitch giving his last message, I suddenly became conscious of my unfitness to be on the platform. I saw the barrenness of my life and ministry. I saw the pride of my own heart. How humiliating it was to discover that I was proud of the fact that I was booked to speak at five conventions that year. That night, in desperation on the floor of my study, I cast myself afresh on the mercy of God. He heard my cry for pardon and cleansing and, as I lay prostrate before Him, wave after wave of divine consciousness came over me, and the love of the Savior flooded my being: and in that hour I knew that my life and ministry could never be the same again. If in small measure God has been pleased to use me, it is all because of what He did for me that night.[3]

God met with him and brought him back into that glorious experience of the fullness of the Holy Spirit that he once knew. The Lord placed a burden on his heart to evangelize again, as he once did. Realizing that God was calling him back into evangelism, his joy seemed to fade. Duncan had unwillingness in his heart to return to a ministry of evangelism. He found himself struggling with the question, 'How would I support my family?' His wife had promised their daughter a new coat for her birthday. As he was praying, at 02:00 a.m. in the morning Sheena opened the door, lay down on the rug and, after praying with him, said, 'Daddy, whatever it costs, just go through with God.' Sheena continued, 'Daddy, I believe you are fighting the question whether you should go back to the Faith Mission. I am fully persuaded that God is asking you to go back.' Then Sheena spoke the words that sounded to Duncan like the voice of God Himself, 'Daddy, perhaps you are wondering how you can look after us. I know that you promised to buy me a new coat for my birthday but, Daddy, Mother will be quite willing to fix my old coat. You needn't buy me a new coat.'

He had no choice but to surrender and obey God's calling, resign from his position and trust God for the future. In that moment when Duncan had said 'Yes' to God, flood tides of glory came over him again and again. In a vision he saw thousands of people from the Highlands and Western Islands drifting into hell. He heard a voice calling to him, 'Go to them! Go to them!' Duncan had a new awareness of the reality of Jesus in his personal life, and it was evident in his preaching from then on. He became the instrument of the Hebrides Revival in 1949.

God At Work!

When God is doing His work, He not only works with one person or place but in several areas, so that His will, agenda and purposes can be accomplished. As we have already established in the previous chapter, the Holy Spirit has been at work in every person's life in numerous ways long before a preacher speaks the word of truth to him or her. *When God leads us to somebody, he has been there before us.* God could have spoken to Duncan Himself, but He chose to do so through his daughter. He had been working behind the scenes in her heart and life, as He burdened her to pray for her father and revival. He also laid it upon her heart to ask him the question that led to Duncan's surrender to God's plan. Sheena herself had struggled with whether asking the question was the right thing to do. Later on she willingly surrendered her own desire for a new coat to the will of God. Duncan also struggled with God. While God was working, bringing Duncan back to Him in the town of Falkirk, God was also working in the hearts and lives of some people on the Isle of Lewis in the Hebrides islands. They were praying for revival and invited Duncan to preach on their island. God wanted to bless them by sending revival and drawing them to Him. God was at work, at the same time, in the lives of Sheena, Duncan and the people of Falkirk.

This is a principle that is also clear in the life of Moses. He was deep in the desert, minding the flock of Jethro, his father-in-law, when God's call came. God revealed Himself and the burden He had for the people of Israel. God had a job for him. However, Moses did not feel qualified for the task that God had given to him. He struggled to say yes and eventually accepted the call. God told him, 'I will be with you' (Exodus 3:12).

He also told him:

> I will give this people favor in the sight of the Egyptians; and it shall be, when you go, that you shall not go empty-handed. But every woman shall ask of her neighbor, namely, of her who dwells near her house, articles of silver, articles of gold, and clothing; and you shall put them on your sons and on your daughters. So, you shall plunder the Egyptians.' (Exodus 3:21–22)

Moses did as the Lord told him. It was in Egypt, after the first nine plagues, that God spoke about this again. And the Lord said to Moses:

> I will bring one more plague on Pharaoh and on Egypt. Afterward he will let you go from here. When he lets *you* go, he will surely drive you out of here altogether. Speak now in the hearing of the people, and let every man ask from his neighbor and every woman from her neighbor, articles of silver and articles of gold. And, the Lord gave the people favor in the sight of the Egyptians. Moreover, the man Moses *was* very great in the land of Egypt, in the sight of Pharaoh's servants and in the sight of the people. (Exodus 11:1–4)[4]

God was at work at the same time in the life of Moses, the people of Israel and the Egyptians to work out His plan and purpose.

So it was also with Jesus and His disciples. Jesus had come to reveal God's love and to reconcile the world to Himself. Jesus is the perfect model of a person enjoying intimate fellowship with our heavenly Father, of someone walking closely with Him. We have already established that His life was guided by two principles: saying and doing what He had heard and seen. Jesus taught and modeled the same principles to the disciples. In the previous chapter we have seen that Jesus sent the disciples out on their first missionary journey to places where He had already been or to people prepared to receive them. The Father was at work in the life of Jesus, the disciples and the villages and towns where the disciples were about to go.

God originally created people to glorify His name. He created humans in His own image for fellowship with Himself. God had a close relationship with Adam and Eve in the garden. But then they sinned. They disobeyed God. The image was marred, and the fellowship broken. When the time was right, however, God took a decisive step to recreate the potential of people to bring glory to His name.

Was there ever a person whose every thought, word, and deed brought glory to God every hour of every day of every year of their life.

Yes. One.

The Lord Jesus.

In Jesus' prayer to His Father, He said of Himself, 'I have glorified You on earth. I have finished the work which You have given Me to do' (John 17:4).

Therefore, if I am ever to accomplish my ultimate goal in life, to glorify God, I must be transformed more and more into His image, to become like Christ (Romans 8:29). How then do I become like Christ? By being around Jesus, sitting at His feet, listening to His voice, talking with Him, loving Him and doing things together. However, it is not enough merely to hear His Word and call Him 'Lord.' We must also obey what He commands. Jesus said, 'He who has My commandments and keeps them, it is he who loves Me. And he who loves Me will be loved by My Father, and I will love him and manifest Myself to him' (John 14:21).[5]

There is no fellowship and intimacy with God where there is no obedience. Elisabeth Elliot says it best, 'God is God. Because He is God, He is worthy of my trust and obedience. I will find rest nowhere but in His holy will, which is unspeakably beyond my largest notions of what He is up to.'[6]

God is at work in several areas at the same time, and my obedience and commitment to God's call impacts not just my life but also the lives of others. Jesus showed His love for the Father, the disciples and the world by going to the cross voluntarily (John 14:31). He did not flee or hide. He willingly laid down His life and became the Savior of the world.

Moses was chosen to lead the Israelites out of Egypt ...
and he responded.
Sheena was chosen to speak to her father ... and she
responded.
Duncan was chosen to be a revivalist ... and he responded.
Jesus was chosen to reveal God's love and reconcile the
world to Himself ... and He responded that he accepted.
The disciples were chosen, called and appointed ... and
they responded.

And they became a blessing to others!
What about You?
It's time to respond.

What Now?

In the previous chapter we saw how Jesus commissioned His
disciples to go and represent Him on their missionary outreaches.
Just as Duncan Campbell heard the words *Go to them! Go to them!*
Jesus wanted the disciples to go to the villages and nearby towns.
He told them where to go, what to do and what to expect on their
journey.

And He called the twelve to *Himself,* and began to send
them out two *by* two, and gave them power over unclean
spirits. He commanded them to take nothing for the
journey except a staff—no bag, no bread, no copper
in *their* money belts—but to wear sandals, and not to put on
two tunics. Also, He said to them, "In whatever place you
enter a house, stay there till you depart from that place. And
whoever will not receive you nor hear you, when you depart
from there, shake off the dust under your feet as a testimony
against them. Assuredly, I say to you, it will be more tolerable
for Sodom and Gomorrah in the day of judgment than for
that city!" So, they went out and preached that *people* should
repent. And they cast out many demons, and anointed with oil
many who were sick, and healed *them.* (Mark 6:7–13)

The fame of Jesus was spreading all over the region of Galilee. Jesus knew that countless homes and hearts would be open to receive the disciples. Many would be willing to listen and respond to their message. He knew that hundreds of people would be willing to contribute to meet all their needs. However, He also knew that not everyone would listen to them and invite them into their homes. He knew that it would be a step of faith and trusting Him as they reached out and ministered to others and gained preaching experience.

The scene is set.
The actual moment of truth has arrived for them.
They have to make a decision.

The Moment of Truth

The moment of truth had arrived for the disciples. They had received their marching orders. It was time for them to go. They had a decision to make. Their decision would show what they really believed about Jesus, and their commission. Can they rely on the promises, protection, power, and trustworthiness of God? Will He provide in all their needs?

Will it be like He said?

The Bible says, 'But without faith it is impossible to please Him, for he who comes to God must believe that He is, and that He is a rewarder of those who diligently seek Him' (Hebrews 11:6). *Faith is not what God is going to do, or what He has done, but what He is doing at the moment.* According to Manley Beasley, 'Faith is to act on the belief that a thing is so, when it is not so, in order for it to be so, because with God it is already so.'[7] It was time for them to act on that belief, take Him at His word, believing that He will provide all their needs (Philippians 4:19), trust in Him and leave the outcome to Him. This is the kind of faith that pleases God.

Crisis of Belief

The disciples faced a crisis of belief. The word crisis comes from a Greek word that means decision or judgment. Dr. Henry and Dr. Richard Blackaby explain in the *7 Truths From Experiencing God*,

'A crisis of belief is not a calamity in your life but a turning point where you must make a decision. You must decide what you truly believe about God.'[8] It is not because of something bad that has happened but it marks a moment where a person must make a final decision or judgment regarding something. They continue:

> The way you respond at this turning point will determine whether you become involved with God in something God-sized that only He can do or whether you continue to go your own way and miss what He has purposed for your life. The way we live our life is a testimony of what we believe about God.[9]

The people of Judah once faced a great multitude of people who rose up against them in battle. King Jehoshaphat was afraid, and set himself apart from the rest to seek the Lord, and even proclaimed a fast throughout all of Judah (2 Chronicles 20:1–3). They cried out to God, 'We have no power against this great multitude that is coming against us; nor do we know what to do, but our eyes are upon You' (v. 12). As a coalition of armies marched against Jerusalem, the people gathered to seek God's guidance and petition His help (v. 13). During these threatening times of disruption and change, they asked, 'Lord, what do You want to do in this moment?' They were facing a crisis of belief. God told the king, and his people, 'Do not be afraid nor dismayed … for the battle is not yours, but God's. Tomorrow go down against them … for the Lord is with you' (vv. 15–17). They were at a turning point. They had to make the decision to believe in God, trust and obey Him.

I still remember the day that God called me into full-time ministry. We were living in a large company house, I had a secure position and earned a good income. When I told my wife that God had called me into full-time ministry and that I had to resign from my position in the Defense Force, she asked me, 'Under which tree and in what tent will we live?' We did not own our own home. If I resigned, we would have to leave and move out of the house and we had nowhere else to stay. I knew that God had called me, and we had to find a place to stay.

We faced a crisis of belief. We had to make a decision. God had wonderfully provided a house for us to buy. Since then we have found ourselves at many crossroads and faced much decision-making.

It seems that this is a regular occurrence.

Once, during a very busy season of ministry, my vehicle broke down nine times, many of those times late at night or on deserted roads. The vehicle finally stopped running and we were left without any transport. We had no money to replace it, and for two weeks I either walked to my appointments or relied on other people to take me to my meetings. We faced a crisis of belief. We had to make a decision about our situation. We had no other option but to trust the Lord to provide us with another vehicle. I was fasting and praying about the crisis that we faced. During these two weeks the Lord started to lay upon my heart a specific color and model of vehicle. One morning, as I was praying, God gave me the assurance He knew about our need and that He would provide for us. Later that day a friend of our family phoned to say that the Lord had laid it upon his heart to help us. I did not tell him about the model and color, but when the vehicle was delivered at our home it was the model and color that God had laid upon my heart.

It seems to me that life is full of these kinds of moments and turning points, but that God knows and sees the bigger picture. He is working out His plan and purpose in our lives and we must trust Him. Oswald Chambers, author of *My Utmost For His Highest,* once said, 'I must learn that the purpose of my life belongs to God, not me. God is using me from His great personal perspective, and all He asks of me is that I trust Him.'[10]

In stressful, confusing times and situations, we might utter a worried 'What now, Lord?' But if we look to the Lord, believe His words and promises, and trust in His care, our fear or concern will be replaced with peace and victory. The way we respond in that moment of crisis will reveal what we believe of God. *If we trust in Him in the stressful situation, it will enable us to grow in our faith and continue in our next assignment with God.*

However, if we do not trust God, we will miss out on what God has purposed for us.

I am determined in my heart not to miss out on anything that God wants to do in my life or through me. I have also found that the more time I spend in His presence and with Him, the easier it becomes to believe and trust in Him and obey Him. We all need to learn how to be obedient. We are not born with the desire to obey God or anyone in authority. It is a learning process of trial and error, and everyone has to learn that.

The disciples faced their *moment of truth, crisis of belief,* and made the decision to obey Him. They learned that following Jesus required constant adjustment and obedience to His call. They learned obedience from Scripture, by watching their Rabbi, and what some of them had already learned and experienced at first hand.

Learning Trust and Obedience

Learning from Scriptures

The disciples studied the Law of Moses, psalms and prophets throughout their childhood. They would have known that obeying God's commands always came into special prominence with any new beginning in the history of God's Kingdom. Noah, the new father of the human race, acted *according to all that God commanded him'* (Genesis 6:22). The Bible mentions his obedience four times. God entrusts His work to the man who does what He commands.

God chose Abraham to be the father of a chosen race because He knew that he had an obedient heart. We read *by faith he obeyed* (Hebrews 11:8). When God called him, he left his country and followed God, not knowing where he was going (Genesis 12:1–4). He met with God daily (Genesis 19:27) and he willingly offered his son Isaac in obedience to God (Genesis 22:3,12). God gave him a blessing that in his seed all the nations of the earth will be blessed because he obeyed the voice of God (Genesis 22:16–18). God blessed Abraham, multiplied his lineage and even revealed his future.

God blessed Abraham with Isaac. As he grew up, he must have noticed how his father met with God and lived close to Him. When

Isaac went down to Gerar, God warned him not to go down to Egypt (Genesis 26:3–5). Isaac experienced God's blessing because his father obeyed the voice of God. What was his response to God? We read that he stayed put and did not go: so Isaac dwelt in Gerar (Genesis 26:6). When God called him, he surrendered his desire to go down to Egypt and obeyed God.

On Mount Sinai, God gave Moses this message, 'Now therefore, if you will indeed obey My voice and keep My covenant, then you shall be a special treasure to Me above all people; for all the earth is Mine' (Exodus 19:5). We read 19 times that Moses, while building the Tabernacle of the wilderness, the place where God was to dwell, acted 'according to all that the Lord commanded him' (Exodus 40:16). In contrast, the disciples would have remembered how their forefathers wandered in the wilderness for 40 years because of unbelief and disobedience (Hebrews 3:18). They must have been reminded about all the kings and prophets who obeyed and those who did not. What blessings and benefits were bestowed upon them and what curses and hardships came as a result of not listening to the voice and commands of God (Deuteronomy 11:26–28).

I believe the apostles' training as students of the Law, and later by the example of Jesus and His impact upon them, made them value the importance of obedience. James later on warned, 'But be doers of the Word, and not hearers only, deceiving yourselves' (James 1:22). Peter reminds us, 'elect according to the foreknowledge of God the Father, in sanctification of the Spirit, for obedience and sprinkling of the blood of Jesus Christ.' And, 'as obedient children, not conforming yourselves to the former lusts, as in your ignorance; but as He who called you is holy, you also be holy in all your conduct' (1 Peter 1:2, 14–15).

Learning from Jesus

In the New Testament, we immediately think of our Lord Jesus and the importance He placed on obedience as the one reason He came into the world. He always confessed to men, 'I seek not mine own will, but the will of the Father which hath sent me' (John 5:30). In His teachings, we find that He demands the same obedience He had rendered to the Father from everyone who desires to be His disciple. *Obedience opens the door to all that God has to give of His Holy Spirit, His wonderful love and blessings.* We reveal our love for God, to Him as well as to the world, through our cheerful obedience. We should ask ourselves if obedience has a special place in our hearts and lives. Our love for God is the inspiration for every action of obedience to Him.

Jesus *learned* obedience

The Lord Jesus learned obedience through everything that He suffered. His sufferings were real and intense. Such as it was in Gethsemane, when our Lord came to grips with death, the ultimate horror that all mankind faces.

> Then Jesus came with them to a place called Gethsemane, and said to the disciples, "Sit here while I go and pray over there." And He took with Him Peter and the two sons of Zebedee, and He began to be sorrowful and deeply distressed. Then He said to them, "My soul is exceedingly sorrowful, even to death. Stay here and watch with Me." He went a little farther and fell on His face, and prayed, saying, "O My Father, if it is possible, let this cup pass from Me; nevertheless, not as I will, but as You will." Then He came to the disciples and found them sleeping, and said to Peter, "What! Could you not watch with Me one hour? Watch and pray, lest you enter into temptation. The spirit indeed is willing, but the flesh is weak." Again, a second time, He went away and prayed, saying, "O My Father, if this cup cannot pass away from Me unless I drink it, Your will be done." And He came and found them asleep again, for their eyes were heavy. So, He left them, went away again, and prayed the third time, saying the same words. Then He came to His disciples and said to them, "Are you still sleeping and resting? Behold, the hour is at hand, and the Son of Man is being betrayed into the hands of sinners. Rise, let us be going. See, My betrayer is at hand. (Matthew 26:36–46)

Jesus did not resist the will of His Father but yielded Himself to it. When the Father called His Son, Jesus gladly and willingly surrendered to do His will, and modeled obedience through His sufferings. We read that Jesus, 'though He was a Son, yet He learned obedience by the things that He suffered' (Hebrews 5:8).

Jesus *modeled* obedience

Jesus was committed to knowing and doing the will of His Father. His mind was submitted to doing the task that His Father entrusted to Him.

> The Lord God has given Me The tongue of the learned, That I should know how to speak A word in season to him who is weary. He awakens Me morning by morning, He awakens My ear To hear as the learned. The Lord God has opened My ear; And I was not rebellious, Nor did I turn away. I gave My back to those who struck Me, And My cheeks to those who plucked out the beard; I did not hide My face from shame and spitting. "For the Lord God will help Me; therefore, I will not be disgraced; therefore, I have set My face like a flint, And I know that I will not be ashamed. He is near who justifies Me; Who will contend with Me? Let us stand together. Who is My adversary? Let him come near Me. Surely the Lord God will help Me; Who is he who will condemn Me? Indeed, they will all grow old like a garment; The moth will eat them up. "Who among you fears the Lord? Who obeys the voice of His Servant? Who walks in darkness and has no light? Let him trust in the name of the Lord And rely upon his God." (Isaiah 50:4–10)

When Jesus came to earth as a man, He submitted Himself to the Father in everything, 'Behold, I have come to do Your will, O God' (Hebrews 10:9). In the wilderness, when He was tempted to use His divine powers for Himself, He refused to do so. He was totally dependent on His Father and the power of the Holy Spirit to help Him. He said, 'My food is to do the will of Him who sent Me, and to finish His work' (John 4:34). It was the principle He lived by. Everything that Jesus said and did He was taught by the Father (John 5:19, 30; 6:38; 8:28; 12:48–50). Jesus prayed about guidance (John 11:42). What He received from His Father, He shared with those who needed encouragement and help (Matthew 11:28).

Jesus *taught* obedience

Peter experienced this first-hand when he came to Jesus and said that everyone was looking for Him (Mark 1:37). Jesus ignored his request and told him to continue with the journey to the next town (v. 38). Jesus taught the disciples to obey His Word. In the Great Commission, He told them to make disciples, and teach them all that He had commanded them. Avery Willis, in his book *Master Life*, explained that the disciples had one thing in common.[11] They did what Jesus asked them to do. They were selfish and impulsive at times, but even when Jesus asked them to do things that did not make sense, they obeyed. They were handing out fish and loaves of bread to crowds before seeing the miracle of multiplication (Mark 6:35–44). They looked for men with water jugs, an unlikely sight (Mark 14:13–16). They went fishing to get a gold coin out of a fish's mouth—another miracle indeed (Matthew 17:27).

Jesus *expects* obedience

Jesus not only taught the disciples to be obedient to the will of the Father but expected this of them. During His entire ministry, from the beginning to end, He said that obedience was the very essence of salvation. No one could enter the Kingdom, 'but he that doeth the will of My Father which is in heaven' (Matthew 7:21). In His final discourse, Jesus explained that our love for God and obedience to Him go hand in hand.

> If you love Me, keep My commandments. He who has My commandments and keeps them, it is he who loves Me. And he who loves Me will be loved by My Father, and I will love him and manifest Myself to him. Jesus answered and said to him, if anyone loves Me, he will keep My word; and My Father will love him, and We will come to him and make Our home with him.
> (John 14:15, 21, 23)

> If you keep My commandments, you will abide in My love, just as I have kept My Father's commandments and abide in His love. (John 15:10)

Obedience is born out of love; it is inspired by it, and it opens the way for a love relationship with God. It opens the door to all that God has to offer us. Our obedience is an expression of our love and devotion to Him.

Jesus *warns against* disobedience

There is no fellowship with Jesus without obedience. Jesus clearly spelled out the danger of disobedience.

> But why do you call Me "Lord, Lord," and do not do the things which I say? Whoever comes to Me, and hears My sayings and does them, I will show you whom he is like: He is like a man building a house, who dug deep and laid the foundation on the rock. And when the flood arose, the stream beat vehemently against that house, and could not shake it, for it was founded on the rock. But he who heard and did nothing is like a man who built a house on the earth without a foundation, against which the stream beat vehemently; and immediately it fell. And the ruin of that house was great. (Luke 6:46–49)

Learning from Experience

Peter learned that Jesus, and a word by Him, made all the difference. He and his friends also experienced this at first hand on the shore of Lake Galilee.

> So it was, as the multitude pressed about Him to hear the Word of God, that He stood by the Lake of Gennesaret, and saw two boats standing by the lake; but the fishermen had gone from them and were washing *their* nets. Then He got into one of the boats, which was Simon's, and asked him to put out a little from the land. And He sat down and taught the multitudes from the boat. When He had stopped speaking, He said to Simon, "Launch out into the deep and let down your nets for a catch." But Simon answered and said to Him, "Master, we have toiled all night and caught nothing; nevertheless, at Your word I will let down the net." And when they had done this, they caught a great number of fish, and their net was breaking. So,

they signaled to *their* partners in the other boat to come and help them. And they came and filled both the boats, so that they began to sink. When Simon Peter saw *it,* he fell down at Jesus' knees, saying, "Depart from me, for I am a sinful man, O Lord!" For he and all who were with him were astonished at the catch of fish which they had taken; and so also *were* James and John, the sons of Zebedee, who were partners with Simon. And Jesus said to Simon, "Do not be afraid. From now on you will catch men." So, when they had brought their boats to land, they forsook all and followed Him. (Luke 5:1–11)

The people were thronging around Jesus and Jesus had no place to sit or stand to teach them. He noticed two empty boats drawn up by the shore, one of which belonged to Simon Peter (Luke 5:1–3), where they were busy cleaning the nets. Jesus previously enlisted Peter, Andrew, James, and John, but then they had gone back to being fishermen (Mark 1:21–39). Here Peter let Jesus borrow his boat. Jesus sat down in it, rowed out a little and taught the people from it. This simple request by Jesus became a stepping stone to a bigger blessing. Peter's obedience paved the way for what was going to happen next, and from this example we learn how essential it is to obey Jesus even in the smallest matters. Our response is important as it leads to more and bigger blessings. Jesus had prepared Peter for that moment.

First, Peter had to make his boat *available* to Jesus (Luke 5:3), and because he did so many were blessed that day. Jesus was able to sit, and the crowds were able to hear Him and listen to His words. Peter must have been pleased that the great teacher Himself had used his boat. Although Jesus taught the crowds, He was also interested in Peter as a person. Peter was forced to listen to Jesus' teaching but was about to experience so much more.

Jesus then *took command* of Peter's boat and told him to launch out into the deep (Luke 5:4). Jesus was a carpenter by trade (Mark 6:3), and one would think that carpenters did not know much about fishing. It was a well-known fact that, in the Sea of Galilee, fishing took place at night, in the shallow water, towards the north, where the Jordan River flows into the sea, and not at daytime in the deep water. That day Peter learned that sometimes God asks us to do something that does not make sense in our human understanding of things.

When God tells us to do something that doesn't make sense to us, trust Him —because it makes sense to Him.

Jesus *commanded* Peter to let down the nets for a catch (Luke 5:4). Peter tried to argue (Luke 5:5) as He and his friends had been trying to catch fish all night long. They said there were no fish there. They had tried but did not catch anything and were already cleaning their nets. As we know, if nets are not washed and stretched out to dry, they rot and break. Peter thought he knew more about fishing than Jesus and might have felt embarrassed with such a great crowd watching them. Maybe Peter wanted to make a point. Anyhow, he let down the net and to his astonishment they had more fish in that net than he could handle. He tried to cope by himself but the net started to break, and he had to call for help (Luke 5:6–7). Then the boat was so full it even started to sink. Peter and the people were astonished at the amount of fish that they had caught. When Peter saw what was happening, he fell down on his knees and said, 'Depart from me, for I am a sinful man, O Lord!' (Luke 5:8).

It is important to see how the Lord taught Peter to trust Him step by step: put out a little from the land, launch out into the deep and let down your nets for a catch. It is often the way the Lord works in our lives. A simple step of obedience brings about a blessing and lays the foundation for the next step of obedience, which again leads to a bigger blessing. What did Peter learn?

- Peter learned that God takes ordinary things or people and does extraordinary things with and through them.
- Peter learned that God wanted him to trust and obey His instructions whether or not they made sense to him.
- Peter learned that God wants us to respond and obey Him regardless of the results or what people may think.
- Peter learned that God sometimes tells you just enough to know what to do next.
- Peter learned that we do not experience the provision of God is because of our unbelief and unwillingness to submit and surrender to Him.

Charles Stanley, in his book *Living The Extraordinary Life,* says that there are several truths that will help you understand this significant moment in the life of Peter from a divine perspective:[12]

- Obeying God in small matters is an essential step to God's greatest blessings.
- Our obedience is always beneficial to others.
- Obeying God may require doing some things that appear to be unreasonable.
- When we obey God, we will never be disappointed.
- Our obedience allows God to demonstrate His power in our lives.
- Obeying God always results in deeper understanding. Obeying God will result in dramatic changes in our lives.

If Peter did not obey the first seemingly insignificant command, the miracle would not have happened. But he was willing to submit to the authority of Jesus, even though he did not understand all that Jesus was doing. Jesus told them, 'Do not be afraid. From now on you will catch men' (Luke 5:10). They left their nets and followed Jesus and, from that moment, all three men were to live by faith, trusting the Lord for their physical needs (Luke 5:11).

What is God asking you to do right now?
Remember that no request is a small matter.
It is a stepping stone.

Enemies Of God's Will

When Jesus called His disciples to go, He had something specific in mind. They were to go out and preach, heal the sick and cast out demons. Jesus wanted the disciples to experience His blessings and it must have given Him tremendous joy to see them go. He knew that they could have refused to go and they would have missed out on the opportunity to grow and become a blessing to others. However, regardless of what God has called, and gifted us to do, He wants us to be aware of the dangers and hindrances that we will face in fulfilling His will. At some point we will be tempted to become sidetracked, stray from our original commission or leave our post and follow another road than the one that He intends for us to be on.

At this point, the disciples had not been with Jesus for a long time, but they had already seen the impact that His life and ministry had on the crowds of people. His popularity was growing. Apart from the miracles and healings, the people were looking for a leader or person who could set them free from the oppression of the Romans. Even the disciples were blinded by this desire, hoping that Jesus would redeem Israel (Luke 24). Despite this, they saw Jesus walking away from crowds and popularity (Mark 1). Jesus taught them a few invaluable lessons in this time.

First, *they had to learn* that not every opportunity or open door that will come their way was necessarily God's will.

Second, *Jesus warned them* to take nothing with them and trust Him to provide for them. They could easily look at the crowds and see 'money' and consider accumulating riches for themselves.

Third, *they learned* about facing the temptation to make a name for themselves. This temptation is a very real threat to this day.

Fourth, *they learned* how to avoid becoming consumed by position, power and success. Pride was the temptation that the enemy used in the Garden of Eden to lure Eve into questioning and disobeying God. It seems to me that pride always contains a personal hook, one that is selfish and not God's desire for us. Pride is the opposite of humility and is opposed to the things of God.

Last, *they had to learn* how to submit to God's Word and not to become distracted by their own will, plan and agenda. The danger of ignoring God's will, and following our own agenda, is very real in the lives of all followers of Jesus. One of the greatest tests of temptation for any aspiring follower or leader is to be able to walk away from a success story in obedience to God's will. Can we truly follow His example or are the hooks of ambition and pride too firmly embedded in us? May our eyes be eternally fixed on the last word and commission received from the Lord. We must stay the course of our commission. We can easily drift off course by following our own agendas.

In Closing

At the end of World War II, when Japan surrendered to America, the Japanese emperor came forward to make a formal declaration. Instead of saying, 'We surrender,' he pulled out his sword and presented it to General MacArthur, the commander of the victorious Allied forces in the South Pacific. Basically, what he was saying was, 'I will not fight you anymore. We are giving up our weapons and submitting to you.'[13] They had enough troops and ammunition to keep fighting, but they submitted to one who was greater and stronger. It would have accomplished nothing for Japan to keep fighting, destroying their people and their resources in doing so. By surrendering, they implied that they recognized it was in their best interest to surrender to the Americans.

What is the *sword* that we have to surrender? It involves an unconditional surrender of our will to Jesus Christ, the Lord of our lives. It continues in a commitment to do the Lord's will and agenda. It is when we surrender our will and life that we take our hands off the control button and forsake all to follow Him (Luke 14:33). Jesus' love for us was so great and wonderful that He actually gave Himself for us and to us (John 3:16; Ephesians 5:25). His surrender gave us eternal life and the ability to know the Father and Himself (John 17:1–3). His surrender enables our nature to change. He 'gave himself for us that he might redeem us from all iniquity, and purify unto himself a peculiar people, zealous of good works' (Titus 2:14).

The more I think about the wonder of Jesus, the more I want to give myself to Him. Paul said, 'I have been crucified with Christ; it is no longer I who live, but Christ who lives in me; and the life which I now live in the flesh I live by faith in the Son of God, who loved me and gave Himself for me' (Galatians 2:20). Jesus expects the same from us. He wants us to love Him above all (Luke 14:26) and not allow self-love to rule our hearts. Not until we are willing to lay down our very lives for Him are we in the place where He wants us to be. There is a price to pay to follow Jesus. Jesus laid down three conditions for us to follow Him.

Then, calling the crowd to join his disciples, he said, "If any of you wants to be my follower, you must give up your own way, take up your cross, and follow me. If you try to hang on to your life, you will lose it. But if you give up your life for my sake and for the sake of the Good News, you will save it. And what do you benefit if you gain the whole world but lose your own soul? Is anything worth more than your soul? (Mark 8:34-37 *NLV*)

Jesus called the crowd together with His disciples, and said to them, "If anyone wishes to follow Me [as My disciple], he must deny himself [set aside selfish interests], and take up his cross [expressing a willingness to endure whatever may come] and follow Me [believing in Me, conforming to My example in living and, if need be, suffering or perhaps dying because of faith in Me]. For whoever wishes to save his life [in this world] will [eventually] lose it [through death], but whoever loses his life [in this world] for My sake and the gospel's will save it [from the consequences of sin and separation from God]. For what does it benefit a man to gain the whole world [with all its pleasures], and forfeit his soul? For what will a man give in exchange for his soul and eternal life [in God's Kingdom]?
(Mark 8:34–37 *AMP*)

First, *we must deny ourselves* and surrender ourselves completely to Him. Denial of self is not *self-denial*. The latter means occasionally forgoing certain foods, pleasures, activities or possessions. But denial of self means complete submission to the Lordship of Jesus so that self has no rights or authority at all. It is the total surrender of self. Andrew Murray calls it the life of absolute surrender. It is when we lose ourselves that we actually find ourselves. When we live for Jesus, we become like Him.

Second, *we must take up our cross* and willingly identify with Him in suffering and death. In New Testament times, when people saw a man carrying a cross, they knew he was going to die. Carrying a cross means to suffer. Jesus has already done that on our behalf. The cross represents a pathway that we deliberately choose to identify ourselves in public with Jesus and His cause. The Apostle Paul stayed on this course until his death in Rome. He said, 'But God forbid that I should boast except in the cross of our Lord Jesus Christ, by whom the world has been crucified to me, and I to the world' (Galatians 6:14).

Third, *we must follow Him obediently.* Here following Jesus means trusting Him, walking in His footsteps (1 Peter 2:21), and obeying His commands (John 15:14) out of gratitude for what He has done for us (Ephesians 4:32–5:2) and out of our love for Him (John 14:21–23). What was the driving force in the life of Jesus? It was a life of obedience to the will of God. We must become like Him in order to bear fruit and exhibit His likeness (John 15:8).

God is asking us to believe in Him, adjust, surrender, trust and obey in areas of our life that we might never have been willing to in the past. Maybe He is even asking something that seems impossible. Maybe you are in a situation right now where you are following God, but the circumstances still seem dire. You have begun to doubt in God's purpose and agenda for your life in this situation. You have trusted God and want to obey and please Him in all things but what He is asking from you right now does not make sense. But you must decide whether you will believe God in the circumstances.

Any obedience to God is for our good and to accomplish His perfect will in and through us. Remember that God loves you and His will is always best. It is important to develop a patient, unwavering faith in God, surrender to His will and act on it. When a man or a woman obeys God, the Lord Himself will take care of them. The words of Solomon are comforting, 'Trust in the Lord with all your heart, And lean not on your own understanding; In all your ways acknowledge Him, And He shall direct your paths' (Proverbs 3:5–6).

The disciples were willing to *forsake all* and *lay down their swords,* denying themselves, and followed the instructions of Jesus.

So, they went out and preached that people should repent.
And so began the experience of a lifetime.

7

The COMPLETION

To accomplish His purposes

Then the apostles gathered to Jesus and told Him all things, both what they had done and what they had taught. (Mark 6:30)

"Return to your own house and tell what great things God has done for you." And he went this way and proclaimed throughout the whole city what great things Jesus had done for him. (Luke 8:39)

From there they sailed to Antioch, where they had been commended to the grace of God for the work which they had completed. Now when they had come and gathered the church together, they reported all that God had done with them, and that He had opened the door of faith to the Gentiles. (Acts 14: 26–27)

Take Your Glory Lord[1] by Mary Garnett is the life story of an outstanding man of God. William Duma was born on 16 January 1907 and died on 8 October 1977. His lifestyle was simple, but the effect of his life was sublime. His influence lives on in the countless lives that were impacted by him.

He had committed his life to the Lord at the age of 15, although from the age of 12 until he was 20 he suffered seriously ill health. He struggled to come to terms with his illness and searched for answers to his many questions. He slowly learned that he would have to surrender his question 'why' and place it in the center of God's will. Those years of suffering, unanswered prayers, disappointed hopes of recovery, and declining health were a tough training ground for William. He did not realize that God was preparing him for an extraordinary ministry that would need a firm foundation of unwavering faith in the God of the impossible. Despite his illness William, at the age of 15, was committed to going to school and to working in order to support his family. He also committed himself to serving in the small local church of his town. At the age of 20 he decided to fast for seven days to seek God for healing of his many ailments so that he would be free to preach without sickness. Here is the account of that event.

Each morning for seven days, William left Elangeni, where he lived, to go to his hidden sanctuary. He only took with him some honey and lemon water for sustenance. At sunset he would return home. At the end of the seventh day, he left his sanctuary knowing that God had met with him and that the wind of the Spirit had blown upon him. But he also knew that he had not been healed. As he slowly made his way home, William turned to look at the place of blessing where he had hoped to be touched by God. It was there that the burning desire to be healed was replaced by a greater longing—that God Himself should be his only desire. Although his future was no clearer, he had gained one certainty, that he would not miss God's appointed destiny for his life.

At midnight on the seventh day of his fast, unhealed, William got up to pray. His communion with God was so deep that the hours passed unnoticed. In the middle of the night, he felt a touch to his head and knew it was the finger of God. Heat like fire raced through his body, causing him to sweat profusely. He collapsed and, as he lay on the floor, he felt a surge of cold follow the heat and he realized, almost incredulous, that the pain was no more. He described the moment, 'Although I knew God had touched me, I was afraid that the pain would gradually return. I placed my hands on the parts of my body which for years had been torn by pain. I tested and retested myself, then gathered the courage to see if I could walk without pain. I walked, walked faster, then stopped in the joy anchored in certainty—I was healed! Dumb with gratitude

I knelt, knowing my healing was His charter for my life's work. In His good time, it had arrived.'[2]

Later William went to Durban, where he attended Bible school and then started a new job. He attended Bible classes under Miss G. Hitchcock, a gifted American missionary who was much in demand at conventions. William took charge of a small church under the American Board of Missions as an evangelist. It was during this time that he first experienced the healing of someone else. His uncle and nephew arrived at his door on their way to the Zulu Mission Hospital. His nephew had embedded a large needle and thread in his leg by accident. As the boy did not seem to be in great pain, they decided to overnight at William's home and go to the hospital in the morning. That night the boy awoke, crying as his leg went into painful spasms. Shocked, William sat and stared at the boy until a voice spoke to him and said, 'Why are you looking at the boy and doing nothing? Why are you not praying for him?' Shamed into action by the voice, William prayed and the boy began to scream even louder than before. They looked at the area where the needle and thread had entered and, as they looked, the spasms stopped, and the needle and the thread were expelled by a strong force.

In 1939 William took on the task of pastoring the Umgeni Road Baptist Church, a church of only seven people. It was there that the glory of God came down and the mighty ministry of William Duma took root. William constantly pleaded with the Lord to bring this Umgeni church to a place where the Holy Spirit resided, where His mighty miracles would be a common occurrence. God used those times to cleanse William's heart and draw him closer to Himself. God dealt unsparingly with William's sin and clearly showed him that he must never dally in any of the thousands of ways of sin but remain close to Him and reside in the secret place.

In the 1960s, William was flooded with invitations and absorbed in the preparation of campaigns along with all his other commitments. He recalls, 'Through the years, at 04:00 a.m., by appointment with my Lord, I had been fed by the hand of God. The busyness of preparation ate into my early morning appointment with God. Less and less time was spent in deep communion with God. I told myself I was praying earnestly for the campaigns. Vaguely at first, I realized it had tailed off.'[3]

William's busy schedule resulted in physical tiredness, a decrease in his ability to heal others, a prideful heart and the loss of discernment, which led to hard, untruthful attacks by Christian brothers and sisters which nearly destroyed his ministry. Due to the immense pressure, William suffered a stroke and the doctors believed that he would never recover. In his hospital bed he read the story of Hezekiah, 'Reading of Hezekiah's reprieve, I was comforted. The tears I wept and wept into my pillows cleansed my attitude toward the young pastor. I mourned like a dove in Lebanon for the resentment I had allowed to make a travesty of my ministry. I grieved for the spiritual capital which had drained away because my first eager communion with God at daybreak had been shortened, if not replaced, by campaign planning. Those recollections broke my heart and I wept into the pillows. Healed, I returned to my church and my beloved people not the same Duma.[4]

What was the secret to his life? He was essentially a man of prayer. He saturated his service with prayer and intercession, the secret to the healing ministry. The many hours spent in the presence of God showed on his face and was evident in the power of his preaching and healing. God revealed many secrets to him, and he loved to share that with others in the hope that it would bring glory to the Lord.

The Call To Process and Behold The Glory Of God

God's desire for all of His people is to enjoy more of Him and experience His blessings and abundance, though never at the expense of their holiness, for several reasons. First, because *He loves us.* Second, because it brings Him *pleasure.* Third, because it *accomplishes* His purposes. Last, it brings Him *glory.* The early church father Irenaeus once wrote, 'The glory of God is a man fully alive, and the life of man consists in beholding God.'[5]

Several years ago I had a conversation with Dr. Henry Blackaby, author of *Experiencing God,* which had taught me the value of processing and in beholding God, which I will explain in a little while. We were sitting in a restaurant at the Cape Town International Airport enjoying a meal before his flight back to the USA. We were reflecting on his recent visit to South Africa when he said the following, *Francois, you and I have a lot to process because God has spoken to and with us in these days.* I have never heard that word before and wondered what it meant. However, it would only be during his next visit to our country two years later that I would really start to see the need for this, and understand the spiritual value of processing.

Both of us were speaking at a revival conference that took place in the Audenberg Dutch Reformed Church in Worcester. Dr. Blackaby was scheduled to deliver the Saturday morning message at the conference before departing for the USA later that day. During the last few minutes of the meeting, I left the room to fetch the vehicle and waited for him at the exit. I saw the people kneeling and others lying on their faces at the altar when he walked towards me. They were weeping and crying as they prayed and called out to God. When we were both inside the vehicle and about to leave, he turned to me and simply said, *God just met with us.* I will never forget the look on his face. I cannot describe what happened next. The vehicle was filled with the glory and presence of God. The manifest awareness of God's presence was almost overwhelming. We drove the entire 90 minutes to the airport in complete silence. We were both reflecting on what had just happened.

We met Mrs. Marilynn Blackaby, his wife, at the airport and they checked in for their flight. As they were walking through the customs gate, he turned and looked at me and simply nodded his head. Until that moment, we had not spoken a word.

On my way back to Worcester, it dawned on me that he was reflecting on and processing the encounter with God. It was more important to 'process and behold what God had done' than making small talk with me as we were driving. What exactly is processing and beholding? According to the *Merriam-Webster's Dictionary,* the definition of to process is a series of *actions* and *steps* taken in order to achieve a particular end.[6] The meaning of the word behold is to perceive through sight or apprehension, and to gaze upon the beauty of something.[7] It is to take the time to reflect on or perceive what God is saying or doing in that given moment. Second, to make sure that we understand the truth, reason and purpose of God's dealings with us. Third, what steps have we taken to make it our own, and in so doing achieving God's intention. Last, to gaze upon the wonder and beauty of our God, and to thank Him and show Him appreciation for His involvement in our lives.

Since that day in the vehicle, I have come to understand the need for and value of processing a truth or an encounter with God. Over time I have seen several principles from the life of Jesus and His dealings with the disciples in practise. Much of my study and the principles I discuss in this chapter are not new. However, they have helped me to understand *what to do, when to do it, why to do it, and how to do it.*

What To Do?

In the previous chapter, the disciples responded with obedience when they were commissioned to preach. They were paired and sent out on their first missionary journey. We can only imagine what happened when the disciples came back from their ministry assignments. The disciples were on a spiritual high when they returned. They must have been very excited to tell Jesus about what had happened as they finished their mission trips in triumph (Mark 6:7–13). They preached about repentance, they cast out many demons, and anointed and healed many sick people (Mark 6:12–13). What stories they had to tell of their victories and power! So, they gathered around Jesus, and they *told Him all things, both what they had done and what they had taught* (Mark 6:30).

Jesus also had much to share and report. When the disciples departed on their first mission trip, Jesus did not go with them, but instead also left the surrounding villages and towns to visit, teach and preach (Matthew 11:1). It was during that time (Matthew 14:13–21; Luke 6:1–14; 9:7–9) that Jesus also received the news of the death of his nephew, John the Baptist. John the Baptist was beheaded by Herod and Herod was also looking to capture Jesus.

I wonder who spoke first and if they all tried to talk at the same time, just spilling out all their experiences, or whether Jesus had to quieten them down. Maybe He appointed them one by one or *two by two* as a team to give testimony of what they had witnessed and experienced. Could it be that Jesus was smiling, nodding His head as He listened in agreement, enjoying the obvious excitement of the disciples and the successes of their missionary tours?

What was He Looking and Listening for?

Could it be that He was listening, not so much to see and hear about what they had done and accomplished, but what great things His Father had done in and through them.

> He may have wanted to see whether they had done and accomplished what He had sent them out to do.
> Did He want to see if they were able to put into practise what they had learned from Him?

Jesus would also have wanted to know if His Father was glorified through it all. And to give thanks. Later on, Jesus sent out the Seventy on a mission trip. On their return, Jesus took the time to give thanks, 'I thank You, Father, Lord of heaven and earth … for it seemed good in Your sight' (Luke 10:21).

Throughout the Scriptures, we see this pattern: those whom God blesses and uses in order to have the greatest impact are those who live in submission to His authority, sharing what great things the Lord has done, accomplishing His purposes and seeking only His glory.

The First Missionary in Luke 8:26–39

The country of the Gadarenes was on the eastern shore of the Sea of Galilee. A short distance south of the city there was a spot where the steep hills came down close to the water. It is here where Jesus healed a demon-possessed man. When the man was healed, he begged Jesus to let him stay with Him, but Jesus did not allow him to do so. It was a very natural request. The previously demon-possessed man wanted to remain with Jesus, to whom he had become so heavily indebted. He wished to render to Jesus every service that He might require. But Jesus told him, 'Go home to your friends, and tell them what great things the Lord has done for you, and how He has had compassion on you.' We see that true missionary activity always begins at home. Although we are not meant to end there, it does indeed begin at home (Matthew 10:5–6; Acts 1:8, 1 Peter 4:17).

Instead of going with Jesus, the man was ordered to tell his people what great things 'the Lord' had done for him. He went away and told people what Jesus had done for him (v. 20). In Luke 8:39 the word Lord is replaced with God. Jesus is the Lord. He is God. Jesus sent the demon-possessed man's family and friends a missionary. In fact, the best kind of missionary is one who can speak from personal experience.[8] The man departed and did what Jesus told him to do. Soon he told the entire city (Luke 8:39) and then proclaimed in the region of Decapolis all that Jesus had done for him; and everyone marveled (Mark 5:18–20).

Paul and Barnabas in Acts 14:26–27

What a missionary meeting that must have been! The church in Antioch 'sent' Paul and Barnabas on a pioneer missionary journey (Acts 13:3). The Holy Spirt called and commissioned (Acts 13:2–4) them but their home church served as a 'missions hub' by praying for them and supporting them financially. When they returned, they did not just meet with a few individuals or some leaders. Their report-back did not take place over a meal. No, they had 'gathered the church together.' They gave a detailed report of 'all' that God had done.

Paul and Barnabas had many incredible stories to share. They experienced how a magician was confounded and the magistrate converted in Cyprus; the great loss they suffered when Mark parted ways with them in Perga; the lure of the mountains; the blasphemy at Pisidian Antioch, the Jewish and gentile beliefs; at Iconium, the multiplied conversions and malicious contention; deification and death at Lystra; more souls won; the homeward way; skirting perils; and selecting pastors at Derbe. Thus, their story unfolded. They related the decisions, difficulties and dangers they faced in their pioneer work on the mission field, and how they dealt with them. Why did they do that?

First, they *wanted the church to celebrate with them all the things that God had done in them and through them.* Paul wanted everyone to know that it was God who did all of those things and deserved the honor and glory for it (Romans 15:4). This was also the mindset of Paul when he called the elders of Ephesus and told them that he did not count his own life dear as long he could finish his race with joy (Acts 20:24). Paul declares that whatever we do, drink or eat, it must be to the glory of God, 'Therefore, whether you eat or drink, or whatever you do, do all to the glory of God' (1 Corinthians 10:31).

Second, they *wanted them to know all the things that they had learned and endured* on their journey of faith (2 Corinthians 11).

Third, they *wanted them to know that they were accountable to the church in their dealings with people and money.* Being accountable was very important to Paul. He told Timothy, 'The laborer is worthy of his wages (1 Timothy 5:18). He wrote to the church in Corinth, 'So, also the Lord directed those who proclaim the gospel to get their living from the gospel' (1 Corinthians 9:14).

Fourth, although they worked as tentmakers and trusted the Lord to provide for them, they also *wanted the church to know that they were faithful and could be trusted for future missionary trips.*

Last, they w*anted the church to see and realize that they were seen as partners and fellow laborers* in the harvest.

After giving the church their report, they spent the next year in Antioch. Paul and Barnabas needed a complete rest and taught and preached locally. There was not much time to celebrate and enjoy the success of their tour before there was even more to experience. Life with Jesus seemed to have been like a roller coaster ride. They were always on the go. Moving from one experience to another, one miracle to another, one highlight to another. Jesus needed the time to reflect, process and pray about His own preaching tour and the death of His nephew. Jesus not only withdrew Himself from the crowds to prepare for His next assignment, but also retreated as he had finished His assignment to reflect on the doings of the Father. Jesus used these times of solitude to process what had happened.

Jesus wanted the disciples to start learning the value of 'reporting back,' 'reflecting,' 'considering,' 'thinking,' 'processing for themselves what was happening.' Manley Beasley used to say that 'a truth must not only be believed but be lived.'[9] The disciples needed some time to reflect and process what had happened, after reporting back. It is when we take time out that it reveals to God what we really believe about Him. James A. Stewart, who wrote the story of Helen Ewan of Scotland, explained that Helen always started her communion with God with praise and worship. She would then read the Word to warm her heart, remembering these words of her fellow Scotsman Robert Murray McCheyne, 'It is the look that saves but the gazing that sanctifies.'[10] Charles Spurgeon, a well-known preacher from the 19th century, once said, 'As the rain soaks into the ground, so pray the Lord to let His gospel soak into your soul.'[11]

So, they departed to a deserted place in the boat by themselves. But not before they had to deal with another crowd.

What we need to do is to 'take time out' after every encounter with a truth of God. *It gives us the opportunity to reflect on and process the truth or encounter to celebrate what God is doing in and through us.* When God's Word saturates our thirsty souls, we will experience transformation.

When To Do It?

Jesus took His disciples to a quiet place in the vicinity of Bethsaida (Luke 9:10). They crossed over to the northeast side of the sea in a boat. Many people came from Capernaum and soon they were crowded with people hoping to see Him perform some miraculous cures (vv. 10–11). Despite the interruption to His plans, Jesus was patient and kind, welcomed them and helped them. And so, He began to teach them. We read in Mark 6:33–51:

> But the multitudes saw them departing, and many knew Him and ran there on foot from all the cities. They arrived before them and came together to Him. And Jesus, when He came out, saw a great multitude and was moved with compassion for them, because they were like sheep not having a shepherd. So, He began to teach them many things. When the day was now far spent, His disciples came to Him and said, "This is a deserted place, and already the hour is late. Send them away, that they may go into the

surrounding country and villages and buy themselves bread; for they have nothing to eat." But He answered and said to them, "You give them something to eat." And they said to Him, "Shall we go and buy two hundred denarii worth of bread and give them something to eat?" But He said to them, "How many loaves do you have? Go and see." And when they found out they said, "Five, and two fish." Then He commanded them to make them all sit down in groups on the green grass. So, they sat down in ranks, in hundreds and in fifties. And when He had taken the five loaves and the two fish, He looked up to heaven, blessed and broke the loaves, and gave them to His disciples to set before them; and the two fish He divided among them all. So, they all ate and were filled. And they took up twelve baskets full of fragments and of the fish. Now those who had eaten the loaves were about five thousand men. Immediately He made His disciples get into the boat and go before Him to the other side, to Bethsaida, while He sent the multitude away. And when He had sent them away, He departed to the mountain to pray. Now when evening came, the boat was in the middle of the sea; and He was alone on the land. Then He saw them straining at rowing, for the wind was against them. Now about the fourth watch of the night He came to them, walking on the sea, and would have passed them by. And when they saw Him walking on the sea, they supposed it was a ghost, and cried out; for they all saw Him and were troubled. But immediately He talked with them and said to them, "Be of good cheer! It is I; do not be afraid."

Following the feeding of the 5,000, Jesus dismissed the crowds. It was getting late, and many of the people were far from home. While He was doing so, He ordered his disciples to go ahead of him by boat to the western side of the sea. He desired to spend time in private communion with His Father in heaven. The disciples were still on a spiritual high and had not yet had the time to process all that they had seen and experienced. Jesus and the disciples had just experienced one of God's greatest miracles.

When did Jesus 'process' the miracle that took place? It is clear that immediately afterward Jesus went into the mountains to pray.

The disciples got into a boat and hit a storm. Mark 6:44–45 says, Now those who had eaten the loaves were about five thousand men. *Immediately* ...

When the Father did something through the life of the Lord Jesus, Jesus always took the time to process it. Notice how the Scripture says *Immediately* ... How soon should you process an encounter with God? There ought not to be anything more important that should come between you and taking the time to be with God and asking Him about the significance of what He had done in your life.

According to Jesus, the miracles were all done by the Father; it was the Father living out His life in Him (John 14:10). So, when the Father chose to do this incredible miracle, afterward the Father called His Son to meet with Him. So, what did they talk about? I believe the Father warned Jesus that people would follow Him, because they had their own agendas. They wanted to make Him king not because He was the King but because of the miracles (John 6:15), which was exactly what He did not want (John 18:36). The disciples were not free from their own Messianic expectations (Luke 24:21; Acts 1:6). Could it be that the Father also warned Jesus that people would follow Him because He could feed the multitudes? That He had to resist the temptation to draw a crowd. Maybe Jesus remembered the temptation in the Judea wilderness, 'Command that these stones become bread' (Matthew 4:3), and they will want to follow You.

The time with His Father helped Him to understand, process and in a way prepare Him for the next stage of His ministry. We have already established that Jesus can only say and do what He has seen and heard from the Father (John 5:19; 8:28). As you read more in the Gospels, you will see that is what happened. In John's Gospel we read that when He went across the sea, the multitude found Him and followed Him. Jesus then told them, 'Most assuredly, I say to you, you seek Me, not because you saw the signs, but because you ate of the loaves and were filled' (John 6:26). Then Jesus gave His strong message to those people that He was the bread that had come down from the Father.

When He finished telling them, many forsook Him and walked with Him no more (John 6:66).

How soon should you process an encounter with God? Jesus 'immediately' made arrangements for Him to be alone with His Father. It seems that nothing ought to be more important and come between you and 'processing' your encounter or 'meeting with God.'

Why Do It?

Why must we take the time to process or meet with God? Stay with me as we continue to dig deeper. The disciples will never forget that day at the Sea of Galilee. It became a day and night of wonders. First, they experienced the miracle of the multiplication of the fish and bread. Then they saw Jesus and Peter walk on stormy Galilean waters (Matthew 14:28–32). They heard Jesus speak a word and the storm was stilled. Jesus joined them on the boat, and 'gently rebuked them' before they arrived safely at the shore (John 6:21). What a day and night! Let's observe what Scripture records for us about the why of processing:

> And when they saw Him walking on the sea, they supposed it was a ghost, and cried out; for they all saw Him and were troubled. But immediately He talked with them and said to them, "Be of good cheer! It is I; do not be afraid." Then He went up into the boat to them, and the wind ceased. And they were greatly amazed in themselves beyond measure, and marveled.

Then comes this incredible verse:

> For they had not understood about the loaves, because their heart was hardened. (Mark 6:49–52)

Jesus saw them struggling in the storm, and He walked on the water to them. It was the first time He had ever done that. He could have gone past them, but instead He got into their boat. The disciples were absolutely astonished to see Jesus walking on the water and stilling the storm. The Scripture uses terminology that means 'astonished way beyond measure, way beyond what had ever happened.' They missed the significance of this miracle. Why were they so surprised? In all fairness, the human perspective is that they had not had the time to process the day and all that had happened. Jesus had sent them away by boat, while He Himself took the time to process the encounter with His Father.

Taking the time to process what God is doing in your life prepares you for the next encounter and assignment.

Danger of Hardening the Heart

It is clear from Scripture that not taking the time to process and behold, in order to understand leads to the danger of our hearts becoming hardened. Could I suggest that if you have an encounter with God and you do not take the time to process it, your heart will grow cold, callous and hard. You cannot have an encounter with God and ignore it without it affecting your heart. A hardened heart has great difficulty dealing with the next encounter with God.

> For My thoughts are not your thoughts, nor are your ways My ways, says the Lord. For as the heavens are higher than the earth, so are My ways higher than your ways, and My thoughts than your thoughts. For as the rain comes down, and the snow from heaven, and do not return there, but water the earth, and make it bring forth and bud, that it may give seed to the sower and bread to the eater, so shall My word be that goes forth from My mouth; it shall not return to Me void, but it shall accomplish what I please, and it shall prosper in the thing for which I sent it. For you shall go out with joy and be led out with peace; the mountains and the hills shall break forth into singing before you, and all the trees of the field shall clap their hands. Instead of the thorn shall come up the cypress tree, and instead of the brier shall come up the myrtle tree; and it shall be to the Lord for a name, for an everlasting sign that shall not be cut off. (Isaiah 55:8–13)

Whenever God speaks, He is not asking our permission to do something but announcing what He is about to do in your life. It is like the vine and the branches. The branch doesn't have to make an effort to produce fruit. The branch has to abide in the vine, and it will produce fruit. And you have to abide in the Word of God, and He will do what His Word said. Whatever God said, He will do. Isaiah 55:11 says that whatever word goes forth from God will not return empty. It will produce that for which He sent it. It is critically important that you allow the activity of God to come to completion in your life and begin to set in motion some things that God said. God always says and does things for a reason. It is vital that we pray to hear what the significance is of what He has said or done. If we understand the purpose and effect of the Lord's previous task, it will strengthen our faith, encourage and excite us to respond in obedience to the next task. If not, we face the danger of not understanding and become hard of heart.

How To Do It?

How do we process an encounter with God? We have established what we must do, why we must do it, when we must do it—but how must we do it? We have already established that processing is a series of actions in order to achieve a particular end. The Bible is filled with the failures, the doubts of men and women but those are the very people God had saved and used for His purposes and glory. Ordinary people … people just like you and me. But people who took some steps to process and behold.

It was when Moses *turned aside* to look at the bush that was burning that he met with God and received the assignment to go back to Egypt and lead the people out of Egypt (Exodus 3).

It was when Joseph *thought about these things* that he heard the angel of the Lord speak to him and reveal that he would become the father of the future king of Israel (Matthew 1:20). The Greek word *enthumeomai* can be explained as to think and ponder.

It was when Mary saw the angel *and considered the manner of his greeting* that she realized that she had found favor with God and would give birth to the Savior of the world (Luke 1:29). The Greek word *dialogizomai* can be understood as to reason, to have discourse with oneself in silence.

189

It was when the disciples took the time to consider what God was saying or doing in their lives that God revealed to them the next assignment. This gave me the hope that He could use me as well. I have found that reflecting on and answering some basic questions, allowing the Holy Spirit to reveal the truths to my heart, has helped me to process what God is saying and doing in my life. I trust it will help you too.

- What is God saying to me?
- What does this teach me about God, Son or Holy Spirit?
- What does this teach me about the purposes and ways of God?
- Is there a command to obey?
- Is there an example to follow?
- What liberty and freedom will I experience if I respond to God?
- How will this affect my life, family or workplace?
- What do I need to do now?

Jesus Speaking To His Father

I want to conclude this chapter with Jesus processing and reflecting on His life as He talks to His Father. Most scholars have the Lord Jesus pray this prayer in the Upper Room after He had finished giving the disciples His instructions. Jesus first prayed for Himself and told the Father that His work on earth was finished (John 17:1–5). Then He prayed for His disciples, that the Father would keep them and sanctify them (John 17:6–19). He closed His prayer by praying for you and me and the whole church, that we might be unified in Him and one day share His glory (John 17:20–26).

We can actually picture Jesus talking to His Father, with us listening:

Jesus spoke these words, lifted up His eyes to heaven, and said: "Father, the hour has come. Glorify Your Son, that Your Son also may glorify You, as You have given Him authority over all flesh, that He should give eternal life to as many as You have given Him. And this is eternal life, that they may know You, the only true God, and Jesus Christ whom You have sent. I have glorified You on the earth. I have finished the work which You have given Me to do. And now, O Father, glorify Me together with Yourself, with the glory which I had with You before the world was. "I have manifested Your name to the men whom You have given Me out of the world. They were Yours. You gave them to Me, and they have kept Your word. Now they have known that all things which You have given Me are from You. For I have given to them the words which You have given Me; and they have received them and have known surely that I came forth from You; and they have believed that You sent Me. (John 7:1–5)

The Father and the Son are in sweet communion, and the Son is talking about His own life and work on earth. Jesus tells the Father four things about Himself, and all of those sayings commence in the same way. They are the four 'I haves.'

I have glorified You on the earth. What a confession to make! And Jesus could make it, for in all His words and works and ways, He glorified the Father. He sought to glorify Him in all things. So, He asks the Father directly to glorify the Son. The purpose of this request, however, is not one that is self-seeking. The purpose of His request is clear: that the Son may also glorify the Father.

I have finished the work You have given me to do. Jesus came to teach, preach and do miracles, train the twelve disciples and die on the Cross. Jesus completed the assignments of the Father. I wonder if we will be able to say or pray that? Are we striving to complete the task and assignments? When we find ourselves in the presence of the Lord, He will show all of us the original plan He has for our lives, character and ministry.

I have manifested Your name to the men whom You have given Me out of the world. The word 'name' represents the character and personality of someone. Maybe Jesus was saying, 'I have manifested your character unto the men You gave me.' Jesus was the ultimate culmination and personification of God. He was God manifested in the flesh. If we want to know more about God and what He is like, we must look at the life, teachings and ministry of Jesus. Jesus said to him, 'Have I been with you so long, and yet you have not known Me, Philip? He who has seen Me has seen the Father; so how can you say, "Show us the Father?"' (John 14:9)

I have given to them the words which You have given Me; and they have received them. It is during the times that Jesus spent with the Father that He received the words and truths that He taught and preached. This should also be our desire—only to speak and say those things that we have received from the Father during our moments of solitude and quietness with Him.

In Closing

The late Dr. Billy Graham was known as God's Ambassador. He is one of the most recognized figures in the world—a man who, for more than 50 years, spoke in person to over 200 million people on 6 different continents, in 85 countries, and in all of America's 50 states. Millions more have heard him on radio, seen him on television and in film—more than any other man or woman in history. He was part of history in the making and a friend and counselor to presidents and prime ministers and was the driving force behind the evangelical movement of the 20th century. He was welcomed behind the Iron Curtain, in China and North Korea. He was led by his extraordinary example of integrity.

He was once asked by an interviewer from Sydney, Australia, 'What is the secret of your success?' He said, 'The secret is not me. So many people think that somehow I carry a revival around in a suitcase, and they just announce me, and something happens— but that's not true. This is the work of God, and the Bible warns that God will not share His glory with another. All the publicity that we receive sometimes frightens me because I feel that therein lies a great danger. If God should take His hand off me, I would have no more spiritual power. The whole secret of the success of our meetings is spiritual, it is God answering prayer. I cannot take credit for any of it.[12]

Several years ago my wife and I had the privilege to spend some time with Dr. Tom Phillips, Vice-President of the Billy Graham

Evangelistic Association. We toured the famous Billy Graham Library, as well as the ministry headquarters in Charlotte, NC. We were also able to spend some time with Billy Graham's secretary, who kindly showed us his office, the boardroom and the archives. On our way out, we stopped in the reception area, and looked at the television screen that reflects the names of people who and the places that responded to the worldwide invitation to accept Jesus Christ as their Lord and Savior in that given moment as a result of the ongoing ministry of Billy Graham. He once said, 'My one purpose in life is to help people find a personal relationship with God, which, I believe, comes through knowing Christ.'[13]

I remember thinking that he was true to his calling, created identity and purpose in life—to the very end. He finished well.

I thought about Jesus, who had finished the work, the assignment given Him by His Father (John 17:4). He finished well.

I thought about Paul, who had told the Ephesian elders, 'But none of these things move me; nor do I count my life dear to myself, so that I may finish my race with joy, and the ministry which I received from the Lord Jesus, to testify to the gospel of the grace of God' (Acts 20:24). He finished well.

In that moment at the television screen the Holy Spirit reminded me of the words of Hebrews 13:7 in Scripture:

> Remember those who rule over you, who have spoken the word of God to you, whose faith follows, considering the outcome of their conduct.

> *Remember* your leaders [for it was they] who brought you the word of God; and *consider* the result of their conduct [the outcome of their godly lives], and *imitate* their faith [their conviction that God exists and is the Creator and Ruler of all things, the Provider of eternal salvation through Christ, and imitate their reliance on God with absolute trust and confidence in His power, wisdom, and goodness. (Hebrews 13:7 *AMP*)

> *Remember* your leaders who have taught you the Word of God. Think of all *the good that has come from their lives* and try *to trust the Lord as they do.* (Hebrews 13:7 *TLB*)

Remember your leaders … Jesus, Paul, Duma, Billy Graham and others.
Consider their conduct and the outcome of their godly lives.
Imitate their faith. Try to trust the Lord as they did.

I want to be true to my calling, created identity and purpose in life. I want to finish the assignment given to me by God. I want to finish my race with joy and finish the ministry received from Jesus. I want to finish well. I want to finish strong. I want to finish growing and climbing in my walk with God. In doing so, I want to please and glorify Him in all I do and say.

I believe you want that too.
Remember. Consider. Imitate.

Let me make all of this personal. The ultimate purpose of every Christian is to glorify God. We are called to glorify Him. We read in Isaiah 43:7, 'Everyone who is called by My name, whom I have *created* for My glory; I have formed him, yes, I have made him.' There is no greater purpose or joy in life. I have come to realize that life holds no value or meaning apart from getting to know God more intimately (John 17:1–3; Philippians 3:10). Jesus Christ alone can truly satisfy (John 7). If I seek to be with Him, please Him in all that I am and do and find my joy, peace and rest in Him and live for His glory, I will glorify Him in everything.

We are called to *live* for His glory. Not just individuals but also churches exist to glorify God. Paul wrote the church in Ephesus, 'Now to him who is able to do immeasurably more than all we ask or imagine, according to his power that is at work within us, to him be glory in the church and in Christ Jesus throughout all generations, for ever and ever! Amen' (Ephesians 3:20–21).

We are called to *bear fruit* for His glory, 'By this My Father is glorified, that you bear much fruit; so that you will be My disciples' (John 15:8).

Andrew Murray urged all Christians to begin see the true glory of what we are called to live for, 'It is this that Christ has been working for; it is this that He is working for to-day in us; it is this that He thought it worthwhile to give His blood for; it is that His heart is longing for in each of us; this is the very essence and glory of Christianity, 'that God may be all in all.'[14]

So, What is Man's Chief End?

In the Scottish Catechism we read, 'Man's chief end is to glorify God and to enjoy Him forever.'[15] But at the same time, 'God's chief end is to glorify man and to enjoy him forever.' If we live for the glory of God in this life and world, we will complete and accomplish His purposes and share in His glory. Let us seek the glory here on the earth, for nothing else can bring peace and satisfy the soul. The glory of God is a man fully alive, and the life of man consists in beholding God.

> That God may be all in all!
> *Soli Deo Gloria* – To God alone be the Glory!
> Take Your Glory, Lord!

8

The CELEBRATION

To rest and be refreshed

And He said to them, "Come aside by yourself to a deserted place and rest a while." For there were many coming and going, and they did not even have time to eat. (Mark 6:31)

I've learned the necessity of stepping back, looking where I was going, and having a monthly quiet day to be drawn up into the mind of God. (John Stott)[1]

When life is so busy and hectic and humming; you're uptight and frazzled and stressed; slow down for a while and spend time with the Savior and be sure to get adequate rest. (Fitzhugh)[2]

A while ago, during an unusually intense and busy season of ministry, I found myself at a place in my life where I was not content anymore. I was constantly traveling, teaching, preaching and helping people across South Africa and abroad, which caused me to become worn out and exhausted. I was helping people to rediscover the joy of fellowship with God but at the same time I had reached a point of dryness and tiredness in my own spiritual life and walk with God. I was aware that I had been living in overdrive for a number of years, and I wanted to be 'on fire for God' but instead felt disconnected from the reality and presence of God in my life. I longed for more of God in my life, but I had been too busy for too long and felt out of touch with the need of my body, soul and spirit for balance and rest. I had no idea how to connect the internal and external worlds of my life with each other in a meaningful way.

It was during a one-week vacation at the end of another busy year when I experienced my mind and body just shutting down. My body had had enough and protested about my busy life. This eventually forced me to slow down and take the time to rest. Up until that point, I had convinced myself that to stop working would stifle the flow, the momentum; halt the progress I had made up to that point. I felt numb and disconnected from my emotions and my environment. I had never really taken any time to rest. Even during vacations my mind was busy planning and preparing the next assignment. Our ministry was experiencing incredible growth on a global scale at the time. We were helping people and leaders *Connecting with God* and it was clear that the adventure had only just begun. Some days felt like a roller coaster ride.

I had to learn what Mahatma Gandhi once said, 'There is more to life than merely increasing its speed.[3]

It became a very significant moment in my life. It set in motion a process where God had to teach me the value of pacing myself, finding rest, renewal and enjoyment in a busy life. A few months after the initial experience of tiredness we were sitting in a local restaurant, enjoying a meal with some of our friends. They told us that they were concerned about us and afraid that we might lose our anointing and sensitivity to God. They had noticed that we were burning the proverbial candle at both ends. 'Maybe you should take some time off,' they said. Guys like us don't like to 'just take time off.' There is just too much to do. And we had had a week-long vacation a few months ago. I didn't tell them about my experience during the one-week vacation.

'Take a sabbatical,' they said. 'You can go to our house at the seaside.' The very idea of a Sabbath rest or sabbatical was not high on my agenda. However, our friends insisted and in the midst of a busy schedule, my wife and I took a sabbatical for two weeks. We spent time in the house of my friend near the beach. We set aside some time to talk to God about what He was doing in our lives and ministry, and where we were heading as we pursued Him and His work. We fasted from technology and television, enjoyed time walking on the beach, listening to the noise of the birds and the waves. We prayed and followed a Daniel fast.

During this short but desperately needed sabbatical God spoke to my heart and revealed to me that spiritual exhaustion and tiredness does not come from sin but through service (2 Corinthians 4:1, 16), and whether or not we are exhausted will depend on the source of our resources. We can lose heart when we face constant tribulations and hardships (Ephesians 3:13) and when we fail to pray diligently (Luke 18:1).

Oswald Chambers, author of *My Utmost For His Highest*, says, 'God has saved and sanctified us in order to exhaust us.' He continues to explain, 'be exhausted for God, but remember that your supply comes from Him.'[4] *All too often we strive in our own strength instead of abiding in God and staying dependent on His resources.* It is then that we default back to doing things in our natural ability and no longer rely on the power and presence of the Holy Spirit. Spiritual leaders can easily experience this as they draw a crowd on Sundays, but they fail to deliver God's message to the listeners. Some leaders continue to work hard and arrange many initiatives and even 'host show-stopping experiences' for their members but experience a dryness and a sense of being disconnected. The applause they receive drowns out the voice of God.

How Then Shall We Live?

Wayne Muller, author of *How Then Shall We Live,* once said, 'What is the center of your life? Carefully examine where you spend your attention and your time. Look at your appointment book, your daily schedule—this is what receives your care and attention—and by definition, your love.'[5]

I had to re-examine whether I was where God wanted me to be? Was I doing what God called me to do? What is my created identity? Was God glorified through my ministry and my life? Could the Lord commend my work? I had become distracted and busy with ministry, and I realized that I needed to return to the most important relationship in my life: restore my intimacy with God. I needed some time alone with God and to learn to be intentional in my stillness. Once my mind, body and spirit were more rested, my spiritual life began to feel more focused, connected, and integrated again with what God had in mind for me. Since then I have learned to say no to a great majority of things I'm asked to do, so I'm available to say yes to those few things God wants me to do. I could feel how my mind opened up again and how signs of life returned to my mental and emotional worlds.

When Anne Morrow Lindbergh penned her sabbaticals masterwork *Gift from the Sea*, she scribbled with pencil on paper each morning of her summer break and then shared her awakenings with others. As she delved into her own soul, she began to understand that most men and women live in such a way that refilling their creative wells has to be a pursuit in and of itself:

> But as I went on writing and simultaneously talking with other women, young and old, with different lives and experiences – those who supported themselves, those who wished careers, mothers and those with more ease—I found that my point of view was not unique. In varying settings and under different forms, I discovered that many women, and men, too were grappling with essentially the same questions as I and were hungry to discuss and argue and hammer out possible answers. Even those whose lives had appeared to be ticking imperturbably, their smiling clock-faces were often trying, like me, to evolve another rhythm with more creative pauses in it, more adjustment to their individual needs, and new and more alive relationships to themselves as well as others.[6]

I was able to refill my empty, exhausted and dry existence. I once again discovered the joy of rest and working from the place of abiding and receiving God's supply. Didn't He promise to do so in His Word?

> But those who wait on the Lord shall renew their strength; they shall mount up with wings like eagles, they shall run and not be weary, they shall walk and not faint. (Isaiah 40:31)

Overwhelmed

As I have mentioned, I had been traveling extensively and providing spiritual counsel to individuals, leaders and churches; I listened to their heart cries and struggles. Most of them reported that they were stressed and exhausted, in despair about finding a way of life that actually worked. Most of them were longing to enjoy a more intimate walk with God. They wanted to experience a fresh awareness of the presence of God in their lives. The words that summarize these conversations are busyness, hurry and overload. *It seems that most of us are not just overloaded but overwhelmed, overworked, overcommitted and overanxious.* We have no margin in our lives and we are stretched to our limits. Robert Morris, in his book *Take The Day Off*, explains that the culture of self-improvement and self-advancement through individual effort has resulted in tens of millions of people living burned-out, stressed-out lives. A constant stream of busyness can slowly wear away at us over time: physically, mentally, emotionally, and spiritually.[7]

Wayne Muller, in his book *Sabbath*, tells us that in today's world, with its relentless emphasis on success and productivity, we have lost the necessary rhythm of life, the balance between work and rest. Constantly striving, we feel exhausted and deprived in the midst of great abundance. We long for time with friends and family; we long for a moment to ourselves.[8]

We need to find rest, renewal, and delight in our busy lives.

We all need a Sabbath rest. What is that?

We read in Hebrews 4:10–11, 'For he who has entered His rest has himself also ceased from his works, as God did from His. Let us therefore be diligent to enter that rest, lest anyone fall according to the same example of disobedience.' The Hebrew word for Sabbath is *Shabbat,* which literally means 'to cease.' It means to stop. We all need a day or time to stop and cease working, catch our breath and rest. Muller said, 'We need not schedule an entire day each week. Sabbath time can be a Sabbath afternoon, a Sabbath hour, a Sabbath walk.[9]

So, what exactly is a sabbatical? It's a series of Sabbath days put together over an extended period of time that is used exclusively for stillness, rest, quiet, reflection and prayer. What is the benefit of these days of rest? Gordon MacDonald says in his book *Ordering Your Private World,* that it is a time of closing the loop. When God rested, He looked upon His work, enjoyed its completed appearance, and then reflected on its meaning. It's a time of looking backward. We gaze upon our work and ask questions like: 'What does my work mean?' 'Who did I do this work for?' 'How well was the work done?' 'Why did I do this?' and 'What results did I expect?' and 'What did I receive?' It is also a time to look at the present to re-evaluate the truths and commitments by which we are living. Last, it is a time to look at and affirm our intentions to pursue a Christ-centered tomorrow.[10]

Let's face it, we are all just too busy. Many of us are living burned-out lives. Saundra Dalton-Smith, in her book *Sacred Rest,* challenges us to become honest with ourselves. She asked, 'Can you be 100 percent honest with me? With yourself? How is your maxed-out, stressed-out, multitasking life working for you? Is all your activity getting the results you desire?'[11] It is time to recover our lives, renew our energy and restore our sanity. *God desired that all of us not just to experience more of His presence and His power but to experience true rest.* It's when we slow down the pace, stop running, stop working, stop ministering and receive God's gift of rest (Sabbath or sabbatical), we will hear His voice again and be refreshed.

God Himself worked and rested.

God Worked and Rested

Creation

God's first act was to work. He created the universe, the world as we know it today, all the creatures, and mankind. He did it in six days. Then He took a break. We read in Genesis 1:31–2:23:

> Then God saw everything that He had made, and indeed it was very good. So, the evening and the morning were the sixth day. Thus, the heavens and the earth, and all the host of them, were finished. And on the seventh day God

ended His work which He had done, and He rested on the seventh day from all His work which He had done. Then God blessed the seventh day and sanctified it, because in it He rested from all His work which God had created and made.

God worked hard, but He also instituted the practise of rest. He rested on the seventh day and blessed it to be holy. He continued to work on the eighth day. The initial work of the creation was finished but He continued to care, sustain, maintain, protect and provide for His creation.

Sabbath

He finished the work of creation on the sixth day, when Adam was created. He did not work on the seventh day. He ceased from His activity because He had finished what He set out to do, and now it was time to enjoy the fruits of His labor. He blessed and sanctified the seventh day as a day of rest. He allowed Adam to work for six days but also instructed him to set aside an entire day to rest before working again. God then instituted the Sabbath as a day of rest:

> Remember the Sabbath day, to keep it holy. Six days you shall labor and do all your work, but the seventh day is the Sabbath of the Lord your God. In it you shall do no work: you, nor your son, nor your daughter, nor your male servant, nor your female servant, nor your cattle, nor your stranger who is within your gates. For in six days the Lord made the heavens and the earth, the sea, and all that is in them, and rested the seventh day. Therefore, the Lord blessed the Sabbath day and hallowed it.
> (Exodus 20:8–11)

Manna

The children of Israel escaped bondage from the Egyptians and were traveling as pilgrims through the wilderness to the Promised Land. God miraculously provided manna for sustenance during their time in the desert. They would receive the manna every day for six days of each week for the duration of their journey. They were to gather their food supply each day and only to the extent of their need for that day. If they were to take more it would be spoiled. However, on the sixth day, just before the seventh day, they were told to collect enough for two days. The extra manna did not spoil. God wanted them to rest on the seventh day, just as He had rested on the seventh day. If they went out on the Sabbath to look for manna, they found that there was nothing on the ground.

And so, it was, on the sixth day, *that* they gathered twice as much bread, two omers for each one. Then Moses said, "Eat that today, for today *is* a Sabbath to the Lord; today you will not find it in the field. Six days you shall gather it, but on the seventh day, the Sabbath, there will be none." (Exodus 16:22, 25)

Mount Sinai and the Forgotten Commandment

As they continued their journey, they reached Mount Sinai in the wilderness. It is there where Moses received the Law and the Ten Commandments. It was also on that mountain when God made a promise to and concluded His covenant with Moses. There is something special about one of these commands, 'Remember the Sabbath day, to keep it holy.'

Remember the Sabbath day, to keep it holy. Six days you shall labor and do all your work, but the seventh day *is* the Sabbath of the Lord your God. *In it* you shall do no work: you, nor your son, nor your daughter, nor your male servant, nor your female servant, nor your cattle, nor your stranger who *is* within your *gates*. For *in* six days the Lord made the heavens and the earth, the sea, and all that *is* in them, and rested the seventh day. Therefore, the Lord blessed the Sabbath day and hallowed it.
(Exodus 20:9–11)

It is key to the Israelites' success as a people. It was a sign of His presence. He promised that He would be with them, that He would be their God and that they would be His people. So important was it to their well-being and survival that God even established penalties for violating it:

> Speak also to the children of Israel, saying: 'Surely My Sabbaths you shall keep, for it is a sign between Me and you throughout your generations, that *you* may know that I *am* the Lord who sanctifies you. You shall keep the Sabbath, therefore, for *it is* holy to you. Everyone who profanes it shall surely be put to death; for whoever does *any* work on it, that person shall be cut off from among his people. Work shall be done for six days, but the seventh is the Sabbath of rest, holy to the Lord. Whoever does any work on the Sabbath day, he shall surely be put to death. Therefore, the children of Israel shall keep the Sabbath, to observe the Sabbath throughout their generations *as* a perpetual covenant. It is a sign between Me and the children of Israel forever; for *in* six days the Lord made the heavens and the earth, and on the seventh day He rested and was refreshed. (Exodus 31:13–17)

Does God need to rest? The answer is no. God is not subjecting the creation to a rhythm of work and rest because He needs it, but because He knows that His creation needs it. He modeled this principle from the beginning. Jesus continued to model the same principle as He followed in the footsteps of His Father. He also worked and rested.

Jesus Worked and Rested

When thinking about Jesus, we usually have this mental picture of Him teaching, healing people, doing miracles, or constantly being surrounded with crowds of people who needed His help. But Jesus often sent people away or disappeared without warning to retreat to a place of stillness and rest. When the time for work was over, He would simply stop, retire to a quiet place, rest and be alone with His Father.

> And when He had sent the multitudes away, He went up on the mountain by Himself to pray. Now when evening came, He was alone there. (Matthew 14:23)

> At evening, when the sun had set, they brought to Him all who were sick and those who were demon-possessed. And

the whole city was gathered together at the door. Then He healed many who were sick with various diseases and cast out many demons; and He did not allow the demons to speak, because they knew Him. Now in the morning, having risen a long while before daylight, He went out and departed to a solitary place; and there He prayed. And Simon and those *who were* with Him searched for Him. (Mark 1:32–36)

However, the report went around concerning Him all the more; and great multitudes came together to hear, and to be healed by Him of their infirmities. So, He Himself *often* withdrew into the wilderness and prayed. Now it happened on a certain day, as He was teaching, that there were Pharisees and teachers of the law sitting by, who had come out of every town of Galilee, Judea, and Jerusalem. And the power of the Lord was *present* to heal them. (Luke 5:15–17)

Why did He withdraw? It is clear that He submitted Himself and responded to a deeper rhythm[12] that directed His life. He followed and imitated His Father.

Jesus said to them, "My food is to do the will of Him who sent Me, and to finish His work." (John 4:34)

Then Jesus answered and said to them, "Most assuredly, I say to you, the Son can do nothing of Himself, but what He sees the Father do; for whatever He does, the Son also does in like manner. For the Father loves the Son and shows Him all things that He Himself does." (John 5:19–20)

I must work the works of Him who sent Me while it is day; the night is coming when no one can work. (John 9:4)

Jesus placed a very high priority on getting away from the demands of the crowds. He did not seek affirmation of His ministry from the crowds but from His Father. He refused to be tempted by the siren call of success and resisted the temptation to become a celebrity. He would withdraw from the limelight and those who wanted more of and from Him to be alone. Though He was God, the Son humbled Himself before the Father and yielded His will to pray. He walked away from busyness and popularity and received God's rest, power, protection, correction and direction to prepare Himself for what was coming next.

Jesus took numerous sabbaticals. He went away to be re-energized through prayer, quiet meditation, and to spend personal time with close friends. Jesus, like many of us, was unable to spend large amounts of time away from His responsibilities. So, He maintained a wise rhythm in the midst of His ministry life. He took time off after victories and miracles. He took time off after a season of ministry. He took time off before making major decisions. He took time off when He was facing a daunting task or a challenge. He took time of when He wanted to be away from people.

Jesus had done this very thing many times before. The most prominent pattern we see in verses like these that follow is that Jesus 'went out'—often very early or while it was still dark, either at the beginning or the end of the day, depending on what the day demanded of him. We read in the Gospel of Luke:

Yet he often withdrew to deserted places and prayed. (5:16)

During those days he went out to the mountain to pray and spent all night in prayer to God. When daylight came, he summoned his disciples, and he chose twelve of them, whom he also named apostles. (6:12–13)

While he was praying in private and his disciples were with him, he asked them, "Who do the crowds say that I am?" (9:18)

About eight days after this conversation, he took along Peter, John and James and went up on the mountain to pray. (9:28)

He was praying in a certain place, and when he finished, one of his disciples said to him, "Lord, teach us to pray, just as John also taught his disciples." (11:1)

During the day, he was teaching in the temple, but in the evening, he would go out and spend the night on what is called the Mount of Olives. (21:37)

… went out and made his way as usual to the Mount of Olives, and the disciples followed him. (22:39)

The last night of Jesus's life was filled with beauty and memorable moments. He washed His disciples' feet. He foretold His death. He exposed a betrayer in their midst. He told Peter that he would deny Him. But at the climax of this historic night, Jesus did something remarkable, which John 18:1–2 details for us:

When Jesus had spoken these words, He went out with His disciples over the Brook Kidron, where there was a garden, which He and His disciples entered. And Judas, who betrayed Him, also knew the place; for Jesus often met there with His disciples.

The disciples knew the rhythms of Jesus' life and whereabouts so well that Judas knew exactly where to look for Him in order to betray Him. Jesus knew what was coming, but still found it important to spend time in solitude with His Father, as was His custom. Jesus' life and ministry illustrates just how committed He was to following a predictable pattern of living.

Jesus knew how to balance *work* and *rest*.

He knew how to live … and we do not. That is why most of us struggle with the pace of life, exhaustion and the feeling of being overwhelmed. As in the Fitzhugh quotation at the start of this chapter, *when life is so busy and hectic and humming; and when we are uptight and frazzled and stressed, it is time to slow down, spend some time with Jesus and get some rest.*

He invites us to walk with Him and watch how He does it.
He wants us to learn the unforced rhythms of grace.
It's time to receive God's gift of rest.
It's time for a break.

He instructed them, *Come aside by yourself to a deserted place and rest a while.* So, off they went across the lake by boat to get some rest (Mark 6:31–32).

Time For A Break

Jesus called and commissioned the disciples for ministry and he gave them the authority to preach the Gospel, cast out demons and heal the sick (Mark 6:7–13). When they left on their preaching tour, He also traveled in the region to preach in the cities (Matthew 11:1). Jesus came back in time to receive them when they returned. They were filled with excitement about their newly acquired power and crowded around Jesus to report on all they had done and taught (Mark 6:30).

> But it seemed that Jesus didn't have much time for their ministry reports.
> They had to learn one more lesson.
> They needed to learn the importance of rest.

In today's world, with its relentless emphasis on success and productivity, we can easily be sidetracked by success, popularity or busyness. However, Jesus was more concerned with helping them to understand the balance between work and rest. According to Ruth Haley Barton, in her book *Strengthening The Soul of Leadership,* the reason why Jesus didn't have much time for reports was because He wanted them to establish rhythms that would sustain them in ministry.[13]

One of the clearest pictures of learning the unforced rhythms of grace is found in God's dealings with Israel. Paul tells us in Romans 15:4, 'For whatever things were written before were written for our learning, that we through the patience and comfort of the Scriptures might have hope.' And again in 1 Corinthians 10:11, describing their wilderness experiences, he says, 'Now all these things happened to them as examples, and they were written for our admonition, upon whom the ends of the ages have come.'

Daily

First of all, there were *daily rhythms* in receiving sustenance from God's hand. God wanted to teach the Israelites to depend on Him for their daily needs. Through Moses, God taught the Israelites the importance of establishing a daily rhythm that would guide and sustain them as pilgrims on their journey through the wilderness. God told them that in the evening they would have flesh to eat, and in the morning, He would rain bread from heaven. He provided for them, but it came with a test to see if they would believe, trust and obey Him. They had to learn to go out every day and collect what they needed for that day only. God would provide for them daily. He did so faithfully for 40 years in the wilderness.

> Then the Lord said to Moses, "Behold, I will rain bread from heaven for you. And the people shall go out and gather a certain quota every day, that I may test them, whether they will walk in My law or not." Also, Moses said, "*This shall be seen* when the Lord gives you meat to eat in the evening, and in the morning bread to the full." (Exodus 16:4, 8)

Weekly

Secondly, God taught the Israelites a *weekly rhythm* that would distinguish them from the other nations. Even before Moses received the Ten Commandments, they learned about working for six days and resting on the seventh. In Exodus 16:23, the Sabbath is mentioned for the first time. It is called the seventh day. The Israelites also had to learn how to work for six days and rest on the seventh.

> So, they gathered it every morning, every man according to his need. And when the sun became hot, it melted. And so, it was, on the sixth day, *that* they gathered twice as much bread, two omers for each one. And all the rulers of the congregation came and told Moses. Then he said to them, "This *is what* the Lord has said: 'Tomorrow is a Sabbath rest, a holy Sabbath to the Lord. Bake what you will bake *today*, and boil what you will boil; and lay up for yourselves all that remains, to be kept until morning.'" So, they laid it up till morning, as Moses commanded; and it did not stink, nor were there any worms in it. Then Moses said, "Eat that today, for today *is* a Sabbath to the Lord; today you will not find it in the field. Six days you shall

gather it, but on the seventh day, the Sabbath, there will be none." Now it happened *that some* of the people went out on the seventh day to gather, but they found none. And the Lord said to Moses, "How long do you refuse to keep My commandments and My laws? See! For the Lord has given you the Sabbath; therefore, He gives you on the sixth day bread for two days. Let every man remain in his place; let no man go out of his place on the seventh day." So, the people rested on the seventh day. (Exodus 16:21–30)

The miracle of receiving manna daily endured not for a few days and weeks only but for 40 years, except on the seventh day. God wanted them to learn the importance of resting and trusting Him for their provision. They struggled to trust God for their daily bread in the beginning and made many mistakes. However, Moses guided them step by step to realize that God could be trusted to provide enough for all of their needs. God taught them to receive their substance from Him. They learned that on their pilgrim journey they had to live on promises and not on explanations. Roger Steer, in his book *Hudson Taylor—Lessons in Discipleship,* explains that Hudson Taylor trusted God. He believed, as do so many great men and women of faith, that Christians should be taken up less with the nature of faith and more with the reality of God. Hudson was known for saying that you did not need great faith, but faith in a great God. He urged people never to forget three important statements: 'There is a living God. He has spoken in the Bible. He means what He says and will do all that He has promised.'[14] We need to believe in Him and trust Him to be true to His Word.

In Closing

How can we hear His gentle whisper unless we tarry long enough to listen? According to Ruth Haley Barton, in her book *Invitation to Solitude and Silence,* 'The invitation to solitude and silence is just that. It is an invitation to enter more deeply into the intimacy of relationship with the One who waits outside the noise and busyness of our lives.'[15]

It is in those moments of quietness in solitude, silence and stillness with Him that we relax and rest, that we are restored, revived, refreshed, replenished and renewed. This is what we need for ourselves and what we want for those we are leading and shepherding.

But where to find it?

Come to Me, all *you* who labor and are heavy laden, and I will give you rest. Take My yoke upon you and learn from Me, for I am gentle and lowly in heart, and you will find rest for your souls. For My yoke is easy and My burden is light. (Matthew 11:28–30)

Eugene Peterson, in his contemporary English version of the Bible, captures what Jesus was saying in Matthew 11:28–30 this way:

Are you tired? Worn out? Burned out on religion? Come to me. Get away with me and you'll recover your life. I'll show you how to take a real rest. Walk with me and work with me—watch how I do it. Learn the unforced rhythms of grace. I won't lay anything heavy or ill-fitting on you. Keep company with me and you'll learn to live freely and lightly. (*MSG*)

Practising a Rhythm of Life

Since God spoke to me during my two-week seaside sabbatical, I have taken the time to read through the books *Sacred Rhythms* and *Strengthening the Soul of Leadership* by Ruth Haley Barton. I have found the chapter on the *Spiritual Rhythms in the Life of a Leader* helpful. I have taken the time to reflect on the truths explained and personal example of Ruth in establishing and practising my own rhythm of life. It has become essential to my well-being as well as that of my ministry.[16] My daily rhythm includes a time of solitude and silence in the morning until 09:00 a.m. It begins with an early morning cup of coffee and conversation with Jesus as I reflect on some of the thoughts that are in my heart when I wake

211

up. My wife and I enjoy a walk early in the morning, and I also do some physical exercises. It gives me the opportunity to enjoy nature, smell the flowers, listen to the birds and have some time to review my day with God and His schedule. It also helps me to follow a more balanced and healthy lifestyle. During these times I am not available on my phone.

When I get home, I spend some time reading in God's Word, I listen to the Holy Spirit, pray and write down my thoughts in my journal. Writing in my journal has become a way of slowing down my thoughts, my pace. Usually on a Sunday (if I am not preaching or traveling) I spend more time sleeping, relaxing, reading, going to church or listening to a message. If I am traveling or preaching on a Sunday, I try to find another day in the week or at least plan a quiet day of rest once a month. It is not easy to set aside time, especially when traveling or having to catch international flights, but that is my goal.

Following the example of Jesus in Luke 5:15–17, I try to find some additional time before I preach to prepare myself spiritually. After preaching, I generally try to make some time to process (Mark 6:30) and reflect on what God is saying to me or what He is doing in my life. At the beginning of each year I set aside time for longer periods of fasting and prayer. Some of those days will be spent in solitude and silence, when I unplug from all media, communications and normal responsibilities for a few days. I take the time to look back and reflect on the past year. I listen to hear if there is anything new or specific on God's agenda for me. I listen, plan and journal about the year ahead.

I also feel that it is necessary to take a break in the middle of the year and have seen the value of an annual vacation of a few weeks when I have no agenda other than to sit, stare, sleep and rest. I have found that in the relentless busyness of our lives, we have missed a step in the rhythm of balancing work and rest. We need a day or time of rest, when we can find rest, be restored and refreshed. I shared at the beginning of the book how a canceled meeting gave me a day of rest and time for reflection. The day spent in the coffee shop in Aiken, SC, after a change of place, resulting in a change of pace, led to a change of perspective. It also laid the foundation for this book and a new way of living and ministering.

> A Sabbath well spent, brings a week of content,
> And strength for the toils of the morrow.
> But a Sabbath misspent,
> what'er may be gained,
> is a certain forerunner of sorrow.[17]

The choice to rest is not only crucial for the mind, body and spirit but an essential element for a balanced life. Once we respond to a deeper rhythm of rest, we will find the balance between work and rest.

> God rested.
> Jesus rested.
> The disciples rested.
> You can also!

The Conclusion

An invitation to become a MAN or a WOMAN on the MOVE

My own good intentions don't always convert into good actions, so I want to thank you for finishing this book. The fact that you have read to the end shows that you really care about connecting with God and His purpose for your life. I pray that you have been encouraged and challenged by what you've read.

I began this book with a call to be on mission with God. I would like to end with the same call. So far, we have learned that a disciple is a follower and learner of Jesus Christ, who has responded to His call to join a crucial mission—the redemption of the world. He knows where we need to go and what we need to do.

First, we've seen that Jesus *called* the disciples to be with Him; *taught* them what it meant to follow Him; uniquely *equipped, changed* and *empowered* them, and *gave* them what they needed as He *sent* them out to accomplish their mission. They have learned about:

- the importance of being with Jesus;
- hearing Him speak;
- to be changed and transformed;
- the blessing of obedience;
- being commissioned;
- to behold and process a truth; and
- resting. It's also true for us.

Second, Jesus g*ave them the process through which they can participate* in His cause and mission for the world by making disciples (Matthew 28:19–20).

- Go—sow the seed of the Gospel through our words and deeds in our circles!

- Make disciples—when the Holy Spirt causes the seeds to grow in the lives of those we know, we help them to respond to God through repentance.
- Baptize them—we help them to declare their faith publicly.
- Teach them to observe Jesus' commands—we walk in partnership and discipleship with the new believers in Christ to help them learn the truths of God's Word, apply it and begin to make disciples themselves.

As you were reading this devotional book, I hope that God has shown you areas in your life in which you can grow and mature in your walk with God or surrender to the Lordship of Jesus Christ.

I hope that this book has given you hope and challenged you to be and become a better follower of the Lord Jesus and to invest your life in others'. If so, I believe that I have succeeded. But now you face an even bigger challenge and decision—how to grow into the image of Jesus (Romans 8:28), allowing Him to change your life, values and focus into His focus, and to be a person on mission with God.

Warren Wiersbe, in his book *God Isn't In A Hurry,* said that we should be moved, not only by God's power but also by our love for Him and for lost souls. Love is the greatest motive in the world. If we really love Christ, we should want to obey Him (John 14:15). We cannot stand still in the Christian life. We either go forward or gradually slide backward. This is also true for churches. We ought to be witnesses, but instead we are prosecuting attorneys arguing among ourselves. We are supposed to advertise God's wonderful character (1 Peter 2:9) and yet we ourselves are competing among ourselves and arguing about who is the greatest. We must become a church (or a person) on the move. What does that look like?

- We must *become* men and women of vision and spiritual vitality and have an appetite to see God at work.
- We must *receive* our marching orders from Him, saturate ourselves in the Word (teach, preach and obey it). We

do not need new and elaborate programs, but we need lives changed and impacted by the Word.

- We must *not be afraid* of change—life and ministry will change as we are transformed and changed. Even as the world is changing, we will experience new things. We must adapt.
- We must *embrace* and *confront* reality and meet people where they are. Many of us have friends and family who are saved and some are unsaved but we keep them at a distance.
- We must *connect* with them and expose them to the life of Christ within us. If you and I are Christians on the move, then we will help to move His church. If we look at the life of our Lord and the apostles he chose, led and trained, we find the Holy Spirit painting a picture of a church on the move.[1]

Is God stirring your heart to become a Connector, or Disciple Maker who can disciple someone who can in turn disciple others (2 Timothy 2:1–2)? If so, contact us and let us help you *Connect— The Jesus Way.*

May God bless you as you pursue a lifelong relationship with the Master, allow Him to mold you as you are on mission with Him in your home, your church and even the world.

Who is Francois?

Francois Carr, BTH, MCC, D. Min, NDPB, is the Executive Director of Heart Cry in South Africa. He studied Personnel Management in Cape Town and followed a career as Personnel Officer in the South African Defense Force. During this time, he became involved in a youth ministry that prayed for revival in South Africa. He felt the call of the Lord into a revival-related ministry during a youth conference in November 1992. He became the National Coordinator of Revival South Africa, promoting the message of revival whilst serving full-time as Lieutenant Colonel in the South African Defense Force. He studied part-time, obtaining the following degrees: Bachelor in Theology, Masters in Christian Counseling, and his Doctorate in Ministry.

As the Revival South Africa National Coordinator, he planned and organized revival conferences throughout South Africa until he felt led by the Lord to resign from his position in the Defense Force and enter into full-time ministry. He stepped out in faith and became the Executive Director of Revival SA in June 1999. He founded two ministries called Heart Cry and The Connected Life, which focus on helping people to experience more intimacy with God and mentoring spiritual leaders and churches to become a catalyst for revival. Heart Cry co-sponsors conferences in the USA, Europe and Africa.

Francois is well known for his burden to achieve intimacy with God and revival, and is a popular speaker in Africa, North America and the United Kingdom. He authored several books and articles on prayer, holiness and revival.

He is married to Dorothea and has one daughter, Leoné, who is married to Werner Mostert. Francois currently resides in Pretoria, South Africa.

Contact details
PO Box 90262, Garsfontein, Pretoria, 0042, SA
Websites: www.heartcrysa.com; www.connectedlifeministries.com
Email: office@heartcrysa.co.za

NOTES

Note from the Author

1. See www.connectedlifeministries.com for more information
2. General note about resources:

   Over the years I have read hundreds of books, studied course material, attended conferences, listened to sermons and talked with my mentors. I took notes and sought to personalize all that I have learned, making it my own. I taught and preached messages about what I was hearing, reading and learning, including what God spoke to me about, and used some of them in this book. I honestly cannot remember all the conversations, thoughts and notes from articles, resources, emails and websites that have influenced me over the course of many years. I sincerely apologize for unintentionally failing to reference any source. May the Lord Himself bless you and give due recognition to all the people, books, conversations and messages that have had an impact on my life, message, ministry and writing. On my journey I have used various commentaries, concordances and resources as background reading and study material, including those from the original Greek or Hebrew text, that inspired my thought processes. Some of the resources that I have used and found helpful over the years are as follows:

   A.B. Bruce, *The Training of the Twelve,* Hyderabad, India: Authentic Books, 2000.
   A.T. Robertson, *A Harmony of the Gospels,* New York, N.Y.: Harper & Row, 1922.
   G. Campbell Morgan, *An Exposition of the Four Gospel Narratives,* London, U.K.: Oliphants Ltd.
   Herbert Lockyer, *All the Teachings of Jesus* and *All the Apostles of the Bible,* Grand Rapids, Zondervan, 1972.
   Hebrew-Greek Key Word Study Bible, Chattanooga, Tenn.: AMG, 1984.
   J. Vernon McGee, *Thru the Bible with J. Vernon McGee,* Nashville, Tenn.: Thomas Nelson, 1983.

James Strong, *The Exhaustive Concordance of the Bible,* Peabody, Mass.: Hendrickson, 2007.

John Phillips, *The John Phillips Commentary Series,* Grand Rapids, Mich.: Kregel, 1999.

W.E. Vine, *Vine's Expository Dictionary of New Testament Words,* Peabody, Mass.: Hendrickson, 2005.

Warren Wiersbe, *The Bible Exposition Commentary,* New Testament Volumes 1 & 2, Colorado Springs, Colo.: Victor, 1989.

William Hendriksen, *New Testament Commentary,* Grand Rapids, Mich.: Baker Academic, 1973.

Introduction—The Call

1. Karl Barth in Bill Hull, *Conversion and Discipleship* (Grand Rapids, Mich.: Zondervan, 2016), 19
2. See Heb. 12:1; John 17:4; Acts 20:24
3. Henry and Norman Blackaby, *Called and Accountable* (Birmingham, U.K.: New Hope, 2007), 35
4. Robert E. Coleman, *The Mind of the Master* (Shippensburg, Pa.: Destiny Image, 2016), 13
5. See Prov. 16:9; 20:24; Ps. 37:23
6. Francois Carr, *Revival! The Glory of God* (Pretoria, S.A.: Anker, 2004), 83–85

Chapter 1—The Cause

1. Ann Spangler and Lois Tverberg, *Sitting at the Feet of Rabbi Jesus* (Grand Rapids, Mich.: Zondervan, 2009), Blurb
2. Fred H. Wight, *Manners and Customs of Bible Lands* (Chicago, Ill.: Moody, 1953), 7
3. Disciples Path series: *The Mission* (Nashville, Tenn.: Lifeway Press, 2015), 66; Also available at er.jsc.nasa.gov/seh/ricetalk. htm
4. Ibid., 66
5. Ibid., 66
6. See Matt. 26:32; 28:7, 9; Mark 16:9, 12, 14; Luke 24:13–35, 36–48, John 20:11–18, 19–31; 21:1; 1 Cor. 15:5–8

7. Bill Hull, *Conversion and Discipleship* (Grand Rapids, Mich.: Zondervan, 2016), 149–150

8. See Matt. 4:18–22; Mark 1:16–20; Luke 5: 27–28

9. See Mark 3:13–15; Matt. 10:1–4; Luke 6:12–16

10. Steve Addison, *What Jesus Started* (Downers Grove, Ill.: IVP, 2012), 15

11. Rodney Stark, *The Rise of Christianity: A Sociologist Reconsiders History* (Princeton, N.J.: Princeton University, 1996), 3

12. Available at https://www.bbc.co.uk/religion/religions/christianity/

13. See Matt. 20:20

Chapter 2—The Connection

1. Bobby Moore, *Your Personal Devotional Life* (Southaven, Miss.: King's, 2001), 8

2. Ann Spangler and Lois Tverberg, *Sitting at the Feet of Rabbi Jesus* (Grand Rapids, Mich.: Zondervan, 2009), 14

3. Brother Lawrence, *Gathered Thoughts of Brother Lawrence* (Pa.: Judson), 54

4. Brother Lawrence, *The Character of Brother Lawrence* (Pa.: Judson), 36

5. E.M. Blaiklock, *The Practise of the Presence of God* (London, U.K.: Hodder & Stoughton, 1989), 22

6. Joy Davidman in Joyce Huggett, *Finding God in the Fast Lane* (Guildford, Surrey, U.K.: Eagle, 1993), 43–44

7. Available at https://libquotes.com/watchman-nee/quote/lbl6w7p

8. Roger Ellsworth, *When Heaven Calls Your Name* (Leominster, U.K.: Day One, 2008), 56

9. Charles Wesley in Herbert Lockyer, *All the Women of the Bible* (Grand Rapids, Mich.: Zondervan, 1967), 102

10. See Matt. 18:11; Luke 19:10; Isa. 61:1

11. See Mark 3:7–9, 20; 32; 4:1

12. See Matt. 4:15, 25; 11:21–22; 19:1; Mark 7:24, 31; 10:1; John 1:28; 3:26; 10:40; Acts 21:3–7

13. Edwin and Lillian Harvey, *How They Prayed* (Vol 2), (Richmond, Ky.: Harvey Christian, 1987), 16

14. Clarence H. Wagner, *Lessons from the Land of the Bible* (Jerusalem, Israel: Bridges for Peace, 1998), 19

15. Mabel Brailsford in Edith Deen, *Great Women of the Christian Faith* (Uhrichsville, Ohio: Barbour, 1959), 41–42

16. Hudson Taylor in Bobby Moore, *Your Personal Devotional Life* (Southaven, Miss.: King's, 2001), 3

17. See John 5:19; 30; 6:38; 8:28

18. Ken Blanchard and Phil Hodges, *Lead like Jesus* (Nashville, Tenn.: Thomas Nelson, 2016), 25

19. Alexander Whyte in Bobby Moore, *Your Personal Devotional Life* (Southaven, Miss.: King's, 2001), 35

20. Henry and Norman Blackaby, *Called and Accountable* (Birmingham, U.K.: New Hope, 2007), 59

21. Available at https://www.merriam-webster.com/dictionary/koinonia

22. Frank Boreman, *When Scripture Changes Lives* (Waynesboro, Ga.: OM Literature, 1994), 1–7

23. Howard and Mrs Taylor, *Biography of James Hudson Taylor* (London: China Inland Mission, 1965), 271

24. Richard A. Swenson, *Margin: Restoring Emotional, Physical, Financial, and Time Reserves to Overloaded Lives* (Colorado Springs, Colo.: NavPress, 2004), Back-cover blurb

25. Henri J. Nouwen, *The Way of the Heart: Desert Spirituality and Contemporary Ministry* (New York, N.Y.: Seabury, 1981), 45–46

26. Available at https://www.merriam-webster.com/dictionary/disruption

27. Available at https://www.merriam-webster.com/dictionary/complacency

28. Read full transcript of message by Nancy DeMoss Wolgemuth published on 4 November 2011 at https://www.reviveourhearts.com/events/revive-11/potential-pitfalls-ministry/transcript/

Chapter 3—The Communication

1. Available at https://www.somelinesforyou.com/author/saint-bartholomew

2. Garth Stein, *The Art of Racing in the Rain* (New York, N.Y.: HarperCollins, 2008), 101–102

3. Ron Mehl, *What God Whispers in the Night* (Sisters, Ore.: Multnomah, 2000), 97

4. Ibid., 97–98

5. Available at https://www.margaretwheatley.com/articles/listeninghealing.html

6. Charles Swindoll, *Intimacy with the Almighty* (Nashville, Tenn.: J. Countryman, 1996) 38–39

7. Henry and Richard Blackaby, *When God Speaks* (Nashville, Tenn.: Lifeway, 1995),

8. In my research and studies over many years I found several compelling reasons why God wants to communicate with us today.

9. Bobby Moore, *Your Personal Devotional Life* (Southaven: King's, 2001), 2

10. See 2 Chron. 20:7; Isa. 41:8; James 2:23

11. See Ex. 25:9, 40; 26:30

12. See Ex. 33:7–10

13. See Num. 7:89

14. Available at https://www.biblestudytools.com/lexicons/hebrew/nas/leb.html

15. Lois Tverberg, *Walking in the Dust of Rabbi Jesus* (Grand Rapids, Mich.: Zondervan, 2012), 31–41

16. See Matt. 13:14–38; Mark 8:18

17. Peter Lord, *Hearing God* (Bloomington, Minn.: Chosen, 1988), 83–95

18. See Pss. 27:14; 37:7–9; 37:34; 130:5; 147:11

19. James 4:7–8. See also Deut. 8:11–14; 2 Chron. 7:14; Num. 12:6–8; Ps. 34:18.

20. Marilyn Hontz, *Listening for God.* Available at https://www.amazon.com/Listening-God-ordinary-person-learn-ebook

21. Henry and Richard Blackaby, *When God Speaks* (Nashville, Tenn.: Lifeway, 1995), 13

22. See Matt. 10:18–20; John 14:26, 16:7, 8, 13; Rom. 8:26; 1 Cor 2:9–16; Acts 8:29, 13:2

23. Dallas Willard, *Hearing God* (Downers Grove, Ill.: IVP, 1984), Back page

24. Available at https://www.bibletools.org/index.cfm/ fuseaction/Lexicon.show/ID/G991/blepo.htm

25. See Rom. 7:23; 1 Cor. 13:12; Heb. 10:25

26. See Gal. 1:16

27. See Deut. 6:16; Matt. 4:7

28. See 2 Tim. 3:16–17

29. See 1 Thess. 1:5; 2:13

30. See Rom. 8:16; Phil. 4:7

31. Prov. 3:3–13; Rom. 8:26–32

32. See 1 Sam. 13:13–14; 15:23; 2 Sam. 12:7–15; Acts 9:10–18; 10:1–33

33. See Acts 2:17, where Peter quotes Joel 2:28

34. Available at https://www.merriam-webster.com/dictionary/ journal

35. Charles Swindoll, *So You Want To Be Like Christ* (Nashville, Tenn.: Thomas Nelson, 2005), 72

36. Gordon MacDonald, *Ordering Your Private World* (Crowborough, East Sussex, U.K.: Highland, 1985), 144

37. Manley Beasley, *Alive by His Life* (Kalamazoo, Mich.: Master's, 1976), Blurb

Chapter 4—The Change

1. D.E. Hoste, *The Insight of a Seer* (London, U.K.: China Inland Mission), 5

2. Charles F. Stanley, *Living in the Power of the Holy Spirit* (Nashville, Tenn.: Nelson, 2005), Introduction

3. Warren Wiersbe, *God Isn't In A Hurry* (Nottingham: Crossway, 1994), 48

4. John MacArthur, *Twelve Ordinary Men* (Nashville, Tenn.: W. Publishing Group, 2002), 3–4

5. Stuart Briscoe in Ron Dunn, *Extraordinary Victory for Ordinary Christians* (Fort Washington, Md.: CLC, 1976), 11

6. Available at https://dictionary.cambridge.org/dictionary/ english/consistency

7. John MacArthur, *Twelve Ordinary Men* (Nashville, Tenn.: W. Publishing Group, 2002), 25–26

8. Disciples Path series: *The Way* (Nashville, Tenn.: Lifeway, 2015), 66. Also available by Thomas Fields-Meyer, 'Organ

Transplants: Can a New Heart Change Your Life—and Your taste in Music?' *People Magazine,* Vol. 63, No.13, 4 April 2005. Available online at people.com

9. Available at https://www.merriam-webster.com/dictionary/character

10. Available at https://www.merriam-webster.com/dictionary/competencies

11. Bobby Harrington and Alex Absalom, *Discipleship that Fits* (Grand Rapids, Mich.: Zondervan, 2016), 20

12. Dallas Willard, *The Divine Conspiracy* (San Francisco, Calif.: HarperCollins, 1998), 303

13. S.D. Gordon, *Quiet Talks on Prayer* (New York, N.Y.: Grosset & Dunlap, 1941), 229

14. Charles Swindoll, *Moses* (Nashville, Tenn.: Thomas Nelson, 1999), 75–78

15. Avery T. Willis Jr. and Matt Willis, *Learning to Soar* (Colorado Springs, Colo: NavPress, 2009), Inner-cover blurb

16. Some examples of tests in and for life and ministry preparation: Abraham (time), Samuel (Word), Samuel (character), Daniel (integrity), Balaam (motivation), Elisha (servant), Ananias (obedience), Joseph (misunderstanding), Noah (patience), Paul (isolation, frustration), Elijah (discouragement), Nehemiah (vision), etc.

17. Graham W. Scroggie, *The Land and Life of Rest* (Hampton, Tenn.: Harvey Christian, 1998), 83

18. Helen Roseveare, *Living Sacrifice* (Chicago, Ill.: Moody, 1979), 20–21

19. Miles J. Stanford, *Principles of Spiritual Growth* (Lincoln, Neb.: Back to the Bible, 1988), 11, 13

20. Ibid., 13–14

21. Shelley Trebesch, *Isolation—A Place of Transformation in the Life of a Leader* (Altadena, Calif.: Barnabas, 1997), 49

22. Available at https://en.wikipedia.org/wiki/Samuel_Logan_Brengle

23. Available at https://www.marionstar.com/story/life/2017/03/22/pastor-no-brick-no-book/99462382/

24. Charles F. Stanley, *Living in the Power of the Holy Spirit* (Nashville, Tenn.: Nelson, 2005), 44–47

25. Dennis Kinlaw in *One Divine Moment*, edited by Robert Coleman (1970) and David J. Gyertson (1995), (Old Tappan, N.J.: Fleming H. Revell, 1995)

26. Dennis Kinlaw, *Preaching in the Spirit* (Anderson, Ind.: Francis Asbury, 1985), 119

27. Ruth Haley Barton, *Strengthening The Soul of Your Leadership* (Downers Grove, Ill.: IVP, 2018), 19

Chapter 5—The Commission

1. D.E. Hoste in Patrick Fung, *Live to be Forgotten* (Hong Kong: OMF Hong Kong, 2008), 4

2. Available at https://en.wikipedia.org/wiki/Smolensk_air_disaster

3. Available at https://en.wikipedia.org/wiki/2010_eruptions_of_Eyjafjallajökull

4. Available at https://wist.info/kierkegaard-soren/35849/

5. See 1 Sam 23:1–3, 4–5, 10–11, 12–14; 30:8–9; 2 Sam 2:1–2; 5:17–21, 22–25; 21:1

6. J. Robert Clinton, *The Making of a Leader* (Colorado Springs, Colo.: NavPress, 2012), 31

7. See Matt. 26:42; John 4:34; 5:30; 6:38; 8:29; 17:4

8. See also 1 Sam. 19:19–22; 2 Kings 2:3; 2 Kings 2:15

9. Robert Foster, *Discipleship in the New Testament*, Society of Biblical Literature, www.sbl.org

10. See Acts 4:32; 6:2; 6:7; 9:26; 14:21–22

11. *Discipling* is a process of showing believers how to live and act like Jesus Christ and how to participate in the Great Commission as a lifestyle in reaching others. *Discipleship* is intentionally equipping believers with the Word of God, through accountability relationships, empowered by the Holy Spirit, in order to replicate faithful followers of Jesus Christ.

12. David and Paul Watson, *Contagious Disciple Making* (Nashville, Tenn.: Thomas Nelson, 2014), 124

13. Dennis Kinlaw, *Preaching in the Spirit* (Anderson, Ind.: Francis Asbury, 1985), 81, 84

14. Henry and Richard Blackaby, 7 *Truths From Experiencing God* (Nashville, Tenn.: LifeWay, 2007), 9
15. W. Oscar Thompson, *Concentric Circles of Concern* (Nashville, Tenn.: Broadman & Holman, 1999), Back-page blurb
16. Ibid., 30–34
17. Ibid., 30–31
18. Dennis Kinlaw, *Preaching in the Spirit* (Anderson, Ind.: Francis Asbury, 1985), Blurb
19. Scott Morton, *Funding Your Ministry* (Colorado Springs, Colo.: NavPress, 2007), 40

Chapter 6—The Commitment

1. Available at https://www.azquotes.com/author/17431-Charles_ Studd
2. Brad Allen, *Catch the Wind* (Tarentum, Penn.: Word Association), 57–62
3. Duncan Campbell, *God's Standard* (Edinburgh: The Faith Mission, 1964), 61
4. See also Ex. 12: 35–36
5. See also John 14:23; John 15:10
6. Available at https://www.goodreads.com/quotes/266310-god- is-god-because-he-is-god-he-is-worthy
7. Ron Owens, *Manley Beasley, Man of Faith—Instrument of Revival* (Garland, Tex.: CrossHouse, 2009), 37–38
8. Henry and Richard Blackaby, 7 *Truths From Experiencing God* (Nashville, Tenn.: Lifeway, 2007), 36
9. Ibid., 36
10. Oswald Chambers, *My Utmost For His Highest* (Uhrichsville, Ohio: Barbour, 1935)
11. Avery Willis, *Master Life* (Nashville, Tenn.: Broadman & Holman, 1998), 244
12. Charles F. Stanley, *Living the Extraordinary Life* (Nashville, Tenn.: Nelson, 2005), 88–92
13. Wayne Barber, *The Rest of Grace* (Eugene, Ore.: Harvest, 1998), 45

Chapter 7—The Completion

1. Mary Garnett, *Take your Glory Lord* (Roodepoort, S.A.: The South African Baptist Missionary Society, 1979)
2. Ibid., 13
3. Ibid., 131
4. Ibid., 133–134
5. NIV *Once-a-Day*: *Worship and Praise Devotional,* (Zondervan), eBook: 365 Days to Adore God, 1 May, Day 121
6. Available at https://www.merriam-webster.com/dictionary/process
7. Available at https://www.merriam-webster.com/dictionary/behold
8. See John 9:25; 1 Cor. 15:10; Gal. 1:15–16; Phil. 3:7–14; 1 Tim 1:15–17; 2 Peter 1:16; 1 John 1:1–4
9. Manley Beasley, *Alive by His Life* (Kalamazoo, Mich.: Master's, 1976), Back-page blurb
10. James Alexander Stewart, *She was only 22* (Asheville, N.C.: Revival Literature, 1966), 5
11. Available at http://spurgeon.10000quotes.com/archives/156
12. Billy Graham, *God's Ambassador* (Nashville, Tenn.: W. Publishing Group, Thomas Nelson, 1999), 155
13. Ibid., 1
14. Bruce Bennie, *Andrew Murray: Theologian of the Heart* (Morphett Vale, South Australia: Integrity Word Ministries, 2004), 31
15. Available at http://www.shortercatechism.com/resources/wsc/wsc_001.html

Chapter 8—The Celebration

1. John Stott in Roy McCloughry, *Basic Stott (Part three):* Candid Comments on Justice, Gender and Judgment (*Christianity Today,* 8 January 1996), 25
2. Fitzhugh in *Our Daily Bread* (Grand Rapids, Mich.: Discovery House, RBC Ministries, 2009, 30 September)
3. Available at https://www.goodreads.com/quotes/21592-there-is-more-to-life-than-simply-increasing-its-speed
4. Oswald Chambers, *My Utmost For His Highest* (Uhrichsville, Ohio: Barbour, 1935)

5. Wayne Muller, *How Then Shall We Live?* (New York, N.Y.: Bantam, 1996)

6. Anne Morrow Lindbergh, *Gift from the Sea* (New York, N.Y.: Vintage, 1978), 10

7. Robert Morris, *Take the Day Off* (Nashville, Tenn.: Faith Words, 2019), Back-page blurb

8. Wayne Muller, *Sabbath* (New York, N.Y.: Bantam, 1999), Back-page blurb

9. Ibid., Back-page blurb

10. Gordon MacDonald, *Ordering Your Private World* (Crowborough, East Sussex, U.K.: Highland, 1985), 177, 179, 181

11. Saundra Dalton-Smith, *Sacred Rest* (Nashville, Tenn.: Faith Words, 2017), 9

12. According to *Merriam-Webster's Dictionary* rythm is a movement, fluctuation or variation marked by the regular recurrence or natural flow of related elements. Available at https://www.merriam-webster.com/dictionary/rhythm

13. Ruth Haley Barton, *Strengthening The Soul of Your Leadership* (Downers Grove, Ill.: IVP, 2018), 120

14. Roger Steer, *Hudson Taylor—Lessons in Discipleship* (Crowborough, U.K.: Monarch/OMF International [former Inland China Mission], 1988), 51

15. Ruth Haley Barton, *Invitation to Solitude and Silence* (Downers Grove, Ill.: IVP, 2010)

16. Ruth Haley Barton, *Strengthening The Soul of Your Leadership* (Downers Grove, Ill.: IVP, 2018), 133

17. Herbert Lockyer, *All The Teachings Of Jesus* (Peabody, Mass.: Hendrickson, 2008), 157

The Conclusion

1. Warren Wiersbe, *God Isn't In A Hurry* (Nottingham, U.K.: Crossway, 1994), 86–89

Additional Copyright Information

Connected—The Jesus Way

LIFE—DISCIPLE—LEADER

Connected is a 'discipleship-based process' designed to equip and empower believers and churches to become, develop, and replicate effective followers of Christ. They also become workers and leaders of influence who in turn transform their environment. The goal is to encourage and establish a new lifestyle of intimacy with God. It calls all like-minded people to become part of a movement of believers who rediscover how being Connected can transform their church, community, culture, and country!

OUR PURPOSE

God has called us to lead all people to a greater understanding of what it means to enjoy the reality and purpose of as well as intimacy with God.

JESUS' MODEL

The life and ministry of Jesus impacted the people closest to Him, and reached the ends of the earth. His influence grew and stretched beyond Israel to other parts of the world, and still has an impact on people today. We believe we will be most effective by studying and following His methods, strategy, and model.

BE CONNECTED

This journey will take you deeper in your own walk with God. You will rediscover the power and joy of fellowship with God and His people. As you mentor and disciple others to grow to maturity, you will experience the joy of helping believers to encounter God. You will experience greater intimacy and the deeper reality of being Connected with God, as it brings lasting transformation in the lives of ordinary people.

PROCESS

The Connected Process consists of presentations, practical exercises, spiritual coaching, mentoring, follow-up sessions, and self-study. Life and character transformation takes place as you commit to the process and respond to the Holy Spirit. The journey starts with a Retreat, School of Prayer, or participation in an I Connect Cohort using The Call as resource, followed with 9–12 weeks of discipleship through coaching and mentoring. The initial retreat is followed with The Connected Disciple (8 sessions), and The Connected Leader (9–12 sessions), as well as other supplementary materials.

Join a multitude of believers
and
Subscribe today

USA
Connected Life Ministries,
4000 Parris Bridge Road,
Boiling Springs, S.C. 29316
www.connectedlifeministries.com
Facebook: Connected Life Ministries

South Africa
Heart Cry
www.heartcrysa.com
Facebook: Heart Cry SA
Facebook: Francois Carr
Email: office@heartcrysa.co.za

The CALL

Be and become the follower you are meant to be

The Call
The Call Study Guide
The Call: DVD
The Connected Life Manual

For more information
visit www.connectedlifeministries.com

Also by Francois Carr

English
- Revival! The Glory of God
- Prayer for Revival
- Lead your Family in Worship
- My Time with Him
- The Rest-giver
- Running on Empty
- Spiritual Breathing

Afrikaans
- Herlewing! Die Heerlikheid van God
- Gebed vir Herlewing
- Huisgodsdiens
- My Tyd met Hom
- Die Rusgewer
- Is Jy Vol?